Borrowed Dreams

To: Mark

Carpe diem!

Scott

Borrowed DREAMS

The Roughest, Toughest Jobs
on the Planet . . . and What I
Learned from Working Them

T. SCOTT GROSS

OUR TIME PRESS
Center Point, TX

This publication is designed to provide accurate and authoritative information in regard to the subject matter covered. It is sold with the understanding that the publisher is not engaged in rendering legal, accounting, or other professional service. If legal advice or other expert assistance is required the services of a competent professional person should be sought.

Our Time Press
P.O. Drawer 1515
Center Point, TX 78010

Cover and Interior Design by Lightbourne

Library of Congress Catalog Card Number: 99-90179

ISBN: 0-9670252-0-6

First Printing April 1999

Printing number
10 9 8 7 6 5 4 3 2 1

*This book and everything I do is dedicated
to the one I love . . . Melanie.
(But you can call her Buns!)*

Contents

Preface

I love my job.

Here I was, riding into Chicago on the downtown express thinking about really tough jobs. I wanted to pick jobs for this book that few would want.

And, look at me! It's Sunday night and I'm making the same trip, different scenery, that I make so many nights, Sunday or otherwise, about to check into yet another hotel, screwing up my psyche to be pleasant, perhaps even funny, for yet another desk-bored clerk.

Tonight I was to stay at a private club a stone's throw from the famed Chicago Loop. Very old money.

"Am I breaking any rules by not wearing a tie?" I asked the comely desk clerk. She was discreetly stuffing the last bite of something into her mouth as she stepped from behind a wooden screen.

"No, sir. We're having a casual weekend."

Aren't we having a hi-ho time in the old town tonight? Imagine that! No ties on the weekend. The old boys are really pulling out the stops. Okay, not fair. People have the right to dress how they see fit in their own club. What business does a country boy from a town too small to have a traffic light have criticizing someone's dress code? Hell, if wearing a tie makes them feel closer to their money, who am I to suggest that even the weekends be casual?

I had missed Sunday football. (That's a joke. I can count on one hand the number of football games I have seen in two seasons.)

I had missed cutting the grass, riding in sculptured parade around our hill country property, making the place pretty while leaving enough cover for the deer.

I had missed walking the dogs, Bailey and Chablis.

Chablis, scarred from cancer surgery but still willing to dance her little dance when I would have said, "Little girl?," would have cocked her head, brown eyes not yet understanding her limitations, tail wagging as if that would make things all right. "Little girl, would you like to go for a walk?" Then the spin and dance, slower than before, made difficult by the mauling she had taken at the vet when he tried valiantly to make her whole.

And Bailey, the little scamp. Chablis' understudy, her apprentice. Bailey would spring to her feet from her place behind Melanie's chair and do her puppy-clumsy imitation of the big dog's dance. Yes, we would have walked the girls and talked about the harvest moon that now I could see, not from the country road that winds past our house, but instead from a Chicago hotel room. The moon, our moon, was lifting still wet from a dark and somber Lake Michigan.

I can think of one job that is too tough for some. It's my job, my love, my passion that sometimes, when the hour is late and Melanie is far away, seems more like punishment although most would see it as privilege. I will, too, tomorrow when the audience is mine and the applause washes up over the edge of the stage. Then I will be sure that I am doing the right thing.

Now, sitting in another too short chair in front of another hotel desk, a baseball game provides background. I'm not watching. The noise just helps to hold back the loneliness. Could it be a playoff? This is October, must be a playoff. Now, I sit tip, tap, typing away. And I'm not home. And that is the nature of the beast. Long hours of airplane reading, long hours of waiting. Meals skipped and meals eaten alone.

I ran a few blocks just for the exercise and for a chance to sit at the bar at Bennigan's and grab a bite. Chicken Caesar salad, of course. Low fat, but not too. Served by the bartender to avoid sitting at a table alone. I fought off the urge to leave a ten dollar bill and run straight back to the hotel without eating. I stayed but ate like a wolf, shaking the salad from my fork as if I had caught it myself.

Then I ran. I ran to the room and from the happy voices that were laughing with other happy voices, oblivious to the few who ate in embarrassed silence having been seated by a hostess who insisted on reminding them, "Jones. Party of one?"

(Lady, you don't say 'one' and 'party' in the same sentence.)

So I write this book knowing that everywhere there are good folks who are doing what they love and paying a price that may be too dear. Someone once said that never has a person lying on his deathbed been remorseful over having not spent enough time at the office. Got it.

To all the road warriors, the Moms and Dads. To all of those who work the graveyard shift or even the graveyard itself in order to pay the rent, put shoes on the baby, and perhaps have a few bucks left over for a cold brew on Friday. To all of us I raise my glass. Salud! Health! To all of us! May we live this life with our eyes open wide enough to savor the small pleasures that are so easy to leave at home as we hurry our way to happiness!

About the Adventures

There is something comforting about ignorance. Even though what you don't know can hurt you, sometimes it is the not knowing that allows us to accomplish great things.

If I had known how tough it is to be in business for yourself, maybe, just maybe, I would still be working a real j-o-b.

If I had known how hard it would be to write this book, maybe, just maybe, I would have done something else.

If I had known what it would be like to be married to Melanie, my best friend on the entire planet, well, there's an analogy that doesn't work!

Preparing to write this book has been an adventure. I no sooner got started than I realized that being a pilot wasn't enough. To get to the various adventures in a timely manner, I needed to become instrument-rated. So I did.

And that changed my life. Now I rarely travel on the big iron, choosing instead to bypass gate security, luggage check-in and parking hassles, trading them for the thrill and sometimes chill of navigating alone on the proverbial dark and stormy night.

If there is one lesson that I have learned while writing this book, it is that the world belongs to those who get involved. Great leaders are those who pull with the team, sharing personal defeat as well as victory. Great families are made great through sharing. And great lessons are learned by doing, not watching.

I haven't just written this book or reported this book—I have lived this book.

No, I was not ever a real border patrol agent any more than I was a real hotel pastry chef. But I did hike the hills in the darkest of dark and I did haul my fanny out of bed at four in the morning to measure and mix, roll and cut.

And, no, I was not a real sailor nor did I work as a carnie for an entire season sleeping under the rides and doing laundry on the run. But I did haul the lines on ship and I did chip paint on a rolling deck as surely as I hoisted several tons of three- and four-year olds onto the Peter-Paul ride at the far end of the kiddie midway.

And so I came to the final two adventures and discovered to my chagrin that, because they involved pre-hospital emergency care, I could not participate. I could only report.

There seemed to be few options, none of which seemed in keeping with my agreement with you to participate. I could tag along as a reporter but that seemed rather hollow. I could scratch those two adventures and substitute two others. But I really believed that these final two would be interesting and might teach us lessons not to be learned elsewhere.

There was a third option—earn the medical certification that would allow me to participate.

So I did.

It wasn't easy. I found the best instructor anywhere, a paramedic by the name of Bruce Pritchard. Bruce and his friend, mentor, supervisor and partner Leroy Vargas, put me to work on a killer program to learn the basics of trauma care.

I read medical texts until I could read no more. I studied at home, in hotel rooms, on ship and even while flying 95MK. I worked the ER (emergency room) and rode ambulances to prepare for working the ER and riding ambulances. And the labor paid off. So says the patch that I proudly wear on my right sleeve that lets you know that I am an EMT (Emergency Medical Technician)[1], that you can trust me with your life or the life of your child. I do not take this patch lightly even though it is only the most basic of certifications.

To tell you that this book has been a labor of love is an understatement. This book has been a labor...period!

And that's where ignorance comes to play. Had I known what it would take to write this book, it would not have been written. Had I realized how many nights away from home or even how many of my few nights at home would be spent at study or writing, I would have found something else to occupy what I call my life.

And therein lies the final lesson: Had I known, I would not have dared. Had I known, I would not even have dreamed. So to ignorance, I raise a cheer of thanks. When you look at me, you are seeing a fellow who no longer needs to dream a borrowed dream.

I am living my dream.

Enjoy. Carpe diem!

---

1. EMTs have limited skills. They are not certified to dispense drugs other than Oxygen, Glucose, and assist with several patient supplied drugs. They can start your heart if it has stopped. Get you breathing if you aren't, handle bleeding and transport if you have broken most anything. They can even deliver a baby but please try to plan a little better if you are pregnant in the east end of Kerr County!

2

Freedom in My Pocket

The weather guys were wrong. Instead of scattered to broken clouds at 3,500 feet, I was looking at the top of a solid cloud deck that stretched for miles across what should be Houston. I knew the city was there. My charts said so. The navigation radio receivers said so. The GPS navigation system with its 24 geosynchronous satellites said so.

But looking out my cockpit window at 9,000 feet, all I could see was white, white and more white.

Learning to fly, buying an airplane changed my life. First there is the obvious. No more security checks, no lost luggage, no hauling luggage on board (so there wouldn't be any lost luggage), no more crummy airline food or sweaty people overlapping the armrest and taking my space. That's the obvious. The real value came from being able to land at airports not served by the scheduled airlines, often within a few miles of my business engagements instead of across a busy city. Best of all would be the ability to take Melanie, my wife and self-professed 'nagigator' with me. It's like traveling and never leaving home.

But you don't just plunk down the cash and fire up the engine.

Flying, like anything worthwhile, takes training and practice which earns you the right to fly on sunny days. No, if you are serious about flying, if you intend to fly when there is a schedule to meet, you must get instrument-rated, (able to fly when the clouds are low, in the dark of night, in rain or not.)

I had the plane but not the instrument rating. That was coming. For now, I was limited to fair weather flying, unable to legally penetrate the clouds. My rating was for VFR, visual flight rules. The IFR, instrument flight rules, rating was the next big step.

I had started out in Kerrville, Texas, at 5,500 feet, an unpretentious altitude perfect for eastbound VFR flight. As I flew closer to Houston, the clouds nudged closer together and, like a gentle grade on a mile-long railroad track, never announced that they were rising. I'd bump the autopilot 500 feet higher, figuring that would do the job. Then I'd have to go another 500 feet, then another and another. And now the controller was asking me to "descend and maintain 5,500."

Before I could respond that I could not comply, he caught the mistake and added, "Oh, you're VFR. You've got a cloud deck. Fly heading three-five-zero and report when you can safely descend."

Air traffic controllers are the best.

I flew north sending the controller a "negative" in reply to the inquiries about my status that came every few minutes. The "negative" that was intended to sound every bit as professional as the cool, clipped language of the big iron pilots who shared their space with me, began to sound a little more tense as the clock, miles, and fuel wound down.

"Mooney niner-five-mike-kilo."

"Houston Approach. Go ahead, five-mike-kilo."

"Houston, I think I've found a hole I can get through. Five-mike-kilo."

"Five-mike-kilo, descend and maintain twenty-five-hundred. Report twenty-five- hundred."

If there is one thing that scares the bejeebers out of a pilot in instrument flight, it is the possibility of an unintentional spin. Now I was about to spin...intentionally. The hole that had picked me was really several holes in several layers of dark and turbulent clouds. For a moment, maybe just for me, the holes were in rough alignment and inviting me in for a spin.

I powered back, popped the little red speed brakes from their hiding place in the wings and tipped mike-kilo onto her left side, dipping her nose into the cold clouds. Easy girl. Lay over slowly and not too far. Don't drop your nose too low or our spiral will become a spin. Keep your rudder just so.

I thought about Mike, my flight instructor, and all the hours of practice we had flown in a tiny Cessna 150, sort of a Volkswagen bug with flimsy wings. I caught myself talking to the plane, reminding it and me that we wanted to stay in control just like when we spent boring hour after boring hour with Mike as he drilled and drilled us for a moment just like this.

When the clouds ran out, there were about three thousand feet of clear air between us and the tall pines of Houston. A commuter plane a few miles off the left wingtip bumped toward Houston Intercontinental. A 727 was reported as floating to our altitude and the controller vectored us south and out of the way.

I was on the ground. What a relief! I called the office.

"Fine! Great trip! No problem!" I lied and lied and lied again.

"Guess what? Davy Crocker called. He can do your IFR check ride tomorrow at eight," they reported.

Swell! I needed that instrument ticket today. And now, just when a smart person would be deciding to never, ever fly anything for any reason, I've got an FAA check pilot calling my house to pleasantly announce my pending humiliation. (There's nothing like reality to test your confidence.)

Davy Crocker is no ordinary check pilot. The man has more hours in the air than I have on the planet. I immediately dismissed the idea of fooling him and resigned myself to receiving one of the fabled pink slips that discontinue a check ride until the student gets a little more practice.

To my surprise, the oral part of the exam was quick and painless. (I guess all those hours spent watching John and Martha King on the training tapes were finally paying off.)

"Let's go fly."

"Yes, sir! I'll get the plane preflighted and file a flight plan."

Now picture this. We're in IMC, Instrument Meteorological Conditions (further translated as 'you can't see crap.') Davy starts messing with the autopilot and manages to turn the damned thing off about halfway down the glideslope!

My guess is that he intended to do it but when you are flying blind and on your check ride, you don't question the guy in the right seat. You fly the plane.

"No problem. I'll fly this puppy by hand." (I have the idea that confident talk actually improves performance.)

We slid down the glideslope. Davy, fiddling with his handheld GPS; Me, praying that when we popped out of the clouds, we'd see a space between us and the ground and the runway...the end of the runway, not a side view, and hopefully it would even be the right runway. (It was.)

When you practice for your instrument check, you simulate conditions by wearing a pair of glasses that resemble fogged-over safety glasses. The only clear area is roughly where a bifocal lens would be, had they been regular glasses. When you are wearing the foggles, you can't see much beyond the instrument panel.

Mike and I had flown the required forty hours and more with me wearing those damned foggles until I could, for all practical purposes, fly with my eyes closed. And now, all that training was paying off. T. Scott Gross was about to be awarded a certificate to go out and really learn to fly in the clouds. The foggles were about to be retired.

When Davy signed the temporary certificate, I wanted to

step outside and scream for joy. (I saved that for when I got home, just before dinner when I could no longer contain myself. I called Mom and left a message on her machine saying, "Mom! 'Thought you'd like to know that Betty Gross's baby boy can officially fly with his eyes closed!")

Before I left Davy, I mentioned that I was especially proud to have been certified by him, a war hero, a flying ace, a pilot's pilot with a million hours. And Davy leaned forward and shared a story from his early days of flying when he had thought of himself as hot shit, able to fly anything, anywhere, anytime.

He told about attending an airshow in Europe and being excited to watch what he believed to be the world's best pilot perform a complicated and dangerous maneuver.

The pilot flew across the runway, inverted, not more than ten feet off the deck. Then he pulled up into a near stall, rolled over and repeated the move. The crowd was awestruck.

On the second run, the plane lacked the speed it needed to complete the move. Instead of rolling out and making another pass, the world's greatest pilot continued up powered only by his own public relations. The plane nosed straight up and ran out of energy, slowing until nothing was left but gravity and a hundred agonizing feet of altitude. Gravity pulled the plane by the tail until the flying machine turned into a coffin for the world's greatest pilot.

A young Irish admirer standing nearby with his commanding officer cried, "That's impossible! That's the world's greatest pilot! He has twelve thousand hours!"

"Nay, laddie," said his officer. "He dinna have twelve thousand hours. He had twelve hours a thousand times!"

With those words, Davy left me to crow but not too loudly. To think about flying with my eyes closed but never to be disrespectful of the value of training until competence replaces cockiness.

3

Border Rats and Bandits

The glove slid off in the dark and I tasted for blood. Some, not a lot. Mostly the taste of dust from the long, dizzying slip, slide, climb down the steep canyon walls. The descent into a pitch black night had been terrifying, something we would not have done in the full light and reason of day. A half mile away and probably 500 feet below us, our quarry waited, momentarily trapped and confused by the bright beam arcing from a helicopter, itself trapped by the steep canyon walls only feet from its whirling blades.

The pilot, whom we knew only as Foxtrot One and a welcome voice from a static-filled radio, was a pro— perhaps a Vietnam leftover who still flew for country and glory here in the remote mountains on the Mexican border. Even in this moment there was room to admire him. Whoever it was that called himself Foxtrot One either knew his business or had borrowed anatomy belonging to that famous brass monkey.

We had to hurry.

Racing down the canyon walls, we had paused not to breathe or rest but to shine a light into the darkness, feeling with fingers of light for the edge that we knew would be there. Without thought, we raced down in a barely controlled fall. About the time we were certain that the bottom was close, we would find yet another edge, dropping another dark and scary fifty or so feet before starlight, flashlight, and common sense ran out.

Now, lying face down on the dark canyon floor, I knew there was something wrong with the other finger. Nothing that couldn't wait.

Agent BC Brown flashed a light in my direction.

"You hurt?"

"No. But this would have killed a normal man."

Okay. The sense of humor didn't get broken. And other than thinking that my quadriceps might explode, all my main systems seemed to be working. Apparently there are muscle groups not normally available to pen pushers and I had found quite a painful collection.

Almost close enough to touch, Foxtrot One hovered across a small stream, illuminating the night and nearly a dozen aliens or smugglers, we didn't yet know which, in a beam of surreal white light. The light looked solid as it danced from the smugglers into the brush and back again before anyone could think to run.

I remembered the scene in *Close Encounters of the Third Kind* when a huge beam of white light lifted reluctant travelers into the alien spacecraft. Tonight the spacecraft was ours and it was the aliens who were reluctant. Our light could not lift them into the chopper but it managed to hold them, frozen for the moment in time and place.

They were caught in pincers of light, the blinding, terrifying column from the copter and the still bright pinpoints of light moving from both ends of the canyon. Our two small lights flickered through the stunted trees clinging to the water. Two more lights belonging to agents working their way down from the head of the canyon were closer than ours.

"We've got 'em!" came a shout from the other side.

The Border Patrol in this wild section of east San Diego County may as well be stationed in a foreign country, or on another planet. It's not just a matter of language and terrain but a matter of culture, a culture of violence and predation that separates the espresso-sipping suburbanites from the other side of the ridge to the rough and tumble wild, wild west of the Otay Mountains.

You can't have a wild west without cowboys and tonight, I was riding with the best of the best, decked out in dark green uniforms, saddled up in white four-wheel-drive Broncos. The wild and woolly guys of the U.S. Border Patrol work this rugged badlands to keep our border closed, almost, to the smugglers who fight them nightly.

Tonight, at least in Bee Canyon, the bad guys were losing big time. Cowboys, twenty-two; bad guys, zero.

Finally, I had found a job that is exactly like flying— hours of boredom punctuated by moments of sheer terror.

We hadn't planned on leaving home so soon. But there was time on the calendar and after the first of the year, the speaking business jumps into high gear and I am gone, gone, gone. I thought I'd better work in another adventure in this quiet time at the end of the year.

Because it was so close to Christmas, it seemed a better time to stay home, clean the office, burn brush, and eat chili. When Melanie reminded us of the long flight, we knew she was right. We'd better leave early to arrive rested for the adventure to come.

Earl Nightingale once said that the difference between winners and losers is that winners are willing to do the things necessary to succeed while losers find it easier to adjust to a poor living. I think of that every time I see Melanie packing my bags. I'd much rather stay home with her but that's not how books get written. Still, I was missing her before the little Mooney lifted from runway three-zero in Kerrville.

In a few hours, Stu and I were once again bearing down on El Paso, for a fuel and pit stop at Cutter Aviation on the south side of the field.

The controllers let us land on two-six left, the big, long runway closest to the FBO (fixed base operator). I set her down, easily making the first turn.

The ramp rats at Cutter are first rate, getting us fueled and on our way in less than twenty minutes. And less than five minutes after that, we were cleared for take off on that same long runway, two-six. The little Mooney was running like a new pocket watch.

Taking off in El Paso is interesting in that the controllers almost inevitably vector you over the city of Juarez. The first time this happened, the GPS flashed a warning that I was in Mexican airspace. It felt a little discomforting. Had I messed up? Was this going to get me in trouble? Would the Mexicans shoot?

When they finally turn you west again, the tension leaves the cockpit and there is time to see things from this eagle-eyed perspective. To the north are the mountains, Sangre de Christi, blood of Christ. They are tall and devoid of meaningful vegetation. The biggest crop on this mountain is a grove of communication antennae that reach the final two or three hundred feet, grasping for airplanes that can't quite climb fast enough to escape.

By the time we lifted off the runway, the sun had set behind mountains that promise but never quite deliver shade to the town of El Paso. As if to make it easy on the early settlers, the mountains stop just shy of the border presenting a long, flat, rocky face to the folks in Juarez. Every year at Christmas, a huge star of lights is erected on this face looking into old Mexico.

The Mexicans answer in huge letters outlined in white-washed rock set against a mountain of their own:

La Bible es verdad, leerle, "The Bible, it's the truth, read it."

I know that the sentiment of peace and goodwill to all is what the star is supposed to convey. But in some respects the star seems to mock those who are so very close yet so far from enjoying the bounties of living in freedom. And yes, I know, Mexico is a democratic country where officials are elected freely. At least that is the theory. The facts may be different. If money talks in the United States, it shouts in Mexico. There the wealth is held in a death grip by the tiniest minority. And those that do not inherit wealth often seek it through other means. Mordida, the little bite, is the language of the land. Grease a palm and anything can be made to happen.

Mexico frightens me.

So the star shown brightly, white in the early evening, an electric invitation glowing at the very moment that we, as a sovereign nation, were trying to yank in the welcome mat.

It was with this in mind that we turned to the west, flying over some of the most desolate, foreboding yet beautiful country on the planet. I used the half light of a fading day and the help of the autopilot to complete the Christmas spirit. At 12,000 feet I wrote out Christmas cards while thinking what Christmas could mean.

We were high, as usual, when the SoCal controller handed us off to the approach controller in San Diego. The new guy was even busier than the last. (Now, there's a job you wouldn't want. Just admire them and appreciate them but don't even think about becoming an air traffic controller! We're talking the best of the best. Period.)

"Approach. Mooney niner-five-mike-kilo, checking in at one-zero, ten thousand and I've got information Echo."

We got a "Roger" and instructions to fly a vector to the south but no suggestion to go lower. Oh, swell, another slam dunk! This guy was so busy handling big iron that the little Mooney was going to get a vector to the moon and then be left too high to complain.

A Flight Check King Air was creating havoc out of the

busy but elegant movements of aircraft in and around San Diego's Lindbergh Field. (Flight Check is a government group that uses sophisticated aircraft-based electronics to check airplane navigation systems. They make low flights over airports while monitoring navigation beacons and equipment, checking for the dead-on accuracy that tricky instrument flying demands.)

Every pilot loves Flight Check—except when they are in the middle of already busy operations at an airfield that big iron pilots rate as one of the most dangerous in the world. Land in San Diego and experience the odd sensation of flying at eye level with office buildings and parking garages. All the minimum standards for clearance are met but just barely. If you think it's unnerving to see another aircraft off your wing tip, imagine how it feels to spot an entire office building!

"Mooney five-mike-kilo, descend and maintain 6,000 and report when you have the Flight Check King Air in sight."

"Five-mike-kilo, 6,000. We have the traffic."

"He's going to make a low pass over the field. Follow him straight in. Cleared for the visual runway two-seven. When you have the field, contact tower on one-one-eight-point-six."

Oh, boy! We were headed south, too high for comfort, and needed to turn west while descending fast without running up the tail of a King Air. Yee ha!

Stu took pictures of the skyline as we landed. Why not? We didn't need a telephoto lens!

The U.S. Border Patrol has no business being a government agency.

Too accessible. Too professional.

Setting up this adventure was as simple as placing a phone call. In no time at all, a professional public information officer, Mark Moody, was at our disposal. Moody, a patrol agent on temporary assignment, is as polished as any corporate PR representative. And that could be said about any of the gentlemen that we met in a small, neat office less than a mile from the border.

Got a question? Ask. You'll get an answer that is straightforward, no beating around the bush. The Border Patrol, make that the INS (Immigration of Naturalization Service), has learned that the best way to handle the media is to tell the truth, all the truth, all the time. Smart.

And apparently there is little, if anything, to hide. In fact, "Operation Gatekeeper" is a success story that anyone would want to tell.

In the old days, (and we're talking anything before October, 1994), the United States border was wide open. Thinly staffed with poorly equipped agents who would often detain as many as 1,500 illegals in a single night along the 14 mile strip of border known as IB, (Imperial Beach.) If that's the good news, consider that this huge number of detained illegals was estimated to be only ten percent of those who had attempted to cross. Get it? That's over 10,000 or so illegal entrants per night in a single sector!

Today the numbers are vastly different. A big night might find 300 in the Border Patrol net, estimated to be 90 percent of the total.

But this isn't our story. Our story lies to the east of Imperial Beach and the tall fence made of surplus military landing mats that extends all the way into the surf on our western coast ending in 14 miles. It's really something to watch the fence march right into the Pacific Ocean. Here the border and the sea are calm.

The fence, a wall really, is probably ten feet high and solid. Solid but not dangerous.

Agent Moody mentioned that visiting German military officers were shocked that U.S.B.P.(United States Border Patrol) personnel are bound by policy to refrain from shooting. 'Funny, the very sensitivity that keeps us from shooting people trying to get in is exactly why people want to get in.

Still, no one seems to miss the days when illegals gathered by the thousands at the border, waiting, sensing, smelling for the unseen signal that would send them en masse, in what the guards called a 'bonsai', streaming across the border to the siren call of jobs, medical care and promise.

On the north side of the wall, the ground has been graded flat, cleared of hiding potential. On the south side, Mexican poverty backs up to the towering, rusty metal. Traffic here is one way, northbound.

There was a time when the strip was dragged each afternoon with a ragtag collection of old tires. In the morning, fresh footprints would be counted to give the agents an idea of how many had slipped their net. Today, the tires have been hauled into the brush and are rarely used.

Where attempts to dig under have been made, the National Guard has deposited thick, un-pretty plugs of concrete. To complete the picture, huge towers bearing clusters of lights bathe the entire stretch in queasy yellow light. Agents in patrol vehicles are posted within sight of one another. Imposing? You bet! Today the biggest challenge a day shift agent faces is turning his vehicle for maximum shade, following the sun with their vehicles, listening to sports on their radios.

In IB, (Imperial Beach) the only hot spot remaining is along the south levee, that unfenceable, concrete-lined wash where nature and sewerage run to the sea. Here agents sit and watch. An all day staring match on the other side awaits the frustrated dozens, who gather during the day to chuck rocks at a too-close officer, considering the odds and options for a possible crossing should the guard ever falter.

"We used to get our butts kicked every night," said an agent now proud to be on the winning side. "It was awful. Not enough men. Not enough equipment. At shift change, we'd have to drive from our posts so that our replacements could use the vehicle. In the meantime..."

When you slam the gate in one place, like a flood of the more literal version, the pressure will build until a weak spot can be found. Naturally, someone is going to try to make an end run. A lot of someones.

We left the spit and polish of Imperial Beach, a station so well under control that their biggest enemy is boredom, to drive to El Cajon on the other side of the county, the far side of the world. There we watched 30 or so slightly less polished agents muster for the evening shift where a lot of boring news was delivered to the 30 bored agents. The meat of the meeting came last with the assignment of patrol teams and duty stations.

That duty stations would be a matter of preference was no surprise. That officers felt so strongly about whom they drew as a partner was. It quickly became obvious that the group divided neatly into two camps: the gung-ho cowboys and the clock-watching slugs.

'Slug' is exactly the name that the cowboys used to describe the folks who would rather switch than fight.

Now, this isn't a comment that the Border Patrol is riddled with government free-loaders who simply put in their time. It is not. Not by a long shot. But there are, as in any organization, a percentage, hopefully small, who would rather be anywhere but where they are. You know it and so do I. What we wanted to find out is what makes the cowboys tick and if you knew the answer to that question, could you use that knowledge to turn on the terminally tuned out?

Brian C. Brown, ('Brownie' to some) drew the short straw and was assigned to be our ride for the shift. We know that he was picked because he is suspected to be one of the U.S.B.P.'s best. Good choice, that BC Brown.

Brown wore a dark green, stealth-like outfit complemented with the usual leather belt ornamented by every imaginable tool you could hang from a belt. Pistol, two flashlights, handcuffs, you name it. In a matching green 'trickie bag', Brian carried his eight-year-old, woefully out of date, bulletproof vest.

We saddled up in a bright white Bronco, Stu and camera in the back, me riding shotgun.

San Diego doesn't hug the ocean for a few miles and then suddenly stop. It sprawls wider and wider, thinner and thinner, one little community blending into another until it all just sort of runs out.

This is where our story really begins, east of the city, east of the suburbs and bagel stores, east to the mountains where the world changes color after dark.

To the east of Imperial Beach, the Otay Mountains rise several thousand rugged feet from the desert, skirting along the border as if borders meant something to mountains. "Otay" means brushy place. I found that on the internet and, having been there, believe that the Native Americans who named it, probably the Cuyapaipes, were born optimists.

If names tell you about a place, how about these? Engineer Springs, Boneyard Creek, Rattlesnake Canyon, and Mother Grundy Peak? Go figure. Indians and hippies and snakes, oh, my!

The Otays lie in rocky waves, one range after another running east to west. A narrow valley cuts deep behind the first wave of stone and brush about five or so miles as the crow flies north from Mexico. Of course, if the crow walks, actual mileage may vary. It could be seven, eight or more miles from the border to the little valley. A twisted strip of asphalt, State Highway 94 runs along the valley floor past a cafe, a few houses, and a whole lot of nothing.

After a 30 minute drive, we turned off Highway 94 and drove up a small side road to an overlook where Brian clearly had parked before. It was a collecting point, a place where an agent, new on station, could park to watch and wait for a plan to materialize. We weren't on station three minutes when the plan presented itself by radio.

In mid-conversation, Brian held up his hand for silence. Like a pilot who can pick his own call sign out a flood of otherwise useless communication, Brian's brain latched onto something interesting.

A faraway voice reported that a citizen had called in to tell of two pickup trucks loading drugs just up Highway 94.

They were headed westbound toward us. Brian mentally calculated and then shouted to no one in particular, "They should be just passing us now!"

Call it instinct, call it luck, but as Brian shoved the truck into gear and stomped on the gas, a white pickup fitting the description flashed passed. Gravel flew, Stu grabbed for anything attached and I cinched my seat belt tighter.

We roared down the hill onto the highway but not before a white U.S.B.P. van with lights flashing, whipped around the corner in hot pursuit. We were not more than a quarter mile behind.

Brian quickly caught the van that was just as quickly losing the pickup. We were doing nearly 80! One curve laced into another. Suddenly the road straightened and we whipped along the only real estate that could be considered a straight-away, passing a closed cafe and a lone highway patrol officer who was writing a speeding ticket while a truckload of dope clipped by.

What an opportunity! I yelled at Stu, "Roll tape! Roll tape!" and turned to see that there was not a prayer of getting this on video. Stu is dedicated but to a limit. And now I had a pretty good idea of what was that limit.

The caravan was again swallowed by black curves and time, like the road, compressed and stretched, and compressed again.

"Can't you move a little faster?" shouted a frustrated Indy agent into the mike.

"Brian, this is a van!" Then, "He's passing on blind curves!"

"For God's sake, back off! Let him go before he kills someone!"

It was too late. The pickup took one too many frenzied chances. When we rounded the next curve, a short 15 seconds later, there were already signs of the obvious. The white pickup was in the left lane, facing us, front end demolished. A smaller red pickup was facing the same direction sporting similar, near total damage.

The fleeing driver was long gone. The steering wheel of his late model truck had been hit and hit hard. Although there was no blood on the wheel, Stu, a paramedic by training, guessed that the impact had resulted in massive internal trauma, probably pericardial tamponade, an injury that can kill if the heart sac fills with blood and pressures the heart into an arrest.

In the back of the truck, six tightly stuffed U.S. Army duffel bags carried nearly $400,000 worth of marijuana. Heavy. Bulky. Priceless had they made it to the street. Obviously worth the risk to some.

(An editorial comment, please. I don't care how you feel about marijuana. It is illegal. If you want it legalized, then fight for that. In the meantime, if you use it or tolerate it, you are contributing to violence. Period.)

More border agents from the changing shifts arrived within seconds. Brian wisely ordered agents into the woods to serve as guards in the off chance that the bad guys would attempt to recover the goods.

The driver and passengers of the other truck appeared to be little worse for the wear other than the fact that the driver carried no insurance. I guess there is at least some justice.

As the minutes ticked by and the sparse highway traffic grew thick behind the accident scene, emergency vehicles arrived in convoy fashion to complete the picture. Finally, ticket written, the highway patrol officer we had passed earlier, arrived and in a clip lifted from Barney Fife on the old *Andy Griffith Show*, used his public address system to announce, "Clear the area, this is my scene."

A helicopter, Foxtrot One, appeared from nowhere, announcing its presence with a thickening whop, whop, whop long before it was seen.

A clean, white light flashed down from the chopper, darting this way and that as if the operator was thinking with his hands and had not yet decided how and where to begin the search. In an instant, the plan was presented. Foxtrot One began slicing the entire area from highway to hilltop into precise strips of light and dark.

The bad guys were radio-equipped. One radio lay abandoned on the seat of the truck, begging to be picked up. Before they figured out that half of their convoy was missing, a breathless voice, not more than a few miles further west, announced that he had unloaded and asked where number two was.

"In the woods, pal," I answered to myself.

When the traffic cleared, we set out to plan again. Brian thought it might be good to check a canyon he knew where the smugglers might have loaded.

We drove east a couple of miles and pulled off just beyond a bridge.

We parked and walked in the darkness into a narrow, brush-filled canyon.

No drawn gun. No back-up. Just a flashlight.

Lucky us. No smugglers.

The best of the Border Patrol are spiritual descendants of great hunters. They sense the smallest of signs and can follow even the craftiest quarry over rock and ridge. 'Cutting sign' is the term they use. It can be slow going but if you have feet, you can be found.

Back in the truck, Brian told a story of tracking smugglers alone and on foot into these same mountains. Miles from God knows where on a night as dark as it gets, he surprised a group. He quickly brought four under control but guessed that another three or more were hiding nearby in the brush. Not wanting to resort to the pistol, he threw a rock into the brush ahead of where he suspected they were hiding. When the rock rattled the brush, the three remaining bad guys came out, hands held high, one bleeding profusely from a fresh head wound. (In the best bureaucratic fashion, Agent Brown was disciplined for rock throwing!)

This border business is seasonal. As it was only a few weeks before Christmas, business was slow. We drove to the port of entry, our side, north of the Mexican town of Tecate looking for action. Instead we found something other than your stereotypical 'sleepy' border town. There wasn't anything sleepy about Tecate. This town was completely dead.

The Border Patrol has a small station located about 50 yards from the steel border fence, complete with holding cells, restrooms, and vending machines, all in government issue hospital white. Still, it was a good place to get in out of the cold.

Inside we met a rather unassuming agent who, sans bulletproof vest and webbed Harrison equipment belt, would have fit nicely leading the local Sunday school, only this one was making a rather unusual request. Mr. Mild-Mannered BPA (Border Patrol Agent) was asking for permission to "lay up" in a little canyon for "a couple of nights" in hope of catching a band of drug smugglers who seemed to have found a route that made them nearly invincible and irritated the living hell out of the agent who hated to be given the slip.

Funny thing, the Border Patrol agents seem to have little if any animosity for the men, women and children who brave the wilds in search of a better life. But they absolutely hate the thought of drug smugglers crossing their border. It's too bad that the primary mission seems to be to halt illegal immigration. Drug smugglers are definitely not top priority. That's a game that officially belongs to the Drug Enforcement Agency. With the Border Patrol, drug arrests are only to result when they are incidental to interdicting illegals.

Further to the east sitting on the north side of the highway is White Mountain, an imperfect twin to Tecate Peak that guards the south side. We followed nearly hidden mountain tracks for several miles until the truck could go no farther.

"Up there. Check it out. It's one of our guys and he has the only parking spot. You'll have to walk if you want to see."

We started up what was left of White Mountain. (I could see no reason to call it either white or mountain. What is the Indian translation for Big Pile of Nothing?)

In a van, sitting precariously near but not quite on the ridge, sat a lone agent. I walked up quietly and said, "How's it going?"

"Pretty good. Kinda slow." The head never turned. The eyes never moved.

"I didn't mean to walk up on you unannounced but, now that I did, how come you didn't jump out of your skin? How did you know I wasn't a bad guy?"

"If you had been a bad guy, I would be dead. I'm not dead so you must be a good guy. Who are you?"

The eerie green glow of the night scope cast the operator in frightening silhouette. Why would someone sit in the darkness, looking at a television on hormones? Me, I'd be too scared to sit out there alone wondering if—(no, when!)—the bad guys were going to jump out of the brush and...

"So, I guess you drew the short straw?" I shivered as a little gust rose up the side of the peak and found its way under my vest.

"Oh, no. I asked for this duty. Running the scope is a big deal. You have to know the equipment to be able to take full advantage of it and you have to know the terrain like the back of your hand. Once you spot traffic, you have to be able to very precisely direct the response teams. No, this is good work."

The guy was a nut in my book. Cold, lonely, boring as hell.

"It's a little slow tonight," he continued, obviously able to read my mind with a machine designed to see in the dark. "But when it's busy you might have three or even four groups trying to get in at the same time. This position is at the heart of the action even though the action might be ten miles away."

With that he zoomed in on a house in Tecate, Mexico. Closer, then closer again, until we could clearly see right up to their back door. A small truck moved silently across the screen when the operator zoomed back. The infrared technology produced a picture that was for all the world not much different than a daylight picture on a green and white TV. Incredible.

In San Ysidro we had seen tapes of this equipment. Trust me, when this stuff is up and running, the illegals haven't much of a chance. It's mostly gulf war hand-me-down, definitely not the latest generation of technology. It's big and bulky. And when you see it at work, you realize the Iraqi desert rats didn't have a chance.

Too bad. The equipment isn't always up. Tonight was a perfect example. One of the scopes was down leaving a huge gap in coverage that backup systems could only partially fill. As I was thinking that the bad guys had an easy way in, if only they were aware of it, they came right through it. Almost as if they knew.

Dispatch called that a seismic sensor had a "hit." The message scratched at us from a radio on Brian's belt.

"You want to check it out?" Brian was looking closely over my right shoulder, uselessly hoping to see a confirmation on the glowing screen.

"Sure!" And my heart bumped up a notch or two.

We raced down the mountain to catch Highway 94 heading west. A few miles down the road, Brian pulled into a canyon just beyond the line of sight from the night scope post we had just visited. Brown calculated and cursed. If the hit had indeed been interlopers and not just a coyote, it was possible that the party could already be close. He cursed that, by policy, we could not continue on without lights although that was clearly his preference.

"Why not?" I pressed, thinking that headlights on this pitch black night would be roughly equivalent to advertising at Super Bowl.

"Too dangerous," was all he said.

"Are you afraid of running off the track? Even in the dark I think I can pretty much see it." (Maybe all he needed was encouragement.)

"No. We might hurt someone who could be lying in the brush. We won't see them if our lights are out."

Another mile or so, we abandoned the truck. Any further and we would be sure to have been seen, assuming that we hadn't already been heard in the cold air that carried even whispers halfway to forever.

Somewhere in the dark, maybe miles distant, we heard another truck and waited in the black starlight, crouching low to see who or what would follow. A door shut. We heard the click of the latch. Next, (and we're talking several minutes next) came the crunch of gravel beneath boots, followed by silhouettes of broad-brimmed campaign hats. Two of our guys or the bad guys, trying to be clever.

"Who are you?" said the nearest silhouette.

"I'm a writer, riding out with Brian." Trying to whisper seemed useless in the stillness pouring around this barren pile of nothing.

"You got a gun?"

"Naw."

"You want one?" (This was more a threat than a neighborly offer.)

"Why? So I can shoot myself? No, thanks."

The party continued on foot for another quarter mile or so, maintaining nearly complete silence, like tall cats playing a midnight game none of us really imagined would end in anything other than a long walk in the cold night air.

We walked steadily upward, a third of a mile, I guess, until the top of Little Tecate Peak was close enough to be seen resting against a star-black sky. We split. The new guys headed southeast around the mini-mountain. We headed west intending to complete the circle and, with a little luck, squeeze whoever or whatever had sent electronic chills down a seismic sensor located in the valley a mile closer to the border.

Brian began looking for 'sign.' These guys can spot the most subtle of indications that someone or something has been in the area. They know hot sign from cold sign. They can tell man, woman, or child. They know which direction. They're good. Really good.

We whispered and only when necessary. Brian wanted to use his radio to coordinate the pincer maneuver but radios are difficult to use when you are trying to be quiet. Earplugs pretty well mask incoming sound but what do you do about talking?

A cold wind blew up the back of the peak, swirled around and kicked up shirt collars on our side of the mountain. Overhead, the high voltage power lines on tall, metal legs hummed.

Have you ever heard power lines hum? They do. A low, mean-sounding tone, carrying the energy of life over stone cold mountains to little houses everywhere. Televisions brighten, schoolwork gets done, dinners are cooked all because somewhere power surges from tall tower to tall tower, marching quietly across the darkness.

The other team radioed that they were "cutting sign indicating that they seemed to be heading your way." We froze. Brown asked for the time in a whisper that seemed like a roar. He cursed and announced, still quiet in case he was wrong, that there was no way we would win tonight. "They're probably already past us. Damn!" All this in a whisper that implied that there was still a chance.

To the west the peak dropped off suddenly. A canyon, Bee Canyon, ran long and deep, cutting a gash from Mexico to freedom if you were brave enough, lucky enough, or foolish enough to try it. From our perch at the head of the canyon, we watched two flashlights. Obviously another two agents had responded and were looking for sign working from the top of the canyon down.

Brian decided that if these agents were continuing deeper into the canyon, they hadn't yet seen sign. And that could only mean that the bad guys were still south of our cold lookout.

Standing on the canyon edge, Brown called for Fox One.

"He's down for maintenance." I could hear the answer in spite of the fact that Brian was receiving via an earpiece. In the cold night air, sound carried clean and crisp.

Brown was ready to scream when the radio crackled again, this time from the guys who had headed south around the peak. They should be nearly to us by now, and they were.

"We've got sign and it's fresh!" came whispered excitement over the tiny speaker. "They have to be between us."

We squatted low to the ground, waiting for what might happen.

"Forty-eight, Fox One is back up. Do you still want assistance?" That was the message from the earpiece.

"Yeah, send him quick," Brian hissed into the air.

We waited and listened. Brian heard a cough. We both heard what sounded like a boot scuffing against a stone then nothing more. The night ticked by one shallow breath at a time. A red flashing navigation light rose over the horizon to the north and grew larger. No sound, just light. The sound came almost a minute later and it, too, grew bigger and bigger until it filled the night with ear crunching noise.

Fox One was on the radio requesting a beacon. Brian switched on his massive Magnalite, a beam that Fox One could ride all the way to the canyon's edge.

If there were any illegals, smugglers or coyotes in the darkness, they would no longer have to guess as to whether they were being hunted. The hunt had begun in earnest when Fox One swung onto station, acknowledged Brian's warning about the power lines, and then quickly settled deeper and deeper into the canyon.

We were drawn to the edge to watch the massive white beam for the second time that night. It began to wash the canyon from north to south. We assumed that the search at our level was pretty much history. We were wrong.

If a searchlight could think, this one did.

In a matter of minutes, Fox One struck pay dirt. The light stopped dancing, glued now to a spot deep in the canyon about a half mile away. Stuttering in place long enough to be absolutely certain, flitting away then not quite. It was stuck in place on a target we could not see. Aliens? Smugglers? Coyotes?

The radio came alive with two reports at once. The team that was cutting sign around the peak had literally stumbled upon the owners of the cough and boot that we had heard only minutes before. Eleven illegals had plastered themselves to the mountainside not 30 yards from where we had waited.

Had it not been that one of them had a yellow stripe on his jacket, there is a small chance that the trackers may have walked on by in the dark, dark night.

"Forty-eight. Fox One. We have your party in the light."

We took off at a trot toward the canyon, literally running over 11 illegals flattened in the brush. Apparently they had been there all along. The other two agents had come upon them from the opposite direction and were setting about the round up.

Brian had already started down the mountain when he turned to yell over the noise of the chopper, the sound waves crashing out of the rock canyon below. "You want to go?"

"Go? Hell, I didn't come this far just to watch you break your butt in the dark!"

And it started. A controlled fall into the pitch black canyon. Brian tossed me a small flashlight and began the race before I could figure how to work the light.

Jump, slide, skid to a stop. Jump, slide, skid again. Boot heels digging into the dust and rock, hoping each time that I could stop. A hundred yards of this and I was winded. Two hundred yards and my thighs were on fire, muscles burning free of their attachments, mouth sucking dust with every breath.

When we reached the bottom, the brush began to close in. I had to hurry. Agents were coming down the canyon. We needed to squeeze the bad guys from the south. Watch your step.

Too late. A boot slipped and the body followed. My chest smashed into a granite rock the size of a basketball. Thud. Big, dumb, stupid writer boy. What the hell are you doing lying face down in this canyon with your legs on fire?

We gathered them up. Eleven human beings who were never quite sure that they wouldn't be beaten and never quite sure why they were not beaten. But that's the point. That's the reason you would risk your life to live a few miles further north. In this country we don't beat people. We round them up and send them home. And on some other dark night, we may meet them again. Or maybe not. Or maybe they will be smugglers next time, loaded with drugs and violence rather than those pitiful plastic bags carrying bread, water, and toilet paper.

Can you imagine planning to walk for days in the desert carrying only bread, water, and toilet paper?

The youngest in the canyon that night turned out to be 14, sent by his parents to find work. Instead he found himself trapped by the giant mosque blanco, the white mosquito. What kind of desperation would cause a parent to launch a 14-year-old son into these black mountains just a week before Christmas?

The oldest was fifty-seven. He had trouble climbing his way out of the canyon. We held his arm and encouraged him in two languages.

"Viejo! Tiene una problema?" (Old man, do you have a problem?)

"Tengo duele," he gasped. (I have a pain.)

(In Spanish) "What kind of pain?"

"My heart. And I have diabetes."

"You sure picked a godawful route. For a sick man you seem to have your butt in a strange place."

"I wanted to get medicine for my heart. It is so very expensive in Mexico."

"And you think it's cheap here?"

"It's free, it's free."

Okay. Now is your chance to decide Republican or Democrat.

The Republican might say, "Why should we be responsible for the healthcare of a foreign country?" And the Republican would be right.

The Democrat might say, "But this man has grandchildren and naturally wants to live to see them grow up." And the Democrat would be right.

It's a puzzle.

There are two kinds of agents. Cowboys and slugs. The slugs would just as soon sit in their trucks and watch the world and half of Mexico go by.

Sit in at the evening muster and listen to the guys

wrangle over who rides with whom. The slugs and cowboys don't mix. What slug wants to be rousted out of his truck for every little potential nothing? And what cowboy wants to risk his backside with a less than enthusiastic partner?

We rode for ten hours with Brian Brown on a cold and biting night. Not once did he turn on the heater in his vehicle. Why? We didn't ask. It was obvious. Turn on the heater and you may not want to get out. Too often instinct— or other sometimes false alarms—will roust you out of the truck into the night. It is the getting out, even on a hunch, that separates the cowboys from the other guys.

The cowboys just want to go hunting. It's their border. Cross it without permission and you may as well be taking a swing at them personally.

I was absolutely amazed to discover the humanity with which the cowboys treat their prizes. Round them up, tie them up, if necessary, but send them home as good as you found them.

When we rounded up our eleven in the bottom of Bee Canyon, there was only one way to go—up and out. The two smugglers, (coyotes), who had attempted to run were cuffed together. The rest were lined up and herded along the steep trail.

This was no simple task. The narrow trail climbed steadily up the side of the steep canyon wall. At times, this trail shrank to a matter of inches. There we were in the pitch dark, climbing one step at a time, one step from the edge. My wobbly legs gave me a start on several occasions when I would step but my legs did not. I considered sitting on the canyon wall until dawn. Leave the old one with me and I will watch his tired heart beat until the sun comes up and my legs return to function.

It's easy to see what gets men and women like Mark Moody and Brian Brown to pull on their boots and go 'lay in' in some dark canyon. On the border the goal is always in sight. It's top of mind continuously. Step across the border and you are mine.

On the border everyone knows the score. When the sun

comes up, agents check for tracks and count how many made the trip north. Then they compare that with the number caught and, instant score.

When I asked Brian how he kept score, he simply said, "You can count 'em."

On the border there is a definite sense of position that goes beyond rank. Out in the eastern county, it's as simple as good guy/bad guy.

I like to think that we could all work where there is at least the potential of making a difference, where winning is an attainable possibility.

I think about the goofball educators who work on the self-esteem of students, devoting precious class time to baking cookies and other nonsense. What they fail to realize is that self-esteem comes from being able to produce or perform. How could a kid who can't read, write or add have any self-esteem? And baking cookies isn't going to do it. Nope. Human beings in any endeavor thrive on their ability to see results and solve problems.

On the border, the U.S. Border Patrol has done more for management than a jillion consultants could ever do. They've made winning possible again.

Operation Gatekeeper has turned the tide; not just the tide of illegals who used to cross our border with absolute impunity, but also the tide of morale among the good guys. Because now they can win. And they do.

On the drive from the station, I remember Brian saying that he had the best job in the world. I agreed that, while he was close, it was I who had the best job. His could only be second. But now, now that my finger has healed and my legs belong again to me, now that my chest does not hurt so much that sleep is difficult, now maybe Brian has a point.

I can't know for sure about who has the best job. But I would bet that if I called him and asked him to help me write, that he would say no, that he has other things to do.

And I know that if he called me and said that he needed a little help, well, I would be there by nightfall!

4

A Different Kind of Freedom

Three times we threw the little Mooney against the powerful weather front. Three times we failed miserably.

Sometime early in the morning a norther had blown its way across the western plains of Texas, sweeping over the Edwards Plateau, rolling through old San Antonio and on to the east. The house shook and rattled. Rain tapped against the tin roof urgently. By first light, the storm was gone. History.

All that was left was a dawn as crisp and clear as the newest morning ever. It was a great day for flying. There was a lot of lift in the cool morning air and you could see to forever and beyond.

We nearly jumped off the runway as I pointed the Little Girl's stubby nose eastward. Our first stop would be New Orleans. Dinner would be on the western Florida coast.

By the time Austin handed us to Houston Center, we had already heard hints of weather. Actually it was far more than a hint. I watch The Weather Channel as a religious rite and I don't take the little Mooney out of the hangar without a complete weather briefing. Something big was ahead but from here, 11,000 feet over nowhere, the sailing was smooth as a baby's bottom.

The Stormscope started first. A handful of little green crosses popped onto the screen and died in green phospor before more than a few managed to accumulate. Then there were more...and more...and more. The screen glowed brighter and greener by the minute as I keyed the buttons to switch the view from 200 nautical miles and 360 degrees through the full range...120 degrees and 25 miles.

The Stormscope is an instrument you play, clearing the screen, switching through the various ranges in order to get the best view, in hopes the display will not instantly repopulate with those damnable green crosses, each one marking the spot of serious electrical activity. Okay, *lightning*, if you need a more precise word.

"Five-mike-kilo needs to deviate 10 degrees south for weather," we advised the controller and started into the turn even before hearing, "Deviation for weather as necessary approved" followed by, "Advise when on course."

We took 10 degrees to the south. Then another and another. We turned north for a while but no matter what we did, the damned green crosses jumped in our way. Twenty minutes later and Houston was somewhere to the...south? An incredible line of tall and dangerous thunderstorms blocked the way east.

The charts and GPS confirmed that Lake Charles was a few miles north. Somewhere under the thick blanket of clouds was enough runway for a Mooney. We decided to wait out the storm over lunch.

The ceiling was 300 feet. (That means that when you finally slip from the bottom of the clouds, Mother Earth is waiting only seconds away.)

Chirp, chirp. The gentle sound of a perfect landing reminded me that learning to fly on instruments alone was the best thing I had ever done, other than marrying Melanie. She, of course, was sitting in the right seat, keeper of charts and faith, companion and friend, an adventurer who is ready to go anytime I give the word.

In Lake Charles (LCH) we found Steamboat Bills not more than a few hundred yards from the runway and, in terms of charm, service, and catfish po'boys (a wonderful sandwich) about a million miles from Los Angeles.

Four hours and a lot of pilot talk later, we lifted off to try again. Again the sky was crisp and clear. I think the Germans say, "Die luft ist klar und die himmel ist kuhl," or something equally phonetically incorrect!

Over New Orleans, (MSY, Moissant Field), the sky was again dark and full of moisture. First a gentle pat on the aluminum hide of the Mooney and then an incessant drumming as the rain turned from shower to storm while the sky turned to pitch.

"All right, everybody. Listen up!"

Controllers just don't talk like that and rarely do they speak to more than one aircraft at a time. But this controller did and there wasn't a pilot on the frequency who didn't immediately get that this was the entree to something unusual.

"They're closing the airport. Again. Everybody just maintain your course and altitude and I'll start assigning holding instructions. Southwest..." Then followed a litany of holding instructions, one flight after another. Most were commercial flights. Big iron, two pilots.

They say that the toughest thing to do is to fly an airplane single-handedly in instrument conditions. I believe it. There are charts to juggle, instruments to set and check, radioes to monitor, set, and respond. Plus there is the constant need to simply fly the plane. Compound all this with the fact that in a storm, the plane is not exactly behaving itself. If turbulance gets hold of your metal cocoon, it can get too rough to accurately adjust the instruments. That, of course, separates the amateur from the pro, maybe even the quick from the dead, and definitely makes flying a challenge.

And that's what makes instrument flying fun. It's no pushover, point-it-and-go, namby-pamby exercise. You actually get to fly!

When it was our turn, we were vectored deeper into the darkness, straight to the VOR and told to hold with our choice of radial and leg length. The controller was too busy to think for everyone.

"Five-mike-kilo can go to Gulfport if your radar shows a hole in this stuff. We'll take a vector to the east," I reported in.

"Five-mike-kilo, fly zero-seven-zero and contact Gulfport Approach on one-two..."

A hole! And we were headed right through it!

Ta da! Better to be lucky than good.

It was still pitch dark outside the cockpit. Only the low green glow of the instruments provided any comfort. Five-mike-kilo continued to bounce but the ride at least seemed smoother knowing that we had the storm front beat.

"Mooney five-mike-kilo..."

(Gulfport Approach was on the air. I bet they were smiling to think that a little Mooney had skipped through a hole even the big iron couldn't find with all their fancy radar.)

"...we have a report of a tornado 10 miles and two o'clock. Say your intentions."

Say my intentions? My intentions! Land this thing!

"Five-mike-kilo requests a little southern hospitality and vectors to the ILS in Gulfport while we look for the chart."

The controller gave us the turn and permission to descend. Figuring that we hadn't exactly planned this stop, he also provided the frequency that would put us on the glideslope.

The rain began again and the lights of Gulfport disappeared in the mist as we flew in and out of the clouds. The

Little Girl did her thing and gently latched onto the electronic beam that was calling her to the runway. At about 600 feet, we broke out of the clouds. It was like bursting through time to enter another world. This one was crisp and sparkling. The air was smooth and someone had left the lights on. Flashing white strobe lights drew us to the runway outlined in white and red, calling us, "This way! This way!"

I couldn't help but think that this must be what the U.S. looks like to someone hiking across the border east of San Diego. The lights of the city must call loudly. The cry of freedom must look like strobe lights to a pilot looking to land in heavy weather.

Freedom must look different to different people. To writers, it may be the freedom to speak and write freely. To entrepreneurs, it may be the freedom to do business without interference. To old men hiking in the desert, it may simply be the freedom to hold your grandchildren.

I thought about these things for just moment and then turned my attention to the business at hand—getting to the next adventure.

5

Of Men and Metal Monsters

D o you remember the old Donovan song, *What a Day for a Daydream?* Some days I live that song. Today was just such a day.

There we were bumping our way above the plains of Iowa in search of an adventure. The little Mooney was purring like a kitten.

They say that the propeller on an airplane is nothing more than a big fan designed to keep the pilot cool. If it ever stops turning, the pilot will immediately start to sweat. Well, I was a long way from sweating.

First of all, the flight was going perfectly and, at this low altitude, it was all I could do to pay attention to anything but the beautiful farmland rolling out beneath our wings.

Stu was slightly less impressed. He was snoozing in the right seat.

Although there was a moment in Memphis that really got Stu's attention and made him snap to it. We had taxied to the run-up area at the end of runway 36 right. I was completing the pre-flight checklist, verifying that the cabin door is locked.

"Stu, I don't think your door is fully locked."

"Yeh, it is," came the typical Stu tough-guy response.

"Are you sure? It looks like the handle might not be fully rotated."

"Yeh, it is. Go ahead."

So I did. When the list was complete, I called the tower and was immediately cleared for take-off. In an instant we were barreling down the runway. At about 80 miles an hour, I pulled the Little Girl's nose up and she jumped right off the pavement.

We weren't a hundred feet off the deck when there was a loud popping sound and the door jerked open.

The slipstream of air rushing along the smooth shape of the cabin held the door close to the plane but at the same time kept Stu from pulling it shut.

His attention was less in shutting doors than in grabbing seat leather with his posterior, if you get what I mean.

"Tower, Mooney niner-five-mike-kilo has a small problem. Our door popped open and we'll need to land."

The winds were calm so the tower cleared us to land on the long east-west runway that serves the huge Federal Express hub.

There is a cool trick for shutting the door. Yank the ailerons to the left while kicking the rudder to the right. This flies the airplane sideways and causes the air to push directly against the door so it can be locked. It's a cool trick but hardly appropriate at only a couple of hundred feet.

We elected to land. Stu hasn't missed being WIDE awake for a pre-flight checklist ever since! Once he got over that nasty little incident in Memphis, he has been fine about flying. Only occasionally does he look a little green around the gills, feeling into the pocket on the back of his seat to check that the barf bag is convenient.

Today Stu was just fine. His novel lay open across his lap and a beautiful fall afternoon revealed itself as an autumn carpet in front of my pretty, little Mooney airplane, N95MK.

We had taken off from a small field north of Dodgeville, Wisconsin, home of Land's End and beautiful beyond description. The airstrip was closed when we pointed the nose into the wind for the little Mooney to sniff her way into the darkening clouds. It looked like rain, felt like snow. In a matter of minutes, we were zooming along at a low 4,000 feet, plenty of altitude in this flat country, brushing the bases of the clouds that would soon give way to blue skies over Iowa.

The fields below were a patchwork of green, green grass and golden rows of corn stalks. Barn and silo, field and forest. The patterns looked like whimsy but you knew there had to be science at work. Farmers don't have time to waste painting landscape portraits for passing pilots.

Stu opened one eye, then the other when the air traffic controller in far away Chicago offered another frequency, passing me to Dubuque Approach. Stu has taken to watching the instruments and double checking my radio work. Flying single engine instrument, it's always good to have a second set of concerned eyes.

Below, the roads were arrow straight. Shooting past farm after farm and, suddenly, as if to prove an exception existed, they would arch and curve gently. First one way and then another, rolling around an obstacle until they straightened arrow-like again.

In less than an hour we were handed off to Des Moines Approach control. Our target was the regional airport in Ankeny, Iowa. The GPS on the panel promised concrete in less than six miles although I lied to the controller and agreed that the airport was in sight even though all I could see for sure was another hundred miles of Iowa. But I said "field in sight" and switched to the local radio frequency. (The field was in sight, I just couldn't quite pick it out!)

It's pretty easy to find an airport—look for the power

lines. I think there is a rule that before you build a runway, you have to find power lines to run across the flight path. I hate power lines. And there they were...and there was Ankeny. Beyond was the 66 acres under roof that is the John Deere Des Moines Works, the site of our next adventure. I truly couldn't wait!

You could look at my socks and know that the adventure had begun. It was 4:30 in the morning and there I sat, feet on the bed, pulling on white socks to wear with beat-up work shoes. (When was the last time you wore that combination?)

Our ride showed up right on time. Affable, good guy, Dave Hogan had agreed to be our host for this first adventure. A marketing-type based at the plant, Dave is charged with promoting aftermarket parts for everything that is green and runs like a Deere.

Dave is a big guy with Midwestern friendly plastered across a broad and constantly grinning face. We're both 46 although I couldn't help noticing that I am much better looking!

Other than being our driver and self-appointed host, Dave was our ticket into the expansive John Deere Des Moines Works. Dave had talked the union guys into allowing an interloper, a middle-aged writer tending toward the flabby side, to spend a couple of days working with two of Deere's finest work teams. The first of the two was part of an experiment about to go company-wide called CIPP, Continuous Improvement Process Plan. (I think they could have done with one P but who asked?)

We walked in at 6:30, just in time to catch the CIPP meeting. C-I-P-P. Obviously consultant lingo. Who else would have coined such a term? Continuous Improvement Process Plan. In straight English it means...well, here's the problem. It means different things to different people. To the company, it's a way to wring productivity out of an old process. To the employee, it's a way to wring sweat out of workers already pushed to the max. Funny thing, everybody is right. And everybody is wrong.

For a guy who has always thought that unions are for the terminally weak, suddenly unions seemed to have a place. (Maybe it was the white socks.)

But unions are changing. They have to change.

There isn't room in this economy for an us-versus-them relationship in any company. It's obvious that the rest of the world is no longer bowing and scraping, trying to be economically agreeable, settling for the low wage, no-brainer work and leaving the high-tech thinking to Mother America. So what if kids in China wear Chicago Bulls' shirts? They make the shirts. We make only the magic.

As luck would have it, Department 27, the rake and shovel forge, was the first Deere group to fall under the CIPP program. Luckier still, the day I chose to visit was also the day for a CIPP meeting where the entire department would gather to discuss work goals and processes.

We arrived as a slight, white-haired gentleman, a long-term employee named Charlie, showed up with coffee and comment. I got the impression that Charlie had purchased conversation rights with a pitcher of low lead and another of regular. By 6:30 a.m., the room had filled to overflow. The room was small and the team numbered about a dozen. Add in Stu with his camera and me, and you've got a crowd.

The team had been prepared for my visit so introductions were comfortable. Since I work so often as a speaker, 'first days' on the job come pretty easy for me. Besides, these were obviously friendly guys. Anyone in jeans gets extra points in my book and there wasn't a tie to be found in this crowd!

If we want to keep our high paying jobs at home, there will have to be enormous gains in productivity. Otherwise, the other guys, the ones who pay dirt for wages to offset lower productivity, will end up having United States' jobs and our economy for lunch.

That is exactly what the CIPP meeting was about. To say the least, I was shocked to have been included. Call it part of the new spirit of cooperation between management and labor. Call it an oversight—being allowed to participate and video tape was definitely a surprise.

The department supervisor, Tom, kind of slinked in, taking a chair near the door. The rest of the guys (and they were all guys) managed to squeeze past Tom and slide into their seats, observing some unseen pecking order. At 6:30 a.m., these guys start early.

Tom started the meeting.

A CIPP meeting is unlike any I had seen before. First, Tom may have been in command but he was anything but commanding. I've seen the high-priced consultants do a lot worse than this guy when it comes to facilitating a meeting. And facilitating was exactly what he did.

Although Tom clearly had a prepared agenda, the men in the group were free, make that encouraged, to speak their minds which they did with humor and great understanding of the process.

There was gentle banter wrapped around serious and detailed discussion of—get this—numbers. This motley crew only looked like they had closed the bar. These guys were sharp, with eyes peering out from beneath gimme caps, asking questions about productivity and product flow. I was blown away!

I cupped my hands around a 3x5 card that I had stuffed into my shirt pocket for notes and attempted to be discreet when I wrote, "These guys, all of them, understand the numbers, all of them!"

And that about sums it up. This intimate work group, this team, was as number-savvy a group as you will find in any boardroom. Their personal numbers prove the point. Prior to CIPP, the department production was considerably less than what it is today.

Consulting with the workers, (the true job experts), plant engineers had re-organized the process to speed production and greatly improve productivity. In simple terms, more work from fewer people. Although some of the improvement is definitely of the 'work harder' variety, much comes from working smarter, putting new and old tools to work but better.

A few minutes into the morning, Tom excused himself. I looked around the room and decided that this unlikely crew was not about to run a business meeting without leadership. But they did.

To my left sat Squeak who earned the moniker with his godfather voice, a hoarse whisper that occasionally cracks, a mobster in puberty. There was Gary and Keith, just a couple of guys who would look quite at home in the neighborhood bars that were the stuff of my childhood in Kentucky. Good guys with rough edges. Good guys who really want the company to work and be profitable. Good guys who love their families, plaster Mondale-Ferraro stickers on their lunch pails, and who have the courage to spend one day after another facing off against the hot, metal monsters in the shop in order to put food on the table, and once in a while taking Momma out for dinner.

The talk turned to production. Immediately.

One of the principles behind self-managed teams is to use the combined wisdom of the team to wrest more out of the system. An unspoken principle is that of peer pressure. In a union environment, disciplining slackards is difficult if not impossible. A guy can goof off or smart off and, when nailed by the supervisor, go crying to the union steward who will, usually, defend his 'brother' to the hilt from one grievance procedure to the next until the supervisor says 'to hell with it.'

CIPP turns the tables.

I asked a department veteran if the idea of peer pressure really worked.

"No, not really. I don't like to be in the position to discipline people I have to work with."

When individual pay is based in part on team performance, it seems the crew is much less inclined to vote a straight union ticket, always taking sides along a strictly labor versus management line. Now, with pay and performance tightly linked, they aren't as quick to defend the dear union brother. Everyone, management and labor alike, has a vested interest in performance.

"So, peer pressure doesn't work?"

"Well, we have had a few 'little talks' to clear up matters."

And that was all he would say.

You would expect that personal stuff would dominate this part of the meeting. And there was, I admit, a bit of gripes and complaints that in a marriage would be of the you-left-the-toilet-seat-up variety. But mostly the talk remained focused on production and how it was to be handled, what issues would get priority.

Suddenly, the guys realized that we were deep into private business and asked that we turn off the video camera, which we did. We respect that we were invited guests and will not share further than to say that when a department is organized such that one person can slow the entire team, sometimes you have to offer a word to the wise.

Now CIPP has an unusual feature. Once the team hits its production goal, they receive a cash buy-out. That's the good news.

Then the goal is raised. That's the other news.

Working under such a plan makes everyone aware of the system and their role in making the system work. Suffice it to say that eventually such a team will run into the wall that marks the limit at which a human being can be expected to perform. At first improving productivity is easy. Pick the low hanging fruit by rearranging machines and schedules and, ta da! Instant improvement. But once past the easy stuff, improvement usually requires less cleverness and more muscle.

Everybody knows this. And everybody is thinking about it.

Short term, it means big bucks to both the workers and the company.

Think about it. The company has what is probably the most productive department of its kind and guys with little formal education are dragging down $60,000 a year.

But what happens when this crew of seasoned hands begins to reach retirement and a decade of hiring freeze made possible by productivity gains results in a new set of hands at the controls? I can tell you that if the new guys have all the grace of 'writer boy,' meeting production goals will be more than difficult.

(After two and a half years, production is up an impressive 16 percent. Other figures are even more impressive. Machine maintenance is down 32 percent and waste has dropped an astounding 50 percent!)

When the meeting ended, I was hustled to see the safety guy, another friendly Midwesterner who was as gracious as the day was early. I got the safety rundown, and was quickly outfitted with metatarsal protection, ear plugs, and safety glasses. Boy, was I duded out!

By the time I made it to the shop, the place was jumping. Noise like you can't imagine coming from monster-sized machines and clanging metal that sounded like it was being dropped from great heights on purpose. In a matter of minutes, I was tossed an apron and leather gloves by Gary, another Midwesterner who had spent so many years with these belching machines that he had started to look like them.

My first assignment was to work the bar shear, wrestling long slabs of solid steel into the mouth of a huge shear. Apron, ear protection, shiny metatarsal guards over my shoes, heavy gloves and, oh yes! The glasses.

Line it up, ca-chunk, clank and the first piece falls onto a metal conveyor that sounds like an Army tank in heat. It drops lifelessly into a metal hopper that, when full, will be switched like a miniature railroad car and pushed along a track to a waiting blanking shear.

Ca-chunk, clank; ca-chunk, clank. One loud idea after the other. I thought I was really wailing. "How'm I doin'?" was all I could think. "Writer Boy isn't quite the pansy you thought, huh?"

One ton of steel and two eternities later, Gary moved me

to the next machine. An old guy strapped on the side apron that I had left on the machine and within seconds, it took on the rhythm of a machine gun. ('Guess Writer Boy wasn't so fast after all.)

For the rest of the day, I stamped and pressed, packed and hoisted. My face turned black and my back started to burn. All the while I watched to see what there was to see. Lunch was from 11:00 to 11:30, a little early for my blood, and eaten within 20 feet of the belching monsters of the furnace and press. The guys may just as well have been at Denny's. They bent over the newspaper and shoveled their food as quickly as they moved steel, with the same disconnected lack of attention.

After lunch there was a surprise. We had reached the end of a run and were going to have to change over the equipment.

In many, if not most factories, when the tooling must be changed, the engineers are called. This is complicated, specialized, very precise work. Not something left to some factory grunt who doesn't give a hoot about quality. Not here. Not at Deere. And definitely not in Department 27.

The tool shop was called and within minutes, a cowboy riding a forklift arrived carrying a $30,000 metal die perched at the end of its two long forks. The driver, an engineer, gently deposited the baby and offered to assist but, like Tom, the department supervisor, he did not command.

Puwusssh! The huge, 100 ton press hissed and opened its jaws. Like a dentist working on a tiger, the operator shoved a block of solid steel into the maw just in case the sleeping giant were to awake and snap. A work light was found and within minutes, the surgery had begun. One surgeon, five in the gallery.

When the work was done, a cold blank was shoved into the furnace as a test. Out it shot, red hot and dangerous. The operator snapped it up in long metal tongs and deftly laid it against the 'bumps' in the press. Ca-chunk, pusssssh and the plate was transformed, still red hot, shooting down the line. Six sets of eyes watched as another operator snatched it up and passed it to yet another set of tongs and eyes. A die was pressed into the holes that had been punched by the press.

"Not quite. What do you think?" a sweaty player offered as he tried the die for size first one way and then the other.

"It's okay. But the countersink could be a little deeper. Let's adjust and see what happens."

Now here's the point. These guys could have said 'good enough' and gotten on with the business of piecework. But they didn't. These guys are pros. Real craftspeople of the kind to whom this country owes its greatness and reputation for quality. Made in America still means something and always will as long as men like these haunt the dark shops of department twenty-seven.

The department was down for the better part of an hour while the new die was adjusted, then adjusted again. Finally, when the product was perfect, absolutely perfect, the ca-chunk, clank started again in earnest.

I learned a lot in Department 27 and I noticed even more. One thing that hit me like a ton of steel was how these men had jobs for one reason: there wasn't a machine to replace them.

Okay, so I know that they were grateful to have the job and when it comes to Mother Deere, the entire crew seemed fiercely loyal. And why not? They are well treated, well paid, and have now been given a high degree of control over how, when and in what order their work gets done. You can't say that of many workplaces.

But the thing that hits you is that for most of the day, for most of their lives, these men are machines. Turn and grab, twist and press. One gray steel blank following another.

What does the mind do while the body does such work? Does the mind leave the body? And after working as a machine for so many years, what does this do for the man?

At the other end of the line, finished parts drop with a clatter that is simply unnoticed in the din from the rest of the shop although when I first heard it, I asked if we were near a railroad track; it's that loud, like a train hustling through your living room.

Keith reached a gloved hand into the hopper of confused parts and fished out a couple of samples. Then we slipped into a quiet room just off the work area. Quiet spaces at Deere are few and far between. Inside, Keith cozied up to a computer keyboard that ultimately controlled laser-guided measuring equipment, the kind you would expect to find in a pristine laboratory guarded by serious-looking technicians in crisp, white lab coats.

Keith, rough looking, addressed the bank of space age technology to measure the samples for accuracy and hardness.

From the looks of them, you wouldn't expect any of these guys to be monitoring sophisticated computer-based production control equipment. But they did, manipulating the controls with all the grace of the artists that they are. Nor would you expect to see quality control in the calloused hands of the men who produced the product, responsible for blowing the whistle on themselves should their work be ever so slightly out of spec. But they did.

Keith showed me how to read the laser system that measured the parts to a thousandth of an inch. I still don't grasp the importance of such accuracy for something that attaches to a plow. We're digging in dirt, not repairing heart valves!

But I leaned in close, not so much to understand the process as to witness the result. Maybe that is the lesson; that we all need to be connected to our work. That even sweat can be meaningful. And that, so long as it's one of 'our guys' doing the measuring, even if I can't see ole Keith back there, I feel good knowing that what I do counts.

Bingo!

We were right on the money!

I felt as if I had made them myself. In a very small way, I had.

The Rest Of Your Life

"Did you see any job that you would like to do for the rest of your life?"

The union steward was staring at me.

I have the hands of a writer and try as I might, there was no disguising that I was out of my natural surroundings. In spite of the sweat, my Land's End shirt still showed evidence of being laundered and starched. The collars were buttoned down. I wore a braided leather belt. Even the old watch I chose for the duty seemed to tick, "yup-py, yup-py." It was obvious I was new and obvious that I would be a temporary oddity. No doubt something management had cooked up to sample the emotional water in the plant. I guess you could call that 'a spy.' But I wasn't.

I imagined how the workers must feel and wondered if they would open up and talk. Hell, in this thunderous noise, 'talk' would hardly be an issue. I imagined that the attitude would be, 'Well, nobody will say much and besides, let's see if the kid can hang on. It's not likely those skinny arms will move much metal before they give out.'

"That's what these guys do. One job for their entire life," said the steward who was smiling but as serious as a heart attack, still determined to get an answer.

The thought hit me like every ton of metal I had cut, stamped and lifted in the previous eight and a half long hours had suddenly been dropped upon me. One job. Entire life. No, I hadn't thought of it and now that I had, it didn't seem all that attractive.

I thought about the men that I had met. Strong men. Biceps as big as my leg. Even the old farts pushing 60 had bent to the work and pushed more metal through their machines in an hour than I would move in half a shift.

The funny thing is that not one had complained about the work. It was a job. It was their job. And to these men, they were only sorry that there was little likelihood that their children would enjoy, if that's the word, the security of working for Mother Deere.

If they didn't love their work, they didn't hate it either. Here in the heat and noise, the dirt and rough edges of the shovel and rake forge, men lived out their lives pushing metal through machines that were a magnitude bigger and dirtier than the men who fed them, a master/slave relationship without certainty of who played which role.

"Maybe if I could rotate from station to station. Maybe that would make it a little more interesting" I mused. But I knew that I was lying. I couldn't choose this for me. That was the first thought. (To tell you the truth, I have done worse jobs, lots worse.) The work was hard but filling. When the clock allowed you to look for the door, the body was tired but the mind was wide awake, hardly bent after a day of do it and do it again.

Yeah, I could do this. The muscles would respond. The rhythm would get smoother. Yeah, I could do this.

Forty years?

Well, let's not push it.

The forge has a reputation. Like a roach motel, you check in but you don't check out. Not many people volunteer for the jobs that involve cutting thick pieces of metal, heating them in long furnaces until they glow red hot, then smashing them with 100 loud tons until they become the blades you fasten to soil tilling equipment.

One hot part follows another. From gloved hand to the shear cutter. Another gloved hand into the stamp. It's not subtle work. Not snip, zip, and whir. Just smash, smash, and smash again. It's odd that the result of such violence is a plowshare but that is exactly what we were making in the dark recesses of a 50-year-old plant in Department 27 not far from the edge of an Iowa cornfield.

We worked in the field of dreams. Dreams of Winnebagos and endless fishing. Of grandkids and hobbies. Of hustling another eleven tons of metal on the way to retirement.

When I had called my wife Melanie, her first words were, "You sound tired."

No kidding! Actually, this isn't how tired sounds. This is how dead sounds. I was whupped with a capital W.

The fatigue that she thought she heard in my voice had little to do with the fact that I had moved more dead weight in a day than I had in the previous month. Nope, the voice was tired from yelling.

It took me a while to figure why all the guys have such great big voices. They spend their waking hours shouting over the din of hundred-ton presses to get the attention of guys wearing ear plugs! The next time you are sitting in a neighborhood bar quaffing a cold one, look a little closer and take a little longer to cast your judgement on the old boys with still dirty hands. The guys with the big voices aren't looking for attention; they work in the mill! Hell, they think there's something wrong with you!

John Deere...Green!

I had fallen asleep, make that comatose, even before my head hit the pillow. It had been a major struggle to make it to eight o'clock, the magic hour when I get to call Melanie. She wouldn't say so, but the house gets larger when I am gone, growing every night until it is a many-eyed monster that creaks and flaps her awake until the wee hours when boredom and fatigue and sometimes tears lead her to short sleep.

When at last the notebook computer had said its good nights to the crew via modem and the TV winked out, I was beyond zonked. Every muscle I had and a few that must have been on loan ached like there was no tomorrow. But there was tomorrow and damned if it didn't come as early as the day before!

By five a.m., I was up and about, getting set to give Mother Deere another shot at killing Writer Boy. Another pair of white socks, another laundered shirt, only this time the body was different, harder already from a single day of real work. I felt the biceps and imagined more than there was. In the mirror I saw the bruises. Little badges of macho. Reminders that Writer Boy was still alive and ready for more.

Once again, the ever smiling Dave picked us up. What's with a guy who can drive halfway across Iowa to pick you up at God's hour and still look like an Eddie Bauer ad? Is this guy plastic?

Stu was even grumpier than the day before if you can imagine grumpy conjugated all the way to disgust. He shouldered the camera, a light 32 pounds. When you include the battery belt, the weight grows by the hour until, by day's end, it weighs, oh, about a ton.

Not only does Stu get grouchier as the days count by, he gets bigger and bigger until flying in the little Mooney is pretty near like being cast in a block of cement with Jimmy Hoffa.

At the plant we were met by Sam, an affable Hispanic guy who is as Middle America as David Duke. Well, maybe that was a bad example. But get that Sam is pretty much typical Deere...steel-toed boots, work gloves and ear protection.

Sam works a section of a paint department that stretches forever under metal roof and yellowish light.

The business end of the department is a trough of—surprise!—green paint into which an endless parade of parts dip effortlessly only to emerge as green as green can get. A couple of gazillion volts charge the paint and the parts causing the paint to stick pretty much forever.

But that's not what Sam sees or does. For Sam the paint trough could just as well be on another planet. Sam sees nothing much beyond the single line of overhead parts' trolleys that the computer routes into his work area.

Like working in a train yard only upside down, Sam is the loadmaster. Empty trolleys get outfitted with special hangers, then decorated with unpainted parts and sent off to the green monster on the other side of the plant.

Full trolleys, some with warm parts fresh from the drying ovens, switch into his area where he unloads them.

The computer terminal in Sam's area sees all and knows nothing but everything. Sam calls for more parts, the computer says green (yes) or red (no.) Like the Karate Kid gone to work, Sam focuses on the moment. Parts on, parts off. Now, do it again...and again.

Every trolley load means a trip on the forklift, a graceful ballet of steel and men, and they all seem to be men. This is a man's world in yellow light, green parts and gray everything else, including the men who give their lives to the idea of working for a clock.

The whole building is a clock of sorts. Just as a watch counts days in terms of seconds ticked off one at a time, this building counts lives in terms of parts. Parts painted. Parts loaded and unloaded. Parts, parts and more parts. Pay is by parts. Jobs are by parts. Tick, tick, tick. Part, part, part.

The sun doesn't shine, the wind ceases howling. Only the parts and the green, green paint evidence the passage of time.

Sam likes the work. He 'gets his 40' and, that's enough. Hangs out over a few cold ones. Visits his son's Mexican restaurant that Sam assures me is authentic, if there can be such a place in the middle of a white bread state.

While Sam is making 40, the guy in the next department is making hay. A human whirlwind of mindless energy, this character plows straight through lunch, hanging and unhanging, moving more parts per hour than some of his crew will hang in a day.

The supervisor says that the busy fellow will make 25 hours pay this day. In a week, just imagine. In a year, impossible! In a lifetime? He won't live that long. And if he does, will he be able to slow the machine that has gone without rest for so long? Perhaps it will slow itself, automatically reaching some as yet unknown genetic time-out that says "you had dreams to dream and work to do and you spent your total measure hangin' gray and haulin' green."

Here is a study in motivation. One guy 'gets 40.' The other guy is committing suicide in public.

What makes them tick? And why is one ticking with all the rhythm of the tide and the other to the incessant beat of some unknown master? Is it greed? Could it be tragedy or compassion? Who can know what sparks men's souls?

I got another safety session before reporting to the Paint

Department. It may be obvious, monotonous, boring...call it what you want, but it's for darned sure that Mother Deere wants you to keep all your fingers and toes. The very idea of safety was draped like a mantle over everything we did at Deere.

The paint shop is hard work but, unlike Department 27, there is no one about to shove a hot slug of iron down your pants' leg if you can't keep up. This is tough but it's no forge. No Department 27. Nope, the paint shop is for the guys who watch the Bulls and bet on the Cubs. Department 27 is another place altogether.

I left tired but not beat. Bored but not numb.

In the paint department, I could look up occasionally and watch another load of anonymous green parts slide by. There were eleven endless miles of trolley track and no doubt a story for each and every foot. Mother Deere had a winner here. No sweatshop, just hard work well rewarded even if the work itself was not particularly rewarding.

When Dave came to find me, I was ready to go. In the paint shop I had no sense of identity or place. There was no evident purpose to the work other than to feed the monster and tend to her young. Give me the forge where you can see a beginning and an end, where you can count your product and shape it personally, where the team felt like a team after I had left it.

About a mile later we were once again back to my world where people have desks and places to hang their coats and pictures of the family.

Stu wanted to purchase a John Deere Anything for his youngest and Dave wanted me to say 'hello' to the plant manager. On our way out, we met the union steward and his boss from headquarters, a well-fed man with the red cheeks that belong to Englishmen just in from the golf course.

I wondered how many parts the union guy had hung; how many shovels he had fed into the monster presses; how many days his back had hurt all the way through.

And then I guessed that however many days like those

that he had experienced, it was enough so long as he remembered. So long as he stayed in touch with the workers and the work.

How could you not leave this place with a sense of respect? How would it be to manage such a place where profits and people hang in such delicate balance? And what does it say when a man has spent 40 years in a plant, perhaps working the same position, volunteers to work another day, his seventh or tenth in a row?

I would think about these things in the morning when I awoke in El Paso dreaming of green monster trolleys and gray machines that prowl for wayward hands. But now I had a Mooney that wanted to fly and another adventure that called from the West beyond the mountains.

6

Just to the West

The work you do is working you.

Yep, I'm sure of it. If there was a lesson to be learned at Deere, it has to be that shaping metal shapes the soul. As does hanging parts, assembling components, checking inventories. Whatever you do is doing you.

We were tired. Probably too tired to fly when we lifted from the long concrete runway in Ankeny a few miles from the plant. We should have planned on staying another day but neither Stu nor I are much for sitting. And we both knew that no sooner would we have taken off our shoes and flipped on The Weather Channel (for me), CNN (for him), we would have caught our second wind and wondered why we didn't just fly.

So we flew. Tired, but not too tired to squeeze in a few hours of air time. A few hours would get us that much closer to the next adventure.

We flew and, for a while, said very little.

Stu and I talk very little while at work. We save that for dinner when I usually ask, "What do you think?" And we both attempt to give meaning to the things we did and people we met.

We were well beyond Des Moines Approach Control before either of us said a word.

The most amazing thing I had seen was the 125 ton press. Not that it was huge, although that was impressive, and not that such precision could come from a machine that looks to be little more than a collection of used locomotive parts. No, what captured my attention was the operator who spent eight hours or more in endless repetition.

Forty feet away a man toiled lifting metal blanks from a huge metal cart on tracks and placing them onto a metal conveyor. The cart, the blanks, the conveyor, and the man operating it were all gray. As gray as a winter sky, that kind of gray. Not much form. Not much to distinguish one from the other. A few lines on the metal blanks, a few more on the men at either end of the machine.

At one end, the man (and they were all men) lined the blanks onto the conveyor, staggering them much as you would place bricks on a wall. One after another, never leaving a space, an endless march of steel rectangles about the size of a shoe box, about the weight of a lawn mower.

The conveyor disappeared into an oven. I don't know how long but it was long. I do not remember how long it took to cook from one end to the other but it might have been several minutes. It didn't matter. What mattered was that there was no break in the action. Every three or four seconds the gray man at the gray end placed another piece of gray metal on the gray conveyor.

Every three or four seconds the gray man at the other gray end reached out and lifted a now red, glowing blank with long gray tongs. His motions were quick, fluid as if the heat from the nearby oven had melted his muscles. He held the tongs tightly in gloved hands, wearing an apron that might have had color at one time but now had none other than gray. Like the others, the man wore safety glasses and hearing protection. An office this was not.

With a red-hot blank firmly grasped in the long, gray tongs, the man at the far end would pivot, maybe 60 degrees and deposit his catch into the jaws of the 125 ton press. Beneath the metal apron bolted to the machine's face, a gray work boot stepped on a pedal, signalling to the machine that the prey had been caught. With a rumbling hiss, the huge jaws instantly snapped, bending the still red blank over an expensive metal die. It was almost shocking how quickly the jaws would respond to the signal from the pedal on the shop floor. You would think there would have to be a getting ready, a build-up of steam or whatever. But no, this monster was poised, waiting to snap. And it did, with the slightest of provocation.

The press would snap and, just as quickly retreat, a giant trap, opening and then gone, returned to innocence.

The instant the jaws rolled back, a blast of compressed air spit the blank from the face of the die onto yet another gray conveyor.

The process repeated and repeated. Endlessly forever, the man turned and reached, snatched and turned again. Placed and pushed and turned for more.

Man as machine.

Man, there only because there wasn't a machine yet, that could do the job.

"What does he think about all day?" It was Stu or me doing the asking of a question that went unanswered. Who could know what a man thinks whether he is feeding metal onto a conveyor, shoveling it into a press, bending or breaking or painting or whatever? It is metal not mind that counts.

Man as machine.

I promised to watch the next time I played a game like this to see what I was thinking, if anything. I couldn't remember what I had been thinking when I had taken my turn. I do remember that even when I was working on a giant cutter, stamping out God knows what kind of part, all I was thinking about was the motion, getting my hand in, lining the metal up perfectly, getting my hand out in spite of the laser beam that would override the pedal, and then, face turned, stepping on the pedal. I remember that. But I can't imagine thinking about that and only that for an entire shift much less an entire lifetime.

And the big voices. Already I had caught myself yelling on the phone and it wasn't because of a poor connection. I had become suspicious of management, thinking that there was little use to tell them about my experience as they were unlikely to understand while sitting in the office. Without work boots and metatarsal protection, without apron and eyeglass and ear plugs, what could anyone know about the work and the workers who pushed gray metal into gray machines turning their entire lives into a 40-year long gray blur with little memory of the factory, dreaming only of the fishing and the Winnebago?

For now, I let the Little Girl fly herself straight into a setting sun.

An hour or so into the flight, I started to fidget with the charts, dreaming of flying first east then west, stopping at little green airports with tiny restaurants and friendly voices. Somewhere with chicken-fried steak and cream gravy.

To the east there is such a place. Melanie and I had landed there once.

The job was a simple keynote and, perhaps because it was so simple, I decided to up the ante.

When we checked in, I asked for the food and beverage manager.

"Hi! I'm speaking in the ballroom in a few hours and, since I have not yet met my client in person, I was wondering if you could help me play a little surprise."

To make the surprise work, we decided to tell the client

that I was running late, that I was in my room and would be down to speak ten minutes before scheduled and not to worry. There was a break scheduled prior to my speaking, so with a little help from the food and beverage manager, I was fitted with a fine waiter's uniform and introduced to help serve the break. Perfect!

The break went fine. That's not the story.

The story belongs to a pretty, young server wearing a name tag that said, "Desiree."

"Desiree. That's a pretty name. Is that French?"

"It's French. My mom picked it because she loves French."

"Does it translate into English?"

She looked at her feet and said, as if there were reason to be embarrassed, "It means the awaited one."

I let the pause go too long.

It took her a second to say, "And who are you?"

"My name is Scott. It means he who hardly works!"

You would have thought that I had hit her with a board. Her head whipped around. I had her total attention.

"Does it really?" This was more exclamation than question.

"No, but why the reaction?"

"Oh, nothing." She looked back at her feet, retreating to wherever young women go when they feel hurt. "It's just that my fiancee is named Scott, and he hardly ever works. I thought you were talking about him."

"I see." This was my best facilitator's routine. Wait patiently. Don't rush to fill the silence. Let the silence fill itself.

"Ever since he moved in, he just goes fishing with his buddies. Sometimes he does things for his friends but not too often. Mostly he just lays around the house waiting for me to come home to cook dinner."

"Let me guess. You think this will change when you are married?"

"Won't it? Won't he want to get a job and save for a house and, you know?"

I knew. I really knew and the answer was n-o.

"Desiree, I hate to tell you this but what you see is what you get."

She looked at her feet which, to this point, had been getting most of the attention in this conversation.

"Do you mind if I ask you why you want to marry this guy?"

"He's the only one who asked." She said this as if her saying no to this character would have been a sentence to lifelong spinsterhood.

"Quick quiz. Do you think about him constantly? Can you hardly wait to see him when you get home? Are you bursting with pride when he goes to see your mom? Okay, I can tell by your response that your answers are no, no, and no.

"Look, I have a son your age so I could easily be your dad. Do you mind hearing from your dad for just a minute?"

She said no but I'm not certain that she wanted to hear more. It didn't matter. I had more that she was going to hear, no matter what.

"You are not in love 'cause if you were, you would be thinking about your fellow all day. You wouldn't be able to wait until you see him at the end of the day and you would be parading him everywhere.

"Think about your Scott and ask yourself if this is your idea of how you want to spend the next 30 or 40 years, because, trust me, it isn't going to change."

She could barely look up. I knew that I had hit the mark and that it hurt. I felt sorry.

"Has anyone, even your Scott, mentioned that you are a charming, attractive, young woman?"

No answer.

"Well, you are. Now what are you going to do with that?"

Before she could answer, the doors to the meeting room burst open and out poured my audience-to-be. Desiree and I worked side by side, playing with the folks as we served up sodas and fun. She had quite a flair for entertaining. All she needed was a partner who would encourage her.

When the crowd began to shuffle back to the meeting room, I knew it was time to start the clean up and head for my real work. As I tore off my apron and started to say my good-byes, a tall, charming, attractive, and now smiling, young woman swept to my side and took my arm. She put her face close to mine so that there would be no missing her words.

"Thank you. I made an important decision today. Thanks, Dad!"

She hugged me briefly. I handed her my apron and waiter's coat and hoped that she had indeed gotten more from me than dirty laundry. You can never really know about these things, only hope.

I thought about Desiree and her choices as we flew into the western sun and felt instantly warmer. Maybe it was the sun.

7

Big Wheel, Good Night

Whatever is your image of a carnie—the folks who give the carnival life—forget it. Not that it's inaccurate but because it's probably unfair.

I would flip the lever and lift the six lighted arms one more time, around and around and around. I laid on the buzzer attracting an ever growing, late evening crowd. There is art, call it showmanship, even in the running of a kiddie ride.

Sweating through my shirt, I was proud to be doing good work, lighting little eyes, making moms and dads smile. And, even though I had sweat a bucket of water and my contacts were so fogged that I thought of David Carradine in a cheap kung-fu movie, I still mustered the energy to make every ride special.

He was leaning on the rail, all Yuppie and clean. I had just forgotten to hate people who were clean when this ugly mug leaned a little too emotionally close for the moment. He wore one of those braided belts that are too long. (What are they trying to say? "I lost a lot of weight? I can afford more belt than I need? I borrowed this belt from my father?")

"Pretty dummy job, wouldn't you say?"

I didn't even look up. It wouldn't have mattered. My contacts were so thoroughly fogged from a gallon of sweat that it was all I could do to see the little ones held captive by the dragons of Peter-Paul. Instead, I did a slow burn and considered my options, up to and including dismemberment.

Too much effort, I decided.

"You could call it that. I admit it's not exactly rocket science. Are you a rocket scientist?" I wanted to add, 'dumb ass' but did not since I was, after all, wearing a 'show shirt.'

I was hoping that he had a really ugly job or, better yet, was a banker who had been downsized and was attending the carnival on severance pay.

"Yes, I am," gloated Big Boy, leaning even closer to show off expensive dentistry. "I work on the Iridium project. Do you know what that is?"

This sounded like an offer for a lesson in terms simple enough for a carnie to handle.

"I read about that just this morning in the *Wall Street Journal* when I flew my plane into Chandler." I figured I'd let him stew over that one.

"Motorola really bet the farm on that one," I replied, never taking my eyes off the kiddos in my command. "Did you see what it did to your stock yesterday? You guys really took it in the shorts."

Now it was my turn to show off. I had him cold.

"Say, exactly how many satellites will it take to make that puppy work?"

"I'm not exactly sure," came a stammered response that was more surprise than answer. Who would expect a dumb-head carnie to know about advanced communications projects and stock markets?

"Well, I guess it's like working here. They don't let the

little guys know everything. It must be a pretty dummy job, wouldn't you say?"

He leaned away from the gate. I let the kids down. Lard butt walked off not wanting to bother the carnie further with things too difficult to understand.

We had slipped over the mountains early in the morning. The night before we had only made it as far as El Paso. From Iowa we had flown south and west to Amarillo where we took on another 50 gallons of go juice and filed another leg of the flight plan. I had intended to use satellite technology to navigate arrow straight all the way to the Texas border and a Mexican dinner but the United States government had slightly other plans.

Less than three minutes into the blinding sunset, the controller gave us a vector to pick up a victor airway and amended our clearance. He said that the government was jamming GPS signals in a 300 mile area and that we would have to switch to traditional navigation to remain where their radar could find us.

Fine.

As long as we made it to El Paso in time for dinner, I didn't particularly care which way we did it. El Paso is one of my favorite places of all. I love the people in El Paso. I love the food. And when the great summer storms are terrorizing the high desert like gray battleships in the sky, I love that long, beautiful runway, two-six left.

By the time we had El Paso in sight, the night was as dark as coal. The sun hadn't actually set. It simply dropped like a rock and suddenly the light on the pale desert sand was switched off. Stuart, not a fan of flying in the dark, gave up his napping to stare straight ahead, in case I hadn't quite calculated where the granite clouds were waiting.

The controller cleared us for runway two-six left and then, on short final, asked us if we could side step to two-six right so that a Southwest flight, (our other company plane), could use the longer one on the left. No problem, just juke a half mile to the right and set her down gently. No problem, except that the shorter, narrower runway to the right had just been resurfaced and not yet marked. It was blacker than the night. It had end lights and a few other markers but the black surface just sucked up our landing lights.

I could not see the runway surface, only the edges so I flew by the numbers. The trick is to fly the airplane right to the ground, controlling the rate of descent so that when you arrive, the flight ends gently. It works, in theory.

Seventy knots on the button. Nose up just slightly, flaps full out for a stable rate of descent. Then a familiar 'chirp, chirp.' The wheels touched and we landed literally before I knew it. (There is something to be said for following the rules!)

"Stu? You wanna get out and see if we've landed?" I teased.

Before we had the baggage unloaded, the ramp guys had the fuel truck lined up along Little Girl's graceful wing, topping her off for an early morning run to Chandler, Arizona. As we walked across the tarmac, which was dark in spite of the yellow glow of the building lights, I thought about how this work, my work, might be shaping me. And, here under a clear desert sky, I liked the idea.

In El Paso, Stu and I tipped Carlos to haul us to dinner, someplace authentic. Someplace like Forti's Mexican Elder, lost in the barrio and time, where the very idea of Tex-Mex food must have been born. There's nothing like a good meal and cold tea to wash down a long day. We listened to laughter in Spanish and then in English.

That's the thing about happy. It doesn't really come in languages or colors. This laughter was as rich and smoky as the salsa that I scooped into thin, greasy chips. Just the way I like them. I caught myself, lost in the idea of people loving one another, laughing over chips and salsa so that the salsa I dipped tasted even better.

We floated on fair weather clouds all the way from El

Paso to Chandler, Ariz., where we were slam dunked by air traffic control.

The frequencies were crowded with weekend fliers trying desperately to maintain their independence from the big iron pilots at nearby Sky Harbor (Phoenix's main terminal.) From the ground, the two tiny Chandler airports are a world away from Phoenix. But even from as high as a few thousand feet, you can look northwest and see the long parallel stretches of concrete that Southwest and the rest of the usual suspects call home.

So I should have anticipated that our descent would closer resemble an elevator than an airplane. The first Approach Controller told me to hold my request for lower altitude until the next controller down the line accepted the little Mooney into his airspace. This only delayed the problem of fitting the Little Girl into the aerial ballet that is danced through the airspace around every big city.

By the time the second controller accepted the hand off, the GPS display told the story. We were way too high to consider a normal approach.

(Little planes, and maybe big ones, can be easily damaged if the pilot pulls off too much power, causing the engine to cool rapidly. The result is a tortuous battle between the different metals in the engine as they cool, one faster than the other. We're probably not talking one ten-thousandth of an inch but that's all it takes to tear an engine apart.)

I pulled a little power and glued one eye on the temperature gauge. Nose up to lower the speed enough to drop the gear, then, configured nice and dirty, the little Mooney had at least a chance of sinking fast enough to make the Chandler airport just off her nose.

The tower cleared me for a visual landing and agreed that I could swing wide for a long downwind run, in hopes of dropping enough altitude to land without diving.

I almost made it!

With less than a quarter of a mile to the numbers painted crisply on the end of the runway, we were still way too high. I poured on the coals and announced my intention to go around.

(They say that every landing should be planned with the potential for a go-around in mind. I could have made it, but why? Just go-around and do it again. No big deal.)

Tied down and fuel ordered, we hit the tiny restaurant and felt as if we had walked onto the set of *Wings*. We grabbed a quick breakfast before hitting the midway. Already the air was hot and thick, a portent of the day to come.

We called a cab and were instantly lost. Oh, the driver could find the carnival, all right, we just couldn't quite figure how to get in. Finally, luck rolled right past us in the form of a huge semi rig that labored under an even larger, blue weight. A sign on the side said, "Kamikaze" and if that isn't carnival stuff, I wouldn't know what is.

When we first met the folks at Ray Cammack Shows (RCS), they were at the Los Angeles County Fair for a long run, long enough that the show bosses had taken the time to tuck their headquarters' trailers under a huge, yellow canopy, rolling out yards of artificial turf with hundreds of exotic plants for decor, finishing the look by dotting several decorative water fountains among the plants.

Tell me. Does this fit your image of a carnival?

Inside the clean, white trailers with distinctive logos, were offices that rival any you might see in business. Why? Because the carnival is a business. Big business.

By the time we found the office, a small crowd had gathered around the big blue thing that was bound in yards and yards of new blue vinyl and white nylon rope.

It turned out to be a new ride, the Kamikaze, a half million dollars of lights and hydraulics, sound system and computerized controls, all the way from Italy.

"Hi! I'm Scott Gross. I can see you have your hands full. If you have some grunt work, I can make myself useful."

"Start untying this thing. I'll talk to you later. We've been looking for this ride for a week." I had no idea who was giving the order but it was all the invitation I needed to dive right in as one of the boys.

I started untying and sweating. It was more sweat than work. The sun was a killer and it was only ten o'clock.

When the ride was finally unpacked, the boss handed me off to another supervisor, Tony Fiori, who in turn sent me to the commissary for a uniform.

By then, my hands were as black as the shirt was white.

"Ma'am, there's no way I can put this shirt on without getting it filthy. Where can I wash up?"

The lady behind the counter just looked at me. Her office was like a stopper shoved into the side opening of a semi trailer, holding back a mountain of uniform clothing she seemed to be guarding with her life. (I guess she was!) The carnival was her life. She looked at me as if I had just landed and asked to be taken to her leader.

If you have an image of a carnie as dirty, you're right. Sanitation is a huge problem. Carnies aren't dirty people, but they work in some truly godawful dirty places. Think about it. You have an operation that may involve several hundred people and it's located on a lot or a field that only yesterday may have grown corn or oats. Now, transformed in a matter of hours, it has a new, more vibrant life all its own...but still, no water.

"I can give you some Baby Wipes," said the lady planted in the side of the truck. "They're great in a pinch and, out here, everything is a pinch!" Finally the smile came, cascading down a face that had seen a quarter of a century of carnivals and God knows how many carnies.

My instinct was to look for a place to change when I realized that the step to her rolling warehouse was as close as this city boy was about to get to privacy. I whipped off my sweat-stained shirt and replaced it quickly with what RCS calls a show shirt. (You would call it a nice polo shirt.)

A bright yellow hat topped the bill. Suddenly, ta da! I was a carnie.

Lurking in the shade of a once brightly painted trailer, a huge man waited to assign me to my station. In the first few seconds I understood that there would be no punches pulled for Writer Boy. I expected to work a fabulous ride and was immediately disappointed to learn that I was to work Raiders, a conglomeration of playground ideas smooshed onto the back of a mostly yellow semi-trailer, stacked nearly 40 feet high. The whole package was wrapped in the blaring music of a tape loop playing the theme from *Raiders of the Lost Ark*.

A large man with biceps the size of my waist pointed without looking. There may have been a grunt or something but all I remember is being sent out of the shade and south along the midway. Did he actually mouth the words 'Peter-Paul' or was it heat induced telepathy? Whatever, my first day as a carnie was off to a hot start.

I was assigned to the middle level where I worked a position that I can only describe as "encourager."

Below me, Jerry took tickets.

Jerry is a brick shy of a load. He works with Charlie who is a load shy of a brick. These guys fit the appearance of the stereotypical carnie. Dirty, a little short in the pretty department, yet two of the nicest guys that you will meet anywhere.

Young children by the hundreds pushed and shoved their way onto Raiders, past the swinging tackle dummies, up the ramp, charging into the rope ladder, then down the slide, up the stairs and two flights of swinging cable bridges. And finally, with Charlie assisting with the line up, they slid down the covered slide to Mom and Dad and safety.

I worked the middle level, pushing and encouraging little people to tackle a rope ladder that to some must have looked a mile high.

For four hours straight, I lifted and prodded one kiddo after another. Jerry and Charlie, my buds, carried little ones across the rope bridge, even let them sit on their chests and ride them down the slide in those cases when courage ran shorter than the ride.

Children of all descriptions were charmed by the bright lights and loud music of Raiders. It was big and imposing but the little ones recognized things from the local playground and almost all of them felt up to the challenge. Little ones, sweet as candy, dressed in flowered hats and overalls. Little ones, already hard from the city, pierced ears and heavy metal T-shirts. Little ones.

Two fetal alcohol syndrome children limped and scraped their way onto the ride. They stopped cold at the base of the rope ladder, an obstacle bigger than life. It was the kind of thing that would bring a torrent of hateful taunting at school.

I remembered being in second grade and asking for permission to use the restroom one cold winter morning. When I went into the boy's room, there, sitting on a pot with his pants around spindly legs, sat a deaf kid about my age.

I had seen him at school but never had a chance to know him other than that the kids would sometimes tease him, which I thought was unbearably cruel.

As I turned to leave, the school bully swaggered in and, immediately spying a target poised on the pot, raced over and stuck an index finger in each of the helpless boy's ears, taunting and teasing. It was more than I could take. Before I could think, I jumped and punched him.

A bloodied bully ran. I was pretty surprised myself. And Stevie, the deaf kid, now my friend, smiled a thank you.

Now, here I stood. It was 1958 all over again.

Standing by Jerry, the kids' parents lit up yet another cigarette. (People with one addiction usually have two.) I thought I would just jump over the rail and strangle them until I felt better.

The little girl, nine or ten years of age, had tears in her eyes. Her brother was too frightened to cry so I cried for him.

We held hands and climbed the ladder. Sister, brother, friend.

"You can do it," said the encourager in the bright yellow show hat. "I'm right here to help you and when you get to the top, Charlie will be waiting. You can do it."

And they did. And suddenly there was a connection between the work and and the worker. The product was a smile of triumph belonging to two children who would have to conquer greater obstacles than a rope ladder and a swinging bridge and who, for just a moment, suddenly felt worthy and whole.

Kids are amazing. They can mantle. Mantling is the technique used by rock climbers to hoist themselves up to rock shelves. You keep your body close to the rock and do a vertical push-up until you can get a leg over the edge. Kids do this naturally.

And they work together as teams, naturally.

What in the world is it that causes adults to have to relearn so much of what came with the package?

From my vantage point, I could see quite a bit of the carnival and, in between little customers, I caught glimpses of carnival life. Here's a funny thing about the carnival; there is no waste. No wasted effort, or money, or space. Guess what was in the huge lockers under the trailer that is the foundation for the giant slide? Giant bags of giant baking potatoes! It figures that the food joints have to keep supplies somewhere. But who 'da thought?

Guess how the carnie world knows when to call it a night.

When the ferris wheel lights go on, it's time to clean up and close. The wheel is the one thing that can be seen from anywhere in the carnival.

Guess where the mechanic who keeps the bumper boats running calls home? A six by ten curtained 'apartment' in the front end of the semi-trailer that doubles as his shop and is used to transport the ride in between show dates.

Elegant it's not but it is home. And he's proud to show it off. TV, magazines and sleeping bag. What more could you want?

Well, you might splurge for a room at The Palace. The Palace is a semi-trailer outfitted with ten apartments and a landlord's suite in the front. Each has its own lockable door, bunk and locker, lights and air conditioning. The showers, of which there are two, and restroom are shared. Again, it may not be fancy, but we're talking home!

I watched the sun creep across the heating metal and tried to stay out of its reach. Someone thought to fill two huge coolers with ice water and set them on the back of the trailer, a nice thought that would have been even nicer had it included refills.

By noon the water was gone and the scrounge began with one carnie looking out after the other when water or a cup could be found and graciously shared. During the course of the first day, I drank, by my count, nearly a gallon and a half of water and only went to the bathroom once, and that was merely out of habit. In the shade it was 103° and we had little shade. The poor sucker over at the Peter-Paul had no shade at all.

The Peter-Paul is a simple ride with a funny name. When I say 'Peter-Paul', who do you think of? Of course! And what was their most famous song?

The Peter-Paul consists of six dragon carriages stuck to the octopus arms of a mechanical beast. The beast snorts and jerks and swings around a brightly colored center pivot, each arm supported by a powerful hydraulic piston, something you might expect to raise the bed of a dump truck or a part purloined in the night from abandoned construction equipment. Take away the colored lights, the blaring speakers, and the multiple coats of tasteless paint, and carnival rides are little more than factory equipment on LSD. Instead of moving dirt or metal, parts or assemblies, they move children for moms and dads. Kids can't wait, moms and dads can.

Carnival rides shake and spin, rolling and reversing until we are pinned against the padded seats close to the things that frighten us most.

Melanie's dad always warned that laughter brings tears. Yet what is an amusement ride if it isn't an orchestrated attempt to hurl us faster and faster along the border between that which makes us laugh and that which scares us witless?

For kids, the rides are violence in small scale, scary but not terrifying. For most of the two-, three- and four-year olds that I hoisted into the dragons, the Peter-Paul was just fine, thank you. For some of the youngest, even the gentle Peter-Paul was a bit too much and their moms or dads would squeeze in beside them, coaxing them into believing that they really were riding in a dragon and were having fun.

By the time I made it to the Peter-Paul, I had already put in the better part of a day's work further up the midway, with no sign that it was about to end anytime soon. I was beat. Ten plus hours with little break, the last half spent unloading cranky children from the Peter-Paul, only to turn and load again. Non-stop. Only the short duration of the ride afforded a chance to sit, although you couldn't for an instant take your eyes from the beast itself. And there were the twelve to eighteen little ones who depended on you to swing them safely and gently around and around. You had to watch them...like a hawk.

Come to think of it, there was no place to sit. You could lean but that's about all.

Pwushhhh! The giant hydraulic cylinders would hiss. Purple and red, green and yellow dragons dropped a little lower, their red, electric eyes still flashing after a long summer of endless children.

Just as I was thinking that the Peter-Paul must be the worst place to work, my supervisor, all nine feet tall and size seventeen shoes, decided that if one poor sucker on the Peter-Paul was good, two poor suckers would be twice as good. He assigned me as Assistant Sucker.

Funny, but I didn't want to take responsibility for actually running the ride. John, Chief Sucker in the Sun, a quiet man who was lost in the downsizing of the aerospace industry, seemed perfectly content to run the show while I hustled little kids off and more little, dead-weight kids on.

Two or three to a dragon. Seat belts buckled and checked. Checked again and then thumbs up to John. Around and around, barely long enough to catch a breath before the process was repeated, unload and load. Check and check again. Thumbs up.

Around a million o'clock, the big guy, Howard, suggested that I take lunch (or dinner or whatever.) Howard is a former employee of the RTC, Resolution Trust Corporation, the government guys who bailed out the bankers a few years ago. He's a sax player, claims to be a pretty good cook at the barbeque and father to a hundred or so of the carnies who climb up and around the colored metal frames in the kiddie side of the operation.

I headed to Jack in the Box and ordered a quick meal before noticing the sign that announced "restrooms closed." Damn! I was dreaming about a place to wash my hands, maybe rinse my contacts if the place was clean enough. Tough luck, they were closed.

I had passed two portable toilets on the parking lot and now, seeing an employee unlock the restroom to use it, I realized that the restrooms weren't out of order. Like the sign said, they were only closed.

"Excuse me. May I please use your restroom? I would like to wash my hands before eating."

"They're closed. Use the portables out on the lot."

"Yes, I noticed. But there isn't a place to wash in the portable. May I use the restrooms to wash my hands? I'm pretty dirty."

"Sorry. My supervisor said to close the restroom."

"Let's see if I understand this. If you aren't busy, a clean restroom is included in the price. But if you have a carnival in town, restrooms aren't available. Did I get that right?"

"They're closed."

"I don't want to make a big deal out of this and I know I'm just carnival trash, but I happen to know that you are required by law to have restrooms, male and female, handicap accessible, with hot and cold running water, soap and either paper towels or a dryer."

"They're closed."

I ate with dirty hands and a hatred of anyone who could be so callous as to do such a thing. More than the food, which wasn't particularly good, I wanted to wash my hands and feel clean again.

Closed. If I hadn't been the guest of RCS, there would have been a battle and I can promise you those restrooms would have been opened. But for the moment, for the carnies and the hundreds of other guests that brought sales and profits to the party, the restrooms remained closed.

The carnival is pure experience. No brain work, just fun.

Light and sound, color and motion all working together to excite and attract. Good operators blow the whistle, crank the music, and make their surrogate arms and legs dance to the hiss of hydraulic fever. From a distance and especially at night, the carnival is a thing of beauty, pulsating with energy supplied by generator trucks hidden just beyond the colored lights. But up close, and after ten or so hours standing on your feet, the carnival still looks beautiful.

This is good work. Carnival work is work for the soul as well as the body. The body sinks and sags but it's always able to deliver an unexpected burst when needed. True, this is not rocket science but it is people science. Take all your psychology and stuff it.

As for psychology, the folks who milk the midway for a living are the earth's true retail psychologists.

They call them joints, the games that line the midway. The ones made of painted two-by-fours, draped in colored canvas are called stick joints. Every midway carnie dreams of owning his or her own joint. Carnies working the joints are paid strictly on commission. Goof off tonight and forget about eating tomorrow. As salespersons, midway carnies are the best.

Call yourself a customer if you wish, but on the midway and in the eyes of a carnie, you're a 'mark.' Pure and simple, a target of convenience.

Think about it. A carnie has all of about three seconds to

say or do something to grab your attention. 'Think you're that good?

Take your media budget and training programs. Compress them into three seconds and you begin to get a picture of what the carnie does instinctively. Take all of your focus groups and psychographic surveys and stuff them into a twelve-by-twelve booth with a colored awning and see how they would stack up against a carnie with a polished pitch.

If I have to give a name to what they do to make you look, I'd probably call it situational selling, although used car salesmen use a more colorful term, cold spearing. In a millisecond, the experienced carnie sizes up the mark and creates a one-of-a-kind sales pitch.

Bone tired, I shuffled past the joints that should have been closed but were still milking marks for one last dollar. Two young women at the end of the last row of joints were comparing notes when I stopped to shoot the bull.

Their game was simple; pop two balloons with two darts and win a rather odd-looking hat that resembled something Dr. Seuss used to crown characters in *Cat in a Hat* (If you had kids, you'll remember that one! It was basically a hat that no one would want in the morning. Tall and floppy, made of plush something or the other, a stovepipe hat of garishly colored rings.)

The customers loved them.

"So, give me your best pitch," I asked.

"Easy."

"Hey, Bud! I can get you a better hat than that!" She snickered and pointed in half squat, mouth half-covered to make the mockery more dramatic.

A piece of cake. One quick glance and grab onto something, anything that you can use to personalize the pitch. Dr. Frazier Crane should be so astute.

Down the way, a rather earthy-looking carnie was wowing stragglers with a challenge to break beer bottles with a baseball. Everyone wants to break glass and here is this guy giving permission to do it in public. From ten feet away, all you have to do is throw a baseball at a row of beer bottles, stuck neck down into a two-by-six.

Easy. A piece of cake. And isn't the sound of breaking glass exciting?

Color and sound, light and motion, these are the tools of the carnival.

Challenge is a big part of a carnie's pitch. It must be the macho that sells so many suckers.

"Win this for your little lady! Bet you can't do it! Hey! Even girls can do this one!"

And the gut response is a predictable, "Oh, yeh?"

By Saturday, Stu and I were aching to head home. For a while I couldn't quite figure how so many with the carnival could travel an entire season, living on a gravel lot, sleeping in a sleeping bag rolled out under a ride or tucked into a stick joint. Then it occurred to me.

They are home.

Talk to a carnie and you get that the toughest part of the year is the off-season, looking for family that may not exist, searching for something to do; missing 14 hour days and the hard excitement of life on the road.

Me? I just wanted to get off the road. My contacts were foggy. My back had gone numb. When John finally mentioned that he would hang around for any last minute riders on Peter-Paul, I could have kissed him.

I picked up my computer at the office and started the mile long trudge to the hotel. Stu had already left so I started hiking alone.

The occasional car would pass, a few slowing to get a look at the carnie walking into their world. I prayed that I wouldn't hear gun shots. It was that kind of night and crowd. I looked back at the carnival now growing sad and dark and felt that I was walking away from home.

I wondered why anyone would work with the carnival. RCS is by reputation the best in the business yet I still found the work to be tough, unforgiving, almost brutal. I thought about the people that I had met. Too early to call them friends but I know that if I were ever to need help while on the road, a carnie would be a good person to ask.

There are no strangers to a carnie.

I used to think that perhaps Dorothy was right, that there really is a wonderful place just beyond the rainbow. Perhaps if her dreaming had taken her to the carnival and if her heart was juuuusst right, she might have come to believe that the carnival was more like home than home itself. Maybe when the carnies crawl into their sleeping bags under the tilt-a-whirl, or pull a blanket over themselves in the tiny space where they repair the bumper boats, or close the light in their cubby-hole room at the palace, maybe it is they who are dreaming 'there's no place like home, there's no place like home.'

At the corner I stopped for the light and looked back just in time to see the lights on the big wheel blink out.

Time to go home. Time to go home.

8

Island of Iron

The entire east coast lay quiet under a blanket of thick wet snow, so heavy that traffic could barely move. The smoke from fireplace chimneys rose not much further than the chimney itself before crawling along the roof ridges, skulking into the neighborhood making the whole world smell like winter.

A huge, low pressure system had swirled its dreariness across half the continent. Not a problem except that it was the half that we needed to fly. By Memphis we knew the little Mooney wasn't going to make it all the way to Virginia by evening.

En route we had been cheating on Air Traffic Control, dividing our radio loyalties between the controllers in Houston, then Fort Worth, and finally Memphis Center as we listened to the weather boys at Flight Service.

Every time we were able to eavesdrop on another pilot calling for a weather update, the picture continued to morph from unlikely to impossible.

Under the gray skies of Memphis, I checked the engine oil out of habit, wincing when I got a little too close to hot metal. The Little Girl was sitting under the huge canopy at Wilson Air. Those folks are good. Rarely does it take them longer to fuel our little bird than it takes to file another leg of flight plan and look at the weather radar for the umpteenth time.

This time was no exception. The tanks were topped in minutes while I watched the gray skies turn even darker, taking on the ominous shade of a thunderstorm, an event unlikely in this cold and listless air.

Our enemy would be ice. Ice and small planes don't mix. Ice does funny things to the Little Girl's wings and my psyche. And judging from the way Stuart shifted uneasily from one foot to the other, he wasn't that hummed up about flying further. That made two of us; three if the airplane could vote.

So I filed to Lexington, Kentucky, home of bluegrass and thoroughbreds. Southern but not the deep south. Country ham and grits but only if you know where to stop. And I knew.

Lexington Approach couldn't seem to find airspace for us so they gave us the grand tour made not so grand by the fact that it was all in the soup. They cleared us to descend and then held us, captured in ice-laden clouds for what seemed an eternity.

The Little Girl tried hard to ignore the ice that began to grow on the leading edge of her two stubby wings. First a little frost, then clear ice, followed by a little more until it began to look like a lot and it was.

Finally we were turned to intercept the instrument landing system stretching its radio wave arms upward to catch us. Two arms guided us vertically while another welcoming pair funneled us left and right, talking to the autopilot to line us up with the runway.

If ever there is a time for faith, it must be on an instrument landing. Check the frequencies, watch the airspeed.

Not too fast or you will pop out of the murk, unable to run out of speed before you run out of runway. Not too slow or the plane will struggle to hold onto the glideslope and may suddenly pitch up, dropping even more speed, threatening to fall rather than glide.

Check that the pitot heat is on. Now, the landing lights; maybe now the GUMPF check to be certain, again, that the wheels are down.

We broke out with a few hundred feet to spare. I lifted the Little Girl's nose so that she looked cuter than ever, before settling onto the runway.

The mist on the windscreen turned to ice during taxi until, arriving on the ramp, it didn't matter that there was no one waiting to marshall us into a parking position. We wouldn't have seen them anyway. The smart folks were inside. It seemed that no one wanted the icy cold duty of meeting our plane. They were probably surprised to see us. Not many fools were flying this day.

Stu and I found country ham and grits and called it a night but not until we had teased our waitress into bringing us a few extra yeast rolls and a touch of butter.

It still looked and felt like night when the Little Girl lifted gently off the runway, tucked her wheels up under her metal skirts and pointed her nose into the gray overcast. I dialed in the next few waypoints on the GPS and unfolded the maps to guard our progress east into the low pressure system that refused to give up and slide quietly into the Atlantic.

The Appalachians, from a mile high, look like green-backed ruffles lining up north to south, dividing farms and towns, forcing man and beast to look for alternate routes when traveling east or west. We flew at 7,000 feet. Any higher and we would have been into the freezing level.

Our destination was Manassas, Virginia, south of the Dulles International Airport, far enough out to be called country yet close enough to still fall under the spell of Dulles

Approach Control. No problem. This would be another instrument landing and another set of eyes would be as welcome as it was required.

Manassas belongs to history.

On July 20, 1861, Union and Confederate forces were jostling for position, preparing for a battle that would turn the green fields of summer red with blood and fill the shallow hollows with screams of the dead and dying, all in the name of God and freedom, no matter which side you were on.

There had already been skirmishes at such places as Blackburn's Ford and Mitchell's Ford when large numbers of Union soldiers under the command of General McDowell gathered at nearby Centreville. For the other side, whose sons would die just as dead, Confederate Generals Beauregard and Jefferson Davis were masterminding a meeting that would spell death for hundreds if not thousands.

Thirteen hundred of McDowell's troops crept undetected to Sudley Ford on Bull Run Creek. For the South, General Johnston's 1,400 troops joined the 2,500 commanded by General Jackson in nearby Manassas. (The neat little airport that now is home to corporate jets by the dozens, sits pretty much right on top of this gruesome but important piece of history.)

That night the campfires were as cold as supper. There would be no singing and storytelling, just the oiling of guns and the checking and rechecking of equipment.

Long before sunset, McDowell made the decision to attack at first light. But like all decisions, this one did not stand alone nor could it deny the force of facts unknown. Unfortunately, McDowell was unaware that the forces of Johnston and Jackson had joined, creating an irresistible force by McDowell's out-numbered, out-gunned legions.

The resulting debacle gives the word surprise a bad name. Eight hundred and forty-seven are left dead on the battlefield. Two thousand, seven hundred and six are wounded, many of which will later die not of their wounds but of the infection that would inevitably follow. An incredible thirteen hundred and forty-five are listed as missing.

Missing!

The Little Girl touched the hallowed ground now covered with concrete without so much as a nod to what had gone before. It is history. Only history. These are the hills and hollows through which history and Amtrak passes.

Stu helped by dialing in the automated weather report beamed up from Manassas. The wind was calm. The ceilings were higher than expected. The runways were reported as having patchy ice and unknown braking action. Swell!

Under the cloud deck, the little airport with its two parallel north/south runways looked even smaller as it lay quietly in the snow-covered countryside. The airport looked deserted, its legions of planes topped with snow and crusted ice. From our altitude the hot days of summer and the crispness of autumn looked far, far away.

When Approach cleared us to Tower, we were asked to report on the braking action as no other plane had landed since the storm.

Well, if you line things up just right, don't go in like your tail is on fire, and get the flaps up to transfer as much weight as possible to the mains, you should coast to a stop before running out of runway without having to use the brakes.

We did it ju-u-ust right with a thousand or so feet to spare.

At the end of the runway, we tapped the brakes gently, slipped five or six feet, and dutifully reported to the tower that the 'braking action is minimal.'

We rented a car, one of those small jobbies with the godawful paint job that prevents both rust and theft. Our destination was the Amtrak Station, Lorton, Virginia. Stu offered to navigate while I piloted the unsightly metal beast.

We passed stark, white farmhouses, remnants of the days

when men were turning this now white landscape red with blood. We drove tree-covered lanes, their bare branches flocked in white velvet until the country road gave way to highway, highway to freeway, and freeway to parking lot.

Stu broke out the camera.

The whole of the station looked to be as gray as the sky that wrapped the day, romantic in its own special way, its colors soaked up by cloud cover and matching concrete. A small, snow-capped sign announced that we were in the right place, a thought that was quickly confirmed as we drove up the hill and found ourselves face-to-face with three long trains waiting anxiously beneath government-green canopies.

The snow storm had been a fast, wet storm, the kind that flocks the trees and looks and sounds dramatic only to melt away at the first hint of sunshine. Even before the sun made its appearance, the drip, drip, drip of icicles melting at the canopy edge gave the scene a colder than it really was feeling, except for when you walked in just the right spot and the dripping ice scored a bull's eye down your collar. Then, it was as cold as you can imagine.

Stu quickly handled the details and in a matter of minutes, we were settling into separate compartments aboard a stainless steel car that hulked over the platform. Our car was Car 5344. I wondered how they were able to line the cars up in such perfect order as to match the neat printed matching signs that hung at eye-level outside each car entry. Then I realized that they simply backed in the train and changed the car's numbers to match the sign. Still, it was a professional touch even if it was meaningless.

We counted the cars like kids will do, sometimes losing our place as we noticed that some were designed for hauling passengers, others were for dining, and still others were look-alike containers into which the passenger's automobiles were being driven, up the ramp until they were swallowed by a metal friend of Jonah.

Stu made instant friends with a round, black lady made

even rounder by the layers of a new winter coat. In his own inimitable way, Stu is a man of the people, drawing folks to him like white on rice and today he was in fine style.

Carrying a video camera might have something to do with Stuart's charm but not much. If anything, it just speeds an inevitable process. By the time I got both feet onto the platform, Stuart had already been introduced, hugged and invited to tour the cars where his new found, nice and round, by the pound friend worked as a 'coach cleaner.'

How does he do that?

We toured and marveled. Looking up at big boy toys only whetted Stu's appetite. I knew without asking that he had his sights accurately focused on the two shiny engines now idling on a separate side track less than a hundred yards away.

The engines were the latest issue from General Electric, the same people who make televisions and toasters, aircraft engines and, I think, even nuclear submarines. Well, they are even bringing good things to life on the railroad. Although later we would learn that the guys who actually drive the darned things wished that there had been a few less bells and whistles on this particular model.

From my vantage point, looking square into the nose of these monsters, they were pretty darned impressive. I noticed that they even have a cow catcher. (Is that the right term?) You know, the blade that looks like a snow plow suspended in front of the leading wheels. I remember being told that they were added in the early days of railroading to scoop aside range cattle that drifted onto the tracks. Hence, (and don't you love the word, hence?) they are called cow catchers. Well, correctly named or not, this baby had one. And not a single cow in sight. I guess they must be working!

While standing in front of the engines, another fast moving freight train roared by. I tried to think of another way to say it. Everyone says, "roared by." And that's exactly what it did. It didn't skulk by or roll by. It didn't zoom or streak by. The damned thing roared by, shaking the ground like a thundering herd of those cows the other engine had obviously cleared in advance. And, some smart ass engineer on the other train thought that laying on the horn at just the critical moment would be a pleasant tribute to Writer Boy, who was certain that it was the Amtrak train doing the snorting and jumped out of his skin off the tracks just in time for nothing, (thank you very damned much!) I knew what my dad would have said. Something to the effect of, "Blow it out your..."

Oh, never mind. It really was pretty cool.

Maybe I needed a reminder that the real business of railroads is freight. Great, long, heavy, endless trains hauling freight. I should have known. We see it all the time from the air where the trains look more like the model versions except even longer in scale. Out West, we watch mile-long trains hauling coal. In the Midwest, we see them hauling steel and autos, one in one direction and the other going the opposite.

The business of railroads is business and there is no secret that passenger trains, except in a very few well-defined markets, are dinosaurs. Like cow catchers and steam power.

Down the tracks there was a hiss of air brakes and the first movement in the yard was made by a soot-covered, yard freight engine with 588 tattooed on its side. The bell rang its distinctive clang, clang railroad sound. The diesel engines belched and screamed when the engineer called for more juice to wake up the huge electric motors that do the real work.

Did you know that? Diesel trains are really diesel-electric trains. Huge diesel engines burn fuel oil to turn generators which, in turn power electric motors that drive the wheels. This eliminates the need for complex gearing. There is no shifting of gears in a train—there are none!

The engine moved slowly, taking up slack in the couplings one car at a time. Then without notice, the entire train was in motion. Slow motion.

A kiss at the end and a few of the couplings gave back the slack and the train was suddenly longer.

I watched this from my compartment in the other string of cars sitting beneath the still dripping canopy. It was as if the scene were playing somewhere distant and only by special gift was I able to imagine it all. Here I was, warm and comfortable. There it was, cold and perhaps a little dirty. Now, it is all far, far away.

Behind the door in my compartment hung a chef's coat. Someone had been watching the details. Here on the world's longest passenger train, details were in abundance and we would soon discover that someone was watching over them all.

I dressed for dinner though not in the usual sense of the phrase. Chef coat, checked kitchen pants, white socks, work shoes and, of course, a tall white paper hat. Back in my college days when I carried both chef's tools and slide rules, the hats were as tall but made of heavy cloth that we would stretch over tall shortening cans and spray with starch until they were stiff as boards.

Before Melanie and I were married, I worked a second job, cooking at Denny's, the love of my life, for the fun of it. Denny's pretty much sent me through college, a project that I left one credit short of a degree, a fact I like to blame on a little Italian girl who lived too close to campus for my own good.

Melanie noticed my hat one afternoon as I dragged it out of the washer. She offered to finish it for me and smiled her special smile as she left with my shortening can tucked under her arm.

Well, she starched it, all right. She used an entire box of powdered starch on that sucker. You could use that hat as a stool it was so stiff! I didn't have to starch it ever again. Besides, I told her soon after that we were getting married and, since she didn't say 'no,' we did. And I had better things to do with my weekends than to play at Denny's (so I gave up Denny's!).

There is plenty of similarity between a train and a ship in port, lots of 'getting ready.' Everywhere, there are porters with luggage carts, deliverymen with produce on dollies. On the rail to the West, the Buicks and Lincolns that belong to the passengers are being ramped into the mouths of tall, aluminum cars.

In the station, bored ticket agents are aggravating excited passengers precisely because the passengers are excited and the agents, clearly not. The passengers themselves are busy capturing every moment that is Kodak and quite a few that aren't.

Reporting for work for the first time has been an interesting part of each of my adventures. I've had more 'first days' than the average job hopper and I can tell you that the first day is, by far, not just the most important day for the employee. It is the most important day for the company.

The first day is the day when we learn most about expectations and values. What does this company want from me? What values does it hold important? Where do I fit? Or even, do I fit at all? The first day is a decision day. I decide if there will be a second day or if that second day will only be a placeholder while I look for something else, someplace that fits me better and fills me up.

I'm good at first days especially since I know that I have a choice.

Arriving for your first day at work with a 260-pound, camera-toting sidekick always makes an impression! Hey! I could loan you Stuart if you have a big first day coming up. Just let me know how things turn out.

As usual there are the questions. "So why did you choose us? Are we going to be on television? When will the book come out and can I get a copy? What other jobs have you worked and which was the most interesting?"

After a while, I get to actually go to work. And I really do want to work.

I learn that when the train is full, there are about 600 passengers. Dinner is a matter of two or three simultaneous seatings, depending on the load, in three dining cars spaced along the spine of this fast-moving, aluminum snake.

Tonight we'll be feeding 106 in our car. Fifty-two for a first seating at 5:30, fifty-six at the 7:30 seating.

A typical day for the crew is a 12-hour shift that starts at 11:00 in the morning. There is cleaning and stocking to be done, then plenty of pre-dinner prep work, the same as in restaurants that aren't moving at 70 miles an hour.

Day two begins at 5:30 and is all over but the shouting by 9:00 when the train arrives in Sanford, Florida.

On the AutoTrain, everyone eats. It's included.

In coach class the food is served in two diners. It is pre-prepared but it is good and there is plenty of it. Call it airline food, if you will, except there are no folding seatbacks and you don't have to sit, trapped by trash until the flight attendant finally comes back down the aisle.

In sleeper class, we don't use the term, 'first class.' The meals are prepared fresh and, I discovered, they are good. Not gourmet by any stretch of the imagination, but very, very good. Hot, fresh and delicious.

Breakfast is another story. Breakfast is served continental style, whenever you are ready to launch yourself from your berth. On the train, I'm sorry to say, sleeping is better than breakfast.

In Sanford, crew members have a hotel room good for a long shower followed by three or four hours of sleep before heading back to the train for a 2:00 P.M. boarding.

I learn all of this while helping Tiny, the cook's assistant, plate up fresh salads in the north end, lower level of the dining car.

By now I have blended into the rhythm of the work. I notice an occasional eye peeking around the stairway from the dining area above. It seems everyone wants to get a look at Writer Boy. Stuart turns quickly and sprays them with automatic fire from the video camera which almost always sends them into hasty retreat.

Salads done, Tiny heads to his quarters. Since Tiny has dish duty, he will be the last to leave the car tonight. So, with extra help in the kitchen, Tiny is free to turn in his apron and hit the berth for a nap and his favorite jazz album.

Amtrak cooks, I discover, are CIA trained. That's Culinary Institute of America, not what you were thinking. At least that used to be the case. Before someone got the idea that training was a little too expensive, the mostly male kitchen crews were sent to Poughkeepsie to learn the basics of foodservice sanitation plus a tip or two for actually cooking great food. (We're talking a two-week course where they learn the proper holding temperatures, sanitizing routines, and enough basic microbiology to keep passengers from croaking over a mis-handled, raw chicken breast. But we are not talking soufflé, flambé or gourmet.)

The kitchens are gorgeous.

Even if you don't cook, you'd be impressed.

All stainless steel. All electric. A work of art and efficiency in a long, rolling box. There are four convection ovens, a three-foot grill, a steam table big enough for a small cafeteria, two stoves, and plenty of freezer and cooler space so long as you are careful.

There are no fryers, thank goodness. A fryer on a train would be a disaster waiting to happen. Just having a stove is a challenge since there is no way to secure a pot to a stove top. Imagine a pan of boiling water, 200-plus degrees of scalding liquid as the train hits a rough section of track, a sharper than normal curve, or the challenge of an emergency stop. You know what's going to happen to that pot and anyone unfortunate enough to be working north of forward momentum.

Necessity, being the mother that she is, offers a little help. The cooks use metal cleaning pads, wedged under one side of the pot to serve as tiny brillo brakes. It works pretty well.

The cars rotate out every 60 days for what they call e-cleaning. Deep, thorough, and probably needed after two months of non-stop, heavy-duty action.

The kitchen is regulated by Federal inspectors who ride the entire way south then fly home. They check that all food is stored, prepared and held at the proper temperature. They check for proper storage of cleaning supplies, test the cleaning solution strength and make certain that hands are washed.

There's one kind of goofy rule that makes cooks everywhere nuts: You may not wash your hands in a sink that is reserved for washing utensils or preparing food. The opposite is also true. You can't so much as draw water from a hand sink. By law, there must be a hand sink in the prep area and if, through lack of space, there is no room to include a prep sink.

"I've gotta run all the way to the back of the car to get a pot of water when there is good water right over there but, you know those inspectors." And so another cook, this one in a moving kitchen, moans about the rules.

Tonight's menu? New York strip with mushroom red wine sauce. There is herbed chicken picatta, served with wild rice and a vegetable medley. The chicken will bake for an hour and make the entire car smell six ways wonderful. There will be seasoned breaded catfish, also baked and also wonderful. Plus rice pilaf, baked potatoes, and, in case President Bush is with us, steamed broccoli.

When you are free to choose, most go for the big ticket item so it's easy to predict that ninety percent will be eating steak.

For the kids, unless they are smart, there are ChooChoo Chewys (spaghetti with meat sauce, and a side of Oreo cookies, all microwaved to perfection.) Okay, I lied about the perfection part. Let's say, microwaved, until they aren't frozen any more. Ummmm! Good! At least there are Oreos for dessert!

Mike put me to work panning the steaks. Simple work, really. Just open the vacuum pack and remove the individual steaks. These steaks are, in many ways, fresher than fresh. Right after they were cut to uniform size, they were flash frozen and individually vacuum sealed in tough plastic. The immediate freezing and vacuum packaging prevents any further deterioration. Not even your local butcher can do better.

Nearly an inch thick, beautifully marbled and with just a

hint of fat around the trimmed edge, they look good in the pan. They'll look even better on the grill.

Most nights nearly 600 people get fed in three hours. Think about it. Fresh food, well prepared and all in a kitchen that's moving at 70 miles an hour.

Later, fifteen hours to the south, the train will be re-configured and sent home. The quick turn in Sanford allows enough time to drop off the laundry and, if necessary, pick up a few supplies from the small commissary.

"If they don't have it, they'll get it, even if they have to go to the local grocery store."

Suddenly all the lights go out except the emergency lights and I am the only one who seems to notice.

"They're getting ready to connect us all together. The lights will come back on in a few minutes."

Down the stairwell steps a bundle of enthusiasm whose name tag says, "Danny." He is the Service Manager, the boss, and in an instant, it is easy to see why he is the one selected to run the show.

Danny has been riding the rails for eleven years and it's obvious that it suits him. Without prompting, he offers his ideas about what makes the AutoTrain something special. A gentle forward bump pushes the conversation and our section of the train onto the main track.

"We celebrate birthdays and holidays. We spend time together even off the road. A real big plus is that we are separate from the home office. Lorton is just far enough south that it takes an effort to see us. So, if we want to do something, we try it. We've known each other for years. We go through all these wild experiences—late trains, passenger situations—all the different things that have happened. We all say we're going to write a book someday." He manages to say all of the above without any noticable signs of breathing.

"What if it weren't a train? What if it were a diner or a hotel?"

A cute brunette interrupts by dashing in and hugging Mike, saying to Stu, "You should take a picture of us beautiful women, right, Mike?" And she squeezes the round guy a little closer, "That's what we do down here!" She is gone and Danny picks up where he left off, having not so much as skipped a beat.

"It wouldn't be the same."

Now our section is pushed backward toward the waiting sections.

"What is it that would make it different?"

"Because we have to spend so much time together, because we can't get off. I'll be right back. But don't turn that thing off!" Danny checks his hair in the lens of Stu's camera. This guy is definitely not what you would call shy.

Like Santa disappearing up the chimney, Danny slips up the stairwell like so much smoke. There he picks up a microphone and does the railroad version of preflight announcements.

A gentle jolt and our section is attached to the rest of the train.

"Good evening, ladies and gentlemen. My name is Danny, your onboard service chief." Just like the airlines, the speakers have all the fidelity of two cans between an over-stretched string. "We're now leaving the station. We'll be pulling the passengers' sections forward, then we'll be making a normal stop to connect our auto carriers onto the rear of the train. There are 15 auto carriers and 15 passenger cars.

"Tonight we have 126 autos and 254 passengers. Our train is pulled by two General Electric engines with a total of 8,450 horsepower. We're 3,500 feet in length, the longest passenger train in the world.

"The coach lounge is located between the coach cars. For our sleeping car passengers, the sightseer car and the lounge car are located just behind the dining car.

"We have a few safety rules. Keep an eye on children, no running in the aisles and no playing on the steps. You must wear shoes when walking in the cars. Smoking is limited to two designated areas in the lounge cars.

"Dinner tonight will be served in two seatings, 5:30 and

7:30. Our film tonight is *First Wives' Club* and there will be two showings. Breakfast will be served at six in the morning until just prior to our arrival at nine tomorrow."

Then the Cheshire cat smiled and said to me, "And that's it! And no looking either!"

Back downstairs, Danny continued saying, "We work together. If the chips are down, I roll up my sleeves."

"Anything ever happen that is funny?"

"On our last trip, we had a man who wouldn't leave his clothes on. We kept him covered with a sheet until we could stop. A stationperson came on, trapped him and took him off the train.

"One lady had a panic attack. That was weird.

"We've had people die at the dinner table. Well, these are New York/Long Island, well-to-do. They're mostly 65 and older and that's pretty much the age that people die.

"We had a child who refused to eat anything but plain noodles. So we microwaved a ChooChoo Chewy and then washed off all the sauce. How's that for different?"

Before dinner, the crew begins to stop by to see if we can feed them. Some came from other cars. Most asked for their dinner to be served with a slight variation. A few wanted carry out and all were happily obliged.

Like any organization there is a definite pecking order. The conductor is the master of the train, the boss in terms of operation, even over the engineer. Although the engineer has final say over the safe operation of the engines and cars, nothing moves without the approval of the conductor.

"For a while, everyone was hand-picked for this train. There's regular service and then there's AutoTrain." This was said with button-popping, gee-aren't-we-special pride.

The conversation drifted between service and customer: "One of our menus has filet mignon, almost 100 percent choose that."

"Wrapped in bacon?" (That's the way I like mine.)

"No way. This crowd is mostly from New York. They don't eat bacon. They have winter homes in Florida, and summer homes in New York or Connecticut. We're taking people home. They're older people who will need their car when they get there but they either can't drive all that distance or they don't have to."

When the work is good, for whatever reasons, the team doesn't tend to change. Who leaves a job that they love? Even when we had a fast food fried chicken restaurant (and we're talking not much above minimum wage), we rarely turned over an employee. People don't leave jobs that they love and they love jobs where they are loved.

And so it is with the AutoTrain. I'm not sure that this is so much a matter of enlightened railroading—See? That doesn't even sound likely—as it is a matter of the job itself. When people are thrown into a situation where they can't get away, in this case, can't get off, there is a sort of magic bonding that turns teams into families.

Of course, you can't discount that Amtrak pays very, very well but working in the kitchen, listening to the chatter, getting a feel for both the rhythm of the rails as well as life on the rails, I got a picture that looks much different than what you would see in the typical cubicled office. On this train, you can't get off and no one is leaving, for lots of reasons.

By now the car had taken on a gentle rocking motion, predictable yet not. You could depend on the next section of rail to sound and move just like the last. But once in a while, just about the time the rhythm would start to feel natural, the track would throw a literal curve and we'd all grab hold.

About an hour out of Lorton, the steam table had started to take shape. And an hour after that the moist heat of a kitchen at work wrapped around us. The smell of good things cooking was everywhere at once. A couple of bites here, a taste test there and this home-like car would be a great place for a nap!

I got a job that seemed too familiar, preparing the chicken. It was one of those oddball, slightly kinky assignments that only a cook could appreciate. Grab a chicken half and twist the leg into the armpit, or wingpit if there is such an anatomy. (Don't try this at home, I'm a professional!)

Before we knew it, dinner was upon us. As the guest checks began to drop through the chute from the dining area above us, I was assigned the duty of assembling the food on trays and sending them upstairs via a dumbwaiter, not exactly a highly skilled position.

Most of the conversation was about the job at hand. The guys were polite but it was clear that they were keeping an eye on the new kid.

Before I knew it, the entree tickets were being dropped back down the chute with requests for dessert. And not long thereafter, the first seating was over and it was time to clean up, wipe up, and do it all again.

There was a moment, just a moment, between the dinner seatings when we had all the work done and were waiting for the next run to begin. Already, the tables upstairs were beginning to fill. I knew the servers were taking drink orders, delivering salads. But downstairs, which really felt like 'below deck', we were enjoying the calm before the storm.

Chef Cheek (Mike) stood with his arms folded, leaning against the steam table. This would be on the left side of the train as we rode quietly south. Jim stood in shorter imitation of his friend and partner. Neither had a drop on their still fresh chef coats.

Mike and I had just finished a little cook-to-cook talk, discussing the breaded and baked catfish and how surprised we were that this very southern dish was so popular with this not very southern crowd. When Jim sidled up, the talk turned to the train and its effect on their lives.

Mike: "Once you step on board, we don't stop. You don't see a paper..."

Then together, as if to prove they had been partners for a long time, both mentioned, "You don't see a television."

"You don't interact with anyone..." now Mike's conversation belonged to Jim who continued..."there's no phone you can use" and, back to Mike..."I mean we'll get home sometimes and major things can happen that we don't know about."

"So, is this a feeling of being disconnected?"

"Yep. Definitely. Yes," they replied together sort of.

"You're in your own world." Now this was Jim, speaking almost reverently.

"Yeh, you feel like you are in your own little world."

Jim recovers the ball, "Well, look. You don't have any windows down here (except for the loading doors located mid-car and out of sight.) You're down here for 11 hours. We really don't know what's going on. You can't tell if the sun has risen, set, if it's raining, snowing, what the temperature is, right? Until we get to Florida and we see it on CNN."

"We all watch CNN. That and The Weather Channel as soon as we get to our room!"

"Yep, or we'll go as soon as we get off."

"Or we'll call home to see what's going on."

"Or just get the newspaper. Like *USA Today*. It's a high commodity out here. If someone has a newspaper, you see about five other people saying, I'll take that, I'll take that. Like last trip, the Simpson trial, we didn't even know that there was a..."

"Verdict..."

"Until we got to the hotel room..."

"The same as the Super Bowl. We had to hear it from the conductors. I was out here (notice 'out here') when we fired our first missiles at Iraq. The conductors came on the intercom and told us all that the first missile had just been fired on Baghdad. Luckily we were close enough to a city that they were able to rig up a television and get a broadcast. All the passengers filed into the dining car just to see."

"Is this a sense of loneliness?" I was fishing with tasty bait. The idea of isolation had just passed across Mike's clear, brown eyes and washed down the broad face. Jim had been dancing around the word for the past few minutes and when I mentioned it, I knew instantly that I had hit the nerve.

Mike looked down and paused, saying, "Yeh...."

"It's maybe not loneliness...it's just a cutoff..."

"I feel lonely when I go back to bed..." Now we let the gentle rocking of the car fill in the blanks. "...because I like to sit up for a while and talk. When I go back there and everybody's in bed, it's like...geez!"

There is a crew car, usually at the very head or tail of the train. Tonight, heading south, the crew car is behind the two engines. It's plain, lighted like a bus station, but it's home.

"We can sit there without worrying about the passengers."

"A lot of times people will bring a little something from home like cookies or some soup and we'll sit there and have a little late night snack."

There is this thing called Customer Contact Tolerance, a fellow named Ron Zemke coined the term. It is the ability to tolerate, perhaps thrive on intense customer contact. Even the best of us need a little break from customers. After a while the questions are too predictable. The train is no exception.

"Where are we?" said Mike.

"What time is the 5:30 dinner seating?" adds Jim as if he didn't know. And we all laugh, partly because it is a stupid question; partly because we know he didn't make it up.

"How long are we going to sit here? How long does it take to get the cars off? What time is it? You've got to be nice."

With that, the first guest check of the second shift slipped down the chute. I quoted a famous Vietnamese pastry chef, saying, "Let's rock and roll!" And we did.

This time there was evidence of magic. Jim bumped me with his hip, his hands were full, and said, "I'll trade places with you for this run."

In most of these adventures, there was a definite moment when I became a part of the team. This was the moment for the train. After seeing that I did well during the prep phase, growing comfortable with my performance during the first run, the guys accepted me as part of the team and allowed me to work a key position for the second seating.

It is interesting to review the video tapes of the trip.

Between the first and second run, the conversation changed. First run, there was lots of conversation, much of it dealing with the orders at hand. By the second run, there was little conversation. Little was needed. And this time it was less process and more personal.

It was almost 8:00 P.M. and we were all tired. Even Tiny, working the north end of the car, flinging dishes into and out of the washer, was quiet, his CD player stowed. But he was still smiling, still working.

I plated orders, placing dinners on the tray in the same arrangement as on the four quadrants of the guest check. If the upper right quadrant were an order for fish, the fish was placed on the upper right quadrant of the tray. The tray went into the dumbwaiter the same way and the server upstairs placed the orders on the table, system replacing magic.

By the time dessert orders began falling into the kitchen, Mike was hard at work cleaning the steam table. A voice not belonging to Danny announced, "We're now passing through Rocky Mount, North Carolina."

Stu stuck the camera out the window on the cargo door and captured small town America sleepily sliding past. I love the sound as we passed the crossings, the soft-loud-soft Doppler effect of the bell sounding so very lonely.

Tiny burst into a chorus of Day-O Daylight Comes and I Wanna Go Home. For the next 50 miles, we implored "Mr. Tallyman" to let us go home.

Upstairs the last of the passengers dawdled over dessert while the servers got a head start on their side work. Downstairs we were doing the same, plating the last few desserts, traying fruit and bakery goods for breakfast at one end of the kitchen while Mike disappeared in a cloud of steam as he cleaned the grill. Tiny had given up on Jamaican music and was letting the rattle of clean dishes coming out of the machine entertain him.

While we cleaned, the guys filled in a little history.

At one time, there was no sleeping car diner. That made for a long walk down the train to get to dinner so the decision was made to put on a first class dining car. Amtrak purchased a dining car from the Princess Lines. 'Bet you didn't know that at one time, Princess Cruise Lines ran its own train.

What made the cars so special to the crews was that they were two-level cars, much like the ones in use today.

The old cars are referred to as Heritage cars, probably because they're so old. They were half-lounge/half-kitchen and all on the lower level. Because of the need to have a walkway to the next car, the kitchens could not be a full car wide. There was a window in the small kitchen that could be opened, which was good because there was no air conditioning. Talk about heat...a tiny kitchen stuffed with gas-fired, cooking equipment and no air conditioning!

Today this diner is still called the Princess Diner, a reference to the days when the first class diner was a used car from the Princess Line.

The guys were obviously proud of the car and the romance that is associated with cooking at 70 miles per hour. The kitchen may look like Denny's but it's not quite the same.

"You get used to walking, and there have been times when a whole pan has sailed right across the kitchen! But in the past few years, they've added shelf restraints." I never saw one used but it was certainly comforting to know that we had them!

"There have been times when he's plating food on this side, holding a pan on the other side and holding on with his foot!" It's a kitchen trick that works even in kitchens that don't move. Hook your foot under the kick area at the base of the counter and you can lean extra far to grab a plate, flip an egg, or simply hold on.

"We get to know when those curves are!"

"Why do you like this job?" It was obvious that they did. I just wanted to know why.

"I like preparing the food. It gets extremely busy so the trip is over before you know it. It's a lot more creative down here. On the other dining car, it seems like all you are doing is opening packages and I guess that's pretty much what it is.

Here, you feel like you are actually doing something. I'm so glad that they got rid of the prepared food. It feels good when the passengers say, "That was really good!"

"Well, prepared food is a big trend in the industry."

"I hate it!"

Jim: "One reason I came here from the coach car was the prepared food. There was no challenge. It was repetitious."

The passengers are, for the most part, unaware that the food is prepared fresh just a few feet below their table.

Jim: "We sometimes go upstairs in between seatings and we hear the passengers talk. We hear them say, 'That was really good!'"

"I wish the reservations people would explain that it's fresh. Some people order the Kosher dinner because they think they are getting something better. The Kosher dinner actually is pre-prepared! Then they see what everyone else is getting and change their mind!"

"Occasionally someone asks to see the chef. That's why I like working down here. I feel like I am creating something!"

Now Tiny joins the group, wiping his hands on the tail of his apron.

"What do you like about this job?"

"This job? Nothin' to hate! When I worked retail, I was in management. I worked sometimes seven days a week, fifteen hours a day. I had the responsibility of opening the store. I had to worry if employees would show up. I had to hire them and fire them. Here, I just come and do my job.

"This is a family, the AutoTrain family. We don't consider ourselves crew members. This is my family here."

When the work was done, in spite of being tired, there was too little time to sleep before we would leave the train in Florence, South Carolina to work a sister train on the northbound run. So we wandered back to the crew car.

"This is not your standard conductor's hat."

"Naw, man. It's my religion." The eyes turned my way and instantly pegged me as a stranger. Stu says that no matter what uniform I wear, it's never a disguise. Good point.

"Muslim?"

"Yeh, Muslim... "

"It's very cool. I haven't seen one quite like it. Do they come in different colors?"

"I, I buy a lot of fabric..."

"Oh, I see. Anything is fine so long as your head is covered."

"I wear my hat sometimes."

We talked about praying five times a day.

"I'm not in that kind. I'm more in the Mason kind where we teach to love instead of to hate. Some of the same signs and symbols that the Masons use."

We talked about Farakahn.

"I respect him as a person but I don't like some of the things he teaches. I know he's done some rather remarkable things. I don't know much about him...I know he doesn't like me! (laughs)

"I was raised that there is good and bad in everybody so I never got into that."

"How did you get in the railroad?"

"A friend of mine. I was driving a truck and he got me in. I sent them a resume and a few weeks later, they called me for an interview. That was in '91."

"But you're a conductor!"

"Yeah, well, I started out washing windows."

"That's pretty fast! You started cleaning the train and now you're running it!

"I believe that if you want something you've got to strive. I figure that if I am going to work for the railroad, I'm going to become a conductor."

The conductor is like a safety officer, in charge of passenger behavior, signals, etc. The main job is the safe movement of the train. There is always one conductor in the front and another conductor camps out in the trailing car.

"I'm in motels more than I'm at home. I'm on the Extra Board. I'm with different people everyday. I know everybody so I feel more comfortable on this train."

"You're going to retire at this, aren't you?

"Yeah, I'm afraid so. You can't beat the retirement. I would like to get a regular assignment so that I can go to school. Amtrak pays half if you keep a 'C' average."

"It doesn't seem like the supervisors have to do much supervising."

"It's because everybody is an adult. You know what your job is, you go ahead and do it. (On) this train...everybody knows their job. Besides, AutoTrain has an image. These are high class people, we've got an image." (The gist was that when people have an image to uphold, they rise to the occasion.)

"Will this place fill up? Do you get lonesome?"

"No, it gives me time to learn the territory. When I know where we are and someone asks me where we are, I can answer without looking ignorant!"

"We (sic) here in Garwin. The mileposts are named after the nearest town. After a while, I won't need this map no more, I can put this away. If there is an accident, you can know exactly where we're at."

"What's the most interesting thing that's ever happened on a train that you were working?"

"Last week! The train broke down for six hours. The engine quit. We had engine trouble; we sat for six hours. I had four hundred passengers on the train. The conductor and the engineer went to Richmond to get another engine and left me in here with four hundred people. They were complaining; it was something. It was a madhouse. I authorized free coffee, free danish, just keep them quiet!"

"How do they go and get another engine?"

"Cab. They called a cab!"

"One lady was crying because she was going to her mother's funeral. I said, can you imagine being in an airplane and it stop?"

"What was the funniest thing that's happened?"

"This white lady came to me and she said, "Do you know what, sir? You are the handsomest black, bald-headed man I ever seen in my life." Out of the blue! She said, "you are the handsomest black, bald-headed man I ever did see in my life!" It freaked me out! She grabbed me right here...(grabs his backside)...it was wild, it was wild! I told my wife and she just laughed! Now, I wear this hat and take no chances!"

Now here is a dream for the asking. Hey, a truck driver can become a conductor!

And I imagine that there must be conductors who long for the freedom of the highway. Could you work the Amtrak Auto Train? Well, I guess so! I mean, if you wanted to. If you were willing to dream it.

The plan was for us to work the southbound train as far as Florence, South Carolina, then leave the train and catch the northbound train back to Lorton. I'd work in the kitchen on the southbound leg, then, heading north, I would serve breakfast. Piece of cake!

Florence, South Carolina just before midnight. The painted letters on the sign were not quite white. Bathed in the sodium yellow glow of the platform lights, I stepped off the train and felt instantly transported to the set of a B movie, one that Ted Turner had colorized but not particularly well. The air was cold and heavy, still as a blanket of ice.

Stu caught the moment on tape, me, in profile against the sign, the collar on my favorite leather jacket pulled up around my neck. He may have captured the color and sound (there wasn't much, just the diesels at idle) but the cold creeping up my feet and legs wouldn't show on any tape.

A police car swept through the parking lot perhaps a hundred yards away. The cop, looking but not, waited to catch my eye, a gentle warning that whatever I was bringing to Florence, it had better not be, well, you know.

Inside, we waited with a chorus of young black mothers, babies mostly asleep across their laps, waiting for the next iron monster to creep into the station, brake shoes moaning in the early morning hours when most of the world was fast asleep or maybe just peeking with one eye to see if it really were time to look for a new day.

The station had all the charm of an operating room. Clean but hardly comfortable. A few Amtrak promotional posters promised journeys far more glamorous than the tired black women were likely to take, ever. I guessed that they were mostly single but I am as likely to be wrong as right. Maybe there were fathers waiting in some other waiting room, pacing and looking anxiously to the tracks in anticipation of sons or daughters.

The room was warm but not inviting. The tired moms had given up conversation and simply stared at the posters not seeing, spending the least energy holding their babies.

About 1:00 A.M., 40 stainless steel cars slide to a stop at the platform, our car, the furthest from the end, was attached next to the engine out of reach of the platform lights. Green lights began to glow from the doors, a signal I had not yet figured. I rolled a beat-up cart, a bag lady special, toward the square light that fell from the furthest door marking a shadow in reverse on the concrete.

I have seen beautiful things but as we climbed the stairs and counted out the room numbers to find our own, the sight of the bed, really just two seats converted, was the prettiest thing ever. We were tired as tired ever gets and cold nearly to the bone from waiting on the platform. We had worked the Amtrak Auto Train south and, now, catching its northbound neighbor to continue our adventure, we stared straight into the face of exhaustion.

The young black mothers remained in the station waiting for number 98. That train was late. None of the regulars were surprised so none bothered to complain. They saved their energy for staying awake and left the complaining to others.

There would be no young black mothers on our northbound train unless they were part of the crew. Our train was full to bursting with mostly New York Jewish doctors and Mrs., enough to staff a good-sized big-city hospital. The doctor's bored wives in tow were now retired, traveling the rails in a style and freedom that the poor folks left in the Florence waiting room could only imagine.

I was asleep before my head hit the pillow. And good thing. We had a wake-up call for four-thirty. The best we could expect was three hours of sleep and I intended to get it all. In a matter of seconds, I was gone.

The voices were coming from outside. From the fringe of a deep sleep, I tried to listen without waking. The train had stopped. Perhaps it was the voices that had stirred me from that deep, delicious dream. More likely, when the maternal rocking slowed to a stop, the brain took the clue and rose back to the surface.

The voices said that there was no damage and there was something mentioned about a bicycle and a brake hose. I heard the tap of a wrench and fell back into my black, black sleep.

When I came back to life, the train was moving again. Fast. And the tracks felt different. The engineer was an air horn virtuoso obligated to blow us by every cow crossing and intersection of which there seemed to be many.

Across the aisle, Stu was up. I could see him looking with his feet, trying to find his boots without bending over.

In the diner I met a whole new crew but felt as if we had not changed either train or direction. The new team let me serve breakfast. Simple. Nothing more than hauling coffee and charm for a couple of hundred faces over a couple of hundred miles.

"Young man?"

She was talking to me using a term that I had not heard for quite a while. She was pretty in a sophisticated way and about my age. So I noticed for the first time how goofy older men must seem when they refer to a woman as a 'young lady.' Hopelessly contrived and sexist in an innocent way.

"Yes, ma'am?"

"You are simply marvelous. I hope whoever hired and trained you knows they have a gem on their hands." She smiled as if the next request might be for a back rub. I was thinking a couple of bucks worth of tip might be more appropriate.

"Thank you, ma'am. I'll be certain to pass along your compliment. Thank you."

Hired and trained me? What am I? A seal?

———————————

Dog tired. I don't know how tired is dog tired but Stu and I were both all in 'cept our shoe strings. We'd been wheels up at 6:30 A.M. the day before—no two days before. Now we were airborne again. We had flown several hours, all of it hard IMC. (IMC is pilot shorthand for Instrument Meteorological Conditions. In simpler terms, it means "you can't see crap." Solid cloud with visibility limited to the blur of the prop and an eyeful of instruments that you pray are working and will continue to work.)

It was an icy landing and then an equally tough drive to the train. We checked in right after lunch, got off the train just before midnight, and were back on a northbound train in the wee hours of the morning. We had nothing more than a catnap before getting up at dawn. We worked until mid-morning and now, here we are, cranking a cold-soaked Mooney, looking for a shortcut home, knowing that there was none.

At the end of the runway, we completed the run-up and cockpit checks, double-checked that the charts were out and in order, and called Tower that we were ready.

"Mooney niner-five-mike-kilo, cleared for take-off, runway three-six right. Fly runway heading."

I repeated the clearance and slowly applied power. I had two reasons for the slow application of power. First, I didn't want to give a not quite warm engine too big of a thrill. Second, the runway was still patchy with ice and there was no point in getting wild on the take-off roll.

The little Mooney responded perfectly, edging into a gentle roll, picking up speed and perhaps a little ice on her feet in the process. By habit I called out the gathering speed...four-zero, four-five, five-zero, five-five and, as always, it seemed that we were at the magic seven-zero knots sooner than expected. And I let the Little Girl raise her cute nose and sniff for home.

That's when it happened.

At first it seemed like a gentle shudder. We were maybe 30 feet off the runway. I figured that it was ice on the nose wheel. (Sometimes the little Mooney gives a shiver on take-off, the nose wheel rattling a bit, nothing serious.)

Now we were 50 or so feet above the runway. The little Mooney climbs fast even when she's not feeling well and by now, I knew. I knew this was not a matter of ice on the nose wheel. It was too late to shut her down. Besides she was climbing and that's always a favorable sign.

At a hundred feet, flying had lost pretty much all of its glamour. And, in spite of the cold weather, I started to sweat.

"Tower, Mooney niner-five-mike-kilo needs to return to the airport. We're having some sort of mechanical."

"Five-mike-kilo is cleared to land any appropriate runway. Will you require equipment?"

(What a pleasant way to offer the services of the folks in the little red trucks!)

"Negative, but thank you. We'll circle to three-six right."

I pulled the power and a miracle happened. The Little Girl smoothed right out. The big Continental engine started to purr and, like a dummy, I chalked the entire deal up to a fouled plug that had cleared itself. Call it fatigue, if you're generous; stupidity, if you insist.

"Tower, Mooney niner-five-mike-kilo, our problem seems to have corrected itself. We'd like to resume our original flight plan."

"Five-mike-kilo, contact Dulles Departure on..."

We turned to the west, made another scan of the instruments, and everything good to the green, contacted Dulles Departure.

The voice on the other end gave us a new squawk code and heading. We banked slightly, applied power and were certain that the engine was coming right out of its mount!

"Departure, five-mike-kilo needs to return to the airport immediately!"

Back on the tower frequency, we were again offered the red truck hospitality which, again we declined, asking instead for a low pass flyby and a check of our landing gear.

(Don't ask why but I was having the goof ball idea that perhaps there was something hanging from the gear causing a killer shake whenever we increased our speed.)

We weren't having trouble maintaining altitude but I was too skittish to attempt to climb. We skinned past the tower at maybe 100 feet.

"Five-mike-kilo, your gear appears to be down and normal. Cleared to land, your choice."

"Thank you, ma'am. We'll take three-six right, five-mike-kilo."

I banked the plane thinking, "I'm about to put $300,000 worth of shiny, blue metal into a snow covered field. This is not going to be a happy day."

On final approach, I asked Stuart to open his door and reviewed the emergency procedures. "Exit to the rear. If the door won't open, use the cargo door."

Stu opened the door and grabbed seat leather.

I checked the landing gear and flaps a million times and then repeated the process. The Little Girl settled to the runway like the lady she is. We taxied to the ramp. I shut her down and only then began to shake like a leaf.

It was a magneto. Nothing major except if it's your magneto. Having two magnetos kept the little bird flying and, a simple switch of the ignition key to the operating magneto, and the problem, or at least the symptom, would have completely diasappeared. Of course, switching to the wrong magneto, the damaged one, at 100 feet could cause the engine to stop at an altitude much too low for a restart and just right for an unscheduled landing.

We sat on the ground while the folks at the factory searched high and low to find us a replacement part.

Actually, we found a hotel and celebrated the entire adventure properly—with a nap!

———————————

When I was a kid, I often dreamed with my eyes wide open watching the slow moving freight trains as they gained speed and momentum rolling out of the Latonia Yard just south of my Gran's house. We'd chew the hot tar that dripped off the station roof, watch the lead wheels of the engine flatten the occasional penny against the rail, and, for one long summer, we made a record of every train that whistled by. In a pocket-sized notebook, Mark Patterson and I would write the number of the lead engine and a count of the cars. We knew what time to expect them all and it got so that we could wrap an entire day around anticipated departures.

The engines were big and black, crusted in the soot from the towering plumes of black smoke that belched and chugged from their stacks. The engineers hung outside the wide windows inviting what little breeze there was to take the heat of already hot July days. Those were days too hot even for little boys with canteens around their necks and plums from Mrs. Gallagher's yard. Imagine how hot it must have been riding that black iron monster with coal fire in its belly.

One day we saw another kind of engine and didn't understand. It had no coal tender and very little black smoke. This one, said my grandfather, (I called him Boom,) was a diesel-electric. It didn't look, smell or sound like an engine to me. But in a few days this new machine must have worked powerful magic because we began to see long trains of tired-looking steam engines leave the yard, pulled by the new guys, and always in but one direction.

My grandfather said that the steam engines were being replaced, dragged off to the steel mills where they would be turned into new metal and maybe become diesels. To me it seemed like eating your young but there was nothing for a little shaver to do except watch. And, if we had the heart for it, make a record of the lead engine, the time, and the number of old giants that rumbled smokelessly in train.

Sad as that was, the saddest moment came when I learned that the cabooses were next to go. The caboose was always my favorite part of the train. They had tall cupolas where the brakemen would sit, watching the length of the train for hot boxes and other signs of trouble. When a box would start to smoke, the brakemen would signal for a stop and then race along the length of the train where they would open the axle cover to add fresh grease to the over-heated bearing.

The off-duty brakemen would sometimes ride on the little porch at either end of the car. There was a small whistle there, powered by the air lines that ran the Westinghouse brakes. I would wave and they would wave and sometimes toot the whistle which I always interpreted as an invitation to ride...someday.

And in my little dream, I would drift aboard, leaving my hot, sweaty, dirty-faced boy's body lying in the shade of a catalpa tree while I went along on an adventure to places I did not know. I got to blow the whistle and wave at other little boys envious to see me riding on the caboose porch, with my lunch pail and thermos full for adventure.

While the Little Girl waited her turn with the mechanic, I slept and dreamed my little boy dreams smiling to know that when you are wrapped in the long silvery cars of the train, it is the world that does the moving and no one is really leaving home.

9

A Long Day's End

Draw a 650 mile line straight from the nose of the little Mooney and you've got San Antonio. Somewhere about 50 miles shy of the Alamo City sits tiny Center Point, Texas. Home. The thought of home was a good thought, always is. Today the call of home was made stronger by a spring of non-stop travel, mostly for business and nearly all of it at breakneck pace.

Six hundred miles closer but also just off the nose of the Mooney was El Paso. Sitting a hot and arid 4,000 feet above sea level, El Paso was to be our one and only fuel stop en route from a weekend of staff retreat and play in equally hot but infinitely more exciting Las Vegas. If you could look from our perch at 9,000 feet straight through the Sangre de Christi Mountains, you would have seen El Paso. Except for the mountains and a line of killer thunderstorms, El Paso and lunch were just around the corner.

The controller in far away Albuquerque was juggling a dozen or more flights of heavy iron, all requesting altitude changes and course deviations in an attempt to keep the wings up and the passengers calm. The big iron drivers were negotiating their way to the same length of hot concrete that, at the moment, was nothing more than a numerical read-out on our GPS.

I had Stormscope, a four or five inch square of green phosphor screen that danced with bright green crosses, each a lightning strike, a warning in bright green that says "don't fly here." And there was way too much of "don't fly here."

The big boys had radar. Radar shows levels of precipitation but not lightning. If I have to choose, I'll take Stormscope.

A Southwest Airlines pilot asked to deviate into Mexican airspace and was granted a limited right to stray. A commuter plane wanted much the same, saying that the cells in his part of the sky had already built too high to climb over. A Continental pilot, just passing through the sector, advised that he may need to divert to El Paso due to a possible emergency. Swell.

"Stand by," he said. "We'll know more in about two minutes."

In a matter of seconds, he was back on the air declaring a medical emergency, calmly and professionally stating that they were dealing with a "heart attack in progress" and would need a vector directly to the airport, to please have medical personnel and transport available.

And then there was us. One little Mooney punching holes in a layer of cumulus clouds growing taller and darker by the minute.

"Mooney niner-five-mike-kilo, radar shows an area of heavy weather ten miles east of Columbus VOR. Would you like to deviate north to Deming?"

I never refuse an invitation from Air Traffic Control. Even with 20-year-old technology and a dozen or more airplanes to watch, they have never steered me wrong.

"That's affirmative. Thanks for watching, five-mike-kilo."

"Fly heading of zero-five-zero then direct Deming when able. Victor 94 to Newman, direct El Paso."

We read back the amended clearance, turning north as we did. Melanie dialed in Deming and I switched the GPS to slave with the autopilot. In a matter of seconds, our new plan was fact, our old plan forgotten.

Flying in the desert southwest is interesting. Flat, flat desert is punctuated by tall, very barren mountains. Sixty miles of nothing suddenly stabbed by 6,000 feet of rock. One here. Another there. Fly low beneath the cloud deck and watch the mountains disappear into the sky. Nice to see but deadly to those who stray from the airway to discover what pilots only half-jokingly refer to as granite clouds.

When the rains come, and they don't come often, the clouds still continue to float high above the desert floor. That was the way it was today as we sailed along at nine thousand feet, just under the cloud deck, well over the desert brown.

As the afternoon heat poured energy into the atmosphere, the clouds began to cluster and rise, higher and higher, gaining power and nature's anger as they climbed.

And the rain began, not where we were flying but to the left, then the right and then behind us and finally all around us. We looked to the south towards Columbus VOR and saw firsthand the weather that the controller in far away Albuquerque had predicted via radar.

We could easily look under the white and fluffy clouds of stratocumulus. But the air beneath the cumulonimbus, the thunderstorms, grew blacker and blacker, dark as pitch sucking up light like a celestial black hole come to earth.

I asked the controller for lower.

I could see two cells beginning to flank our route to sunshine and El Paso. And I thought that perhaps I could drop under the deck and scoot straight ahead to freedom. Now, this is not always a smart thing to do. Thunderstorms can come complete with down drafts powerful enough to toss an airplane of any size straight to the ground. But the rain, heavy as it was, did not appear to be blowing and besides, that little path just off the nose looked none the worse for the darkening shafts that bracketed north and south.

The controller would not, could not, give us lower even though I could see there was plenty of empty air between us and the darkening desert below. The minimum en route altitude for this stretch of victor 94 was 9,000 feet, exactly the game we were currently playing. So I held my breath and said, "Hold on. This could get a little bumpy."

At 9,000 feet we would only be 500 or so feet into the layer. My out, if we needed one, would be to cancel IFR and descend visually. Then, if we needed still more room to maneuver, we would do a quick 180 and meet the nice people in Deming.

I aimed for a light spot in the clouds knowing, hoping, that it was more than a promise of clear air on the other side.

We slipped into the wall, held on tight, and then, smooth as a baby's bottom, we squeezed out the other side, sailing into the sunshine like we owned the place.

"Mooney five-mike-kilo, are you clear of the weather?"

"That's affirmative, five-mike-kilo." I was breathing again and wondering if I had done the right thing. We were flying tired and fatigue does funny things to judgment. I wondered if fatigue had already worked a black magic with me. But the wondering only lasted a moment before I was invited to contact Approach and find our way to runway two-two, 9,000 plus feet of asphalt and safety.

If there is one thing that makes flying special, it is that you just can't pull over and get out. You are committed. And, you know, if there is one thing that separates the amateur and the pro, the successful and the alsoran, it is often not so much talent as it is commitment. Flying just forces the issue.

Like the carnie who must learn to make home wherever the Big Wheel turns or the crew of the AutoTrain, who no matter what, can't get off, when you are 'out there', there is no turning back.

10

Storm Lake

E l Niño had turned the country on its heels, pumping rain across the Southwest, paralyzing Denver with two feet of wet snow, and shaking a wintry fist everywhere north of Oklahoma. We flew around it, sometimes through it, straying from the flight plan in an effort to turn obstacle into mere inconvenience.

Over southern New Mexico we asked for permission to descend and spent a few hundred miles sniffing the bottoms of storm cells until we ran out of options and were forced to climb.

A day later we skipped around similar storms near New Orleans before nailing a difficult crosswind landing at the little airport by the lake. By Saturday we figured the weather would clear in the nation's midsection where only hours earlier El Niño was still managing to rattle windows in Wichita with cold, gusty winds.

This morning the weather briefers helped draw a mental picture that, with a little boost from The Weather Channel, made me think that we could safely fly.

We planned to fly right up the backside of the system, skirting the massive controlled airspace of Dallas/Ft. Worth, over-flying busy Oklahoma City, and stopping for fuel in Wichita.

At our altitude of 9,000 feet, the wind was out of the southwest at nearly 50 knots giving us a boost to about 235 miles an hour across the ground. In a word, we were honkin'.

By the time we reached Oklahoma, the wind had shifted slyly to the northwest, little by little until it had stolen away every knot that it had given us and taken back a few more as if to prove the point.

Wichita has a reputation as wind-swept prairie and it didn't disappoint. By the time we were close enough to pick up the automated weather broadcast, we were nearly crawling, not more than 150 miles an hour with a falling oil temperature to match.

Approach invited us to fly a heading of 3-5-0 and descend at pilot's discretion to 4,000 feet. We put out our electronic feelers, searching for the invisible radio beams we knew would be reaching out for us from the instrument landing system.

A DC-9 flying ahead of us on the same route advised the controller that 'light ice' had been encountered a thousand feet lower at three.

Approach passed along the message that I had already heard. What do you do? We needed to land for fuel and, even though I always fly with plenty of reserve fuel, the entire Midwest was soaked in cold, damp air. Chances were we'd fly somewhere else to encounter more of the same. Besides, the report was for light ice at 3,000 feet and we wouldn't be staying there very long.

The Mooney has power to spare and if things get too rough, we'd just point her nose upward and climb back to clear air with another plan. More likely we would reach 3,000 feet, grab onto the glideslope, and be looking at the runway in a matter of minutes.

Before we left the house, Melanie had handed Stuart a novel. He's a white-knuckle flyer and she thought it might be good to occupy his attention with something to read.

Good concept, lousy execution. She handed him, *Airframe*, by Michael Crichton. The cover copy begins..."Three passengers are dead. Fifty-six are injured. The interior of the cabin is virtually destroyed. But the pilot manages to land the plane..."

Smooth move, Melanie.

Stuart put away his book as we melted into the clouds looking for runway.

As advertised, we started picking up ice at 3,000 feet, first the leading edge of the wing, and then the windshield.

We dropped out of the cloud layer at about 500 feet, staring right down the centerline of runway one right. The bright orange windsock to the left of the runway numbers stood straight out, pointing menacingly across, not along, the runway. The little Mooney was crabbing to the left, weathervaning into a wind that would have been perfect had the folks in the tower been capable of pushing a button and turning the runways 90 degrees.

I planted the Little Girl on the numbers, fighting the yoke and rudder pedals to keep from being blown clear off the runway. About midway along the strip, I regained control and composure and turned to the FBO. As we taxied along the parallel, we watched two consecutive Citation drivers smoke their even larger tires and felt better seeing them struggle.

While on hold to file the next leg, I doodled a rock/paper/scissors list and watched the clouds sailing across the field grow darker by the minute.

* Anything you can do in boots and jeans
  beats anything done in a tie.
* Any day you can fly, even this one,
  beats any day spent on the ground.
* Mexican food beats anything else
  unless Melanie cooks it.

* Any day spent with Melanie
     beats any other day.

Cleared to take to the skies, we skidded along the same crosswind runway until the little Mooney finally clawed out enough forward speed to leave concrete and crosswind behind.

"Mooney niner-five-mike-kilo, on course direct to Manhattan. Nice paint job. Contact Departure."

"Direct Manhattan. Thanks for the compliment, Departure. So long!"

The gray clouds swallowed us whole, held us close for a few cold minutes, and then spit us out into bright sunshine on top.

Last night we set the clocks back and somebody told the sun. By the time we poked back through the clouds, the sun was well on its way to another day on the other side of the globe. We were left with the chill that always comes in the cold, dry air of dusk this far north.

We set down gently, consuming hardly enough runway to really even need one. Damn! There wasn't a soul to witness this perfection!

Alone on the ramp, we parked next to the only other plane apparent in Storm Lake, Iowa, a Mooney of indeterminant vintage but beautiful nonetheless. It was pointed nose first into the soft orange light that remained. We had heard the pilot announce his arrival when we were still 40 miles out and asked that he let the folks know we were coming, to not head home to watch the ballgame before we made it in.

The rental car was parked out front, as promised, and, no surprise, I found the keys not well hidden inside the gas tank hatch. No note, no contract. Just the keys left by a voice that I had only heard on the phone, never giving either my full name or a credit card, only a promise to bring the car back. And that's the way it is in Middle America, where both values and food are predictably and comfortably white bread.

Tomorrow we would see firsthand how folks in this part of the world get things done. How they make a life out of a flat landscape that stretches to forever; how they depend on neighbors instead of government.

Tonight is the World Series, the second since we started on this project. I'm with Stuart, who is an adventure all in himself. Gruff and rough around the edges, Stuart treats material things as if everything was made out of steel. He tosses and slams and makes me nuts. But he is a gentle giant and there is no one else that I would want to be in charge if there were a crisis.

Stu was a paramedic before the pressures of family and local politics made him think that launching yourself from a warm bed for absolutely nothing made less than zero sense. But if it's my butt that needs saving, he's the one I want to be there. Cool, competent, caring.

Dinner was at the Lakeshore Restaurant, a plain place with plain food served by plain waitresses wearing Lakeshore T-shirts and sporting a Midwestern friendliness that makes any place feel a few degrees closer to home.

Stu and I ate steak. (To hell with fat and cholesterol! We'll walk it off tomorrow.) It was not much more than eight bucks each and it was as hot and delicious as it gets. After seeing the hours posted on the glass door, we made a note to stop back for breakfast.

Breakfast was more of the same only this time, at six in the morning, it was dark outside. The after church families feeling out of place in polyester suits and too-short ties had been replaced by guys in gimme caps and workboots.

"One," droned a monotone voice on the speaker. The voice came from the kitchen and it was trying too hard to sound cool and indifferent. That's cooks for you. All of us are tough guys, too cool to sing or be playful. By nine o'clock when there are a few more waitresses and the sun is up, when the coffee finally kicks in, then maybe 'One,' and 'Seven' or whatever servers are on duty, will be treated to a little more levity from the guy in the stainless cage.

"So you must be number one. Does that mean you are the best waitress or simply the oldest?" I teased.

"Uh-huh," she smiled and poured Stu another round of the hot stuff I never learned to drink in spite of years cooking breakfast in one Denny's or another.

"Uh-huh, what?"

"Both! I started here 25 years ago as a relief. Back then I was so nervous, I couldn't remember my number so they changed it to number one figuring that would be easier. I liked the work and I liked the number and here I am!"

This woman must have started at the age of two because she looked pretty good for someone who had spent two and half decades hauling eggs and dumping coffee. We absent-mindedly watched her make the rounds, dispensing sunshine before dawn in the form of hot coffee and a smile that came naturally.

The Lakeshore was beginning to jump by the time we had sopped up the last of the eggs. The gimme caps had begun to give way to the occasional tie. We decided to leave before the joint turned to sport coats and bankers.

Storm Lake, the town, was named in 1855 when a small group of pioneers first stumbled up the gorgeous glacier lake that is its namesake. Who would have imagined that the herds of deer and elk and the crooked paths that wild beasts follow would someday give way to hogs and arrow-straight rows of corn and beans?

Storm Lake, three thousand acres of crystal clear water is a jewel, wrapped around a pretty, little city that the Chamber of Commerce rather ambitiously bills as "City Beautiful."

I betcha that Mayor Sandra Madsen grew up in Storm Lake. And I betcha she would have never dreamed how life in City Beautiful would someday turn out to be.

We left Storm Lake for Newell, a smaller town outside a small town, in search of the Bodholdts. Good people, we were told, and willing to have unusual company for a while.

The Whitehouse was Camelot in 1961 when Dale Bodholdt met Judy, blonde and slim-hipped, a fireball woman who would give him sons and share life on the family farm in Iowa. They would set up house not far from Grandma B's, raising corn and soybeans, hogs and children, loving them all, waiting for harvest.

Now we sat around the table, father and son, mother and daughter-in-law: partners in America's greatest enterprise, agriculture.

The mailbox announced that Dale and Judy had done well. Neatly applied on the east side of the box in black letters on white stick-on squares modestly revealed that this is where Tony and Lori, Jason, and Kari live, just a few miles from Newell, Iowa (about a century from New York and big cities anywhere.)

The front yard, that green, unplowed space where the house, barns and pens form an island in a sea of crops, was bordered with tall maples. The trees had been planted as if by a surveyor. In soldier-straight order, they marched across the grass alongside the road. The maples, tall, fat and old, were no doubt planted around 1900, the year the spartan-white farmhouse was built.

Not really. This house was never built. It was then as it is now, nearly a century later, a work in progress. The original one room-later-chicken-coop is now a game room where Jason and Kari bide the uneasy truce of brother and sister.

The kitchen has running water, a gift of time installed a few decades ago. And there is the computer, winking its electric eye in the corner.

The house, like the children and family that give it life, is growing and changing.

So it is with life on the farm. Once harsh yet simple, now merely difficult and complicated.

In the yard Sarge is supposed to bark away bad guys. I guess he can tell a friendly face because he nearly begs strangers to forget the house, to come and play instead. He will nuzzle and talk a baleful play-with-me moan until the visitor bends to scratch an ear.

We sit around the table. One that, if tables could talk,

might just tell better stories. There is Tony and Lori, Dale and Judy. Son and daughter-in-law, Dad and Mom, all partners charged with wringing life and a living out of 1,200 acres of gently rolling farmland too close to winter for this southerner.

Lori has dinner on the table. It's noon. Yep. Noon. Dinner is served at noon, lunch comes before supper in what seems to be an unusual schedule of eat and eat again.

On the table there is pork, no surprise. You can, if you wanted, look right out the back door and see where the next pork dinner is waiting. There is corn, delicious, sweet, melt-in-your-mouth corn from the summer garden. Potatoes, baked but tasting mashed, as sweet as the air in springtime. They, too, are straight from the garden, tasting like nothing you will ever find in a restaurant or supermarket.

Grandma made jam. I forget what kind, just good.

There were biscuits and salad, milk and iced tea. Name it and it's yours.

The friendly banter, the reverence for the land, reminded me of a Thanksgiving dinner shared years ago with a family named Klevin that lived in Kingsport, Tenn., that tail of the Blue Ridge Mountains, a neighbor to Bristol and Johnson City. The Klevins were as close to the Waltons as I had ever seen.

It had felt good to stand around their table, joining hands with the rest of the family singing grace in rich, blended voices...'Praise God from whom all blessings flow/ Praise Him all creatures here below/ Praise Him above ye Heavenly host/ Praise Father, Son, and Holy Ghost/ Ahhhh-men.' The words...or was it the melody or was it something else...wrapped around me and let me know that this food would be special.

Years later I would think of the Klevins when I saw *Places in the Heart*. The scene at the end where the murderer and the murdered, where the saints and sinners showed up, both living and dead, at the small town church, the movie maker had told us a marvelous story, all right but as a surprise, presented the moral as an afterthought.

I wonder how many people got it, that there is a place in the heart of God for each of us. Perhaps we won't even have to ask. Perhaps it will be given to us through grace alone.

Then, big Jerry Klevin broke the spell by booming, "Let's eat!" just as now Tony and Lori invited us to join them as if we were neighbors from a little further away than expected.

Lori had called on the radio to remind us 'boys' not to be late, that dinner would be at 'twelve-thirty sharp.' We had been hanging out down at the grain elevator in Newell when Tony hustled us into the pickup. Across the checkerboard landscape, the pick-up bumped and bounced before turning into the gravel drive beside the neat white house just in time.

The kitchen was warm. We used the back door as if there would never be a reason to use the front. We checked our boots for mud, a sin that would have been quickly forgiven but a transgression none of us wanted to test. I pulled off my hat and gloves and denim jacket and tossed them with the others in the pile beside the door. (On the farm, a hat and coat aren't quite the same as in the city. Out here they are not much different than a tool belt, not really clothing just something that is all function, no form.)

Across the table Dale stared into steel blue eyes that belonged to his son Tony, same as his, blue as blue. The arms were hard, muscle born of work not meanness. Short and sinewy; two peas, one pod.

We talked about work and life, friends and neighbors. Although out here, where the sky meets the earth at the end of long, dark furrows, friends and neighbors are pretty much the same thing.

Dale and a neighbor had attended a farm sale, one of those bitter-sweet events where a family farm goes out of business. Maybe the bank finally called the note, having run out of patience and/or excuses, closed her up and called the auctioneer. Or perhaps, if it's any more pleasant, the old Mr. and Mrs. suddenly discovered that they were indeed the old Mr. and Mrs., too old to scratch out another year of hard winters and still more difficult summers. Too old to answer the call of one more season but too young to just die like so many flowers planted alongside the wellhouse. Time to sell out and move to the city. You know, be with the grandkids, take it easy and pretend that you never liked farming the old homestead in the first place.

Dale and friends were at one such event when Dale and Joe decided that another neighbor, also Joe, was due for a little prank. Joe had been cuttin' up all afternoon, thinking he was funny, and he was. And maybe that was all the more reason to pull a fast one.

The two men left the sale early, headed for the neighbors' place. In the barn they cut the bottom out of a five gallon pail used to haul feed to the hogs. Another pail they nailed firmly to the floor of the farrow house, that warm, smelly barn where piglets live until capable of surviving the elements. The bottom-less pail was placed beside it and both were filled with feed.

A dozen years later the simple prank, that vision of unsuspecting Joe yanking on the feed pails and getting a double shot of surprise still had the power to roll us into tearful laughter. And that's the way it is with life in the country; simple pleasures, but not simple people.

Around the table sat a meteorologist, a commodities broker, an accountant, an agronomist, a veterinarian, a banker, carpenter and an engineer, all in the form of four rather ordinary people drawn together by the bond of farm and family, a way of life from which their own personalities were inseparable.

Dinner was followed by generous scoops of ice cream and an invitation to sample several varieties of cookies, all obviously homemade, lovingly stacked in Tupperware.

How is it that we are in Podunk, in the middle of nowhere, still finding people of such sophistication? Dale sits to my left. He's fifty-seven, I think he said. And Judy, his wife and partner, a reminder that beauty is as beauty does, still has that sparkle that turns heads. And my guess is that she will have it to the very end. Yet, sparkle or not, she is talking about yields and management.

"We're members of several associations and that gives us access to consultants," said the blonde woman that Jason and Kari know as Grandma. "When we need a little expert advice or maybe just a disinterested third party to help with our decisions, we call in the hired help. Last week we were debating over whether we should lease a new combine instead of purchasing. So we called one of our consultants.

"The consultant ran the numbers and helped us decide that the lease wasn't in our long-term interest."

"You use consultants? This is a farm. Feed the hogs, plant the corn. Consultants?"

"This is a business," said Grandma.

('My, what big business you have,' thought Goldilocks.)

All this from a group who started the conversation so simply..."You workin' on that machine shed door?" "You bring the boars back?" "Where do you want 'em?"

The rhythm of the day starts early. Kids up. Breakfast. Dinner into the oven.

Lori takes the kids to school and stays, working part time assisting with the English as a Second Language program plus a few other assignments.

We headed to the hogs, bundled to the chin to protect against the crisp, fall air. Actually, the air belonged to winter with a stiff and constant breeze out of the west, blowing 30 degree air until it felt much, much colder, chilling us to our boots in spite of a bright sun and blue, cloudless skies.

First up, feed the animals. On the Bodholt farm that means hogs. Big, fat, hairy hogs. Hogs by the hundred weight. Hogs on the hoof. Hogs on hogs. Big, dirty, ignorant and hungry.

Animal science is just that, science. There is room for compassion but not much. Hogs don't sleep in a bed, they live in mud. Hogs don't get attention other than what is necessary to put bacon on the farmer's table by putting bacon on yours. If you don't like it, then buy the hogs and let them live with you.

Tony had devised a clever way to fill the feed buckets.

Instead of the usual bin and shovel, Tony had the feed delivered into a huge hopper sitting on tall metal stilts. Beneath the hopper ran a small wagon between two metal rails that served as tracks. (Is there a farmer anywhere who cannot weld?)

Place two five-gallon pails on the wagon, roll it into position under the feed hopper, pull back a flat metal sliding door and gravity does the rest, filling the pails without once lifting a shovel.

The hogs knew we were coming, and they were hungry and ready. Pushing and shoving, they rushed the fence as we spread pail after pail against the feedrail and into the mud. The hogs are fed a daily ration of five pounds each, just enough to sustain their massive 250-plus pounds of reproductive bacon. These guys weren't guys at all. They were brood sows, living flesh factories that make ham and pork chops. Hungry?

I wasn't. But the hogs were.

The sows are kept hungry. Not starved. Just not completely satisfied. It makes them more attentive mamas and when you are in the business of breeding, good mamas are what you need.

But keeping them hungry also has a way of eliminating any potential show of manners. Some of the sows' backsides showed bright red blood, a sign that a hungry neighbor had taken a bite of its genitals. Pretty, it ain't.

Four boars were mixed in with the 30 or so females. After feeding at the various pens, our job would be to see how good a job the boars had done.

By 8:30 no one was hungry, certainly not me.

Sarge leaped to his feet, barking to announce a visitor. It was the local vet, here to assist with the pregnancy testing. Coveralls and gimme cap, it was hard to imagine that this was one of the brightest of the bright, one of the select few who had made it into veterinary school. Smart college students become people doctors. But the really smart ones work on the farm.

Think about it. Your family doctor may have wanted a cow for a patient but had to settle for you because, due to the limited number of seats in veterinary school, only the best of the best get the nod. The rest, well, now you know what they're doing.

The truck rattled to a stop and Mr. Greenjeans slid out of the cab, zipping up the coveralls for a little extra warmth.

From paneled boxes on the side of the truck, Dr. Bill unloaded his tools, a mysterious metal box that hung around his neck, a rack full of empty vials, several fat colored grease pencils, and a syringe the size of a house.

And one more piece of equipment, a long metal pole with a loop of heavy cable at the end. This would be used later to fish for hogs, a process that could be called "snout sweeping."

For a moment I am grateful for the cold, clean air. My nose is so frozen that I do not notice the smell of the pig dung that is slopping over the soles of my boots. These boots have walked in some pretty gunky stuff but I think that tonight I will try kicking out of them rather than prying them off by hand.

The vet whips out a bottle of gooey liquid riding in the back pocket of his coveralls. He coats the end of a flat-faced, shiny metal probe and reaches under the hog, feeling for the uterus. This is a sonogram done at the speed of light with no concern about how to decorate the nursery. Male or female, 'doesn't matter. Just find out if this one has been bred or not.

Over the snorting and the clack of hoofs, a small beep could sometimes be heard chirping from the instrument that was hanging around Doc's neck, attached to the probe and veteran of more pregnancies than the stork.

Beep. "This one is." A long orange mark is drawn down the back.

No beep. "Open," says the doc, already looking for the next impatient patient. A long red mark goes on this one.

The hogs are so distracted by the feed that they appear not to notice.

These are big beasts, capable of knocking even a large man to the mud as they body-check their way to a better position along the rail.

Preg testing done, we count. A little more than half. The four boars in the mix still have job security. A few of the older sows do not. The vet looks at one, shakes his head. She is skinny by hog standards and no longer likely to deliver a healthy brood. Breeding is tough on the animals. Between eight and fifteen babies is quite a stress. Just imagine.

"This girl looks like she'll be going to town." You know what that means.

While the vet is here, it makes sense to go ahead and test the herd for disease. The rules require that 30 percent must be tested, 16 of this particular group.

The long pole flashes out, sweeping the ground near the rooting hogs. We've distracted them by tossing out an unexpected ration of feed and the hungry beasts can think of nothing but food which they snort from the mud, salivating profusely at the very thought of more.

Working from the top, Tony would slip the cable loop in the hog's mouth and with a quick snap, pull a sliding outer sleeve on the pole. This had the effect of shortening the loop, tightening it around the snout.

Bingo! Tony gets a strike, lassoing 250 pounds of bacon without looking under the flap on the package to see which has more meat. The hog squeals, so loudly that Dr. Bill has taken to ear plugs, the kind you would expect in a foundry or on a firing range. These brutes are loud. Tightly looped around the snort, the pigs ooze saliva and show the food and mud still clinging to their pink tongues. They aren't being hurt but you would never guess that from the noise.

Tony and the hog both dig in, neither willing to give an inch, a stand-off posture that is perfect for the moment. The vet pushes his way into the crowd, holding the huge syringe in a safe position. None of us wants a surprise.

He reaches down and spears the pig in the carotid artery running the length of the windpipe. If the hog is hurt more, it's impossible to tell over the already loud, pleading squeal. As the blood is sucked into the syringe, Dr. Bill pulls a pair of gun-metal gray pliers from a pocket and zip quick attaches a metal tag through the ear. I add a white mark across the back.

Tony lets loose and jumps back just in case. The hog just as quickly retreats with a menacing glare that means nothing.

By the time we had captured and tested about a dozen hogs, the feed scattered along the rail was gone and the hogs, now wary began to wander deeper into the pen, staying out in the mud watching. When we spotted one without an eartag, we'd move in and attempt an arrest. Of course, even pigs aren't totally stupid, they'd move away, turning their snouts out of range as they brushed by to escape.

Hogs are not purposefully dangerous. They want food and that's about it. Later we would walk past one of the pens nearer the road and laugh to see these huge porcine players all lined up in the shelter, lying on their sides, sleeping in the late afternoon sun.

Pigs in the proverbial blanket. Cute, if a row of 300 pound hams can look cute.

Now that we were good and smelly, Tony decided it was time to finish chiseling a corn field just to the east of the house.

Tony scrambled up the ladder to the cab of the John Deere and fired up the giant diesel engine. The Deere is a huge piece of green equipment outfitted with seven foot tall dual tires. The arrangement adds traction and keeps the machine from sinking into the mud. The front wheels are also powered and taller than an automobile. It looked new as did most of the equipment we would see. We'd come to find out it was in its twelfth season, a tribute to either good maintenance and care or the incredible quality of American farm equipment.

Tony flipped down the armrest making the seat wide enough to accommodate a trainee as green as the tractor.

Air conditioned. Radio. Automatic transmission that can be shifted with or without the use of the clutch. Left and right brakes that allow the driver to lock one wheel completely and pivot the awkward appearing apparatus in graceful pirouette at the end of each row.

Following close behind was a bed of metal disks trailed even closer by a gang of sharp-pointed metal chisels. The disks would cut any remaining corn stalks, the chisels would lift the ground, breaking it into nature-sized chunks so that moisture and fertilizer could penetrate rather than run off.

The winter temperatures would freeze moisture that slipped beneath the surface causing it to further expand, lifting the soil in a natural churn that would mean added abundance when the sun returned life to the soil in early spring.

"Over there," Tony swept a gloved hand to the north, "that's the Land O'Lakes grain elevator where we are members. Our harvest is there.

"During harvest we work these fields every day for a month. I drive the combine, I'll show it to you later. Dad drives the tractor and pulls the wagons along side. We never stop. I just swing the boom over his wagon, start the auger and, while continuing to harvest, empty the hopper into the wagon. When the combine is empty, I wave Dad off and he goes for an empty.

"Mom pulls the loaded wagons over to the elevator and we keep at it sometimes until past midnight.

"Last year we had a great crop. We all did. There was one day when the elevator took in 145,000 bushels of grain. There were grain wagons lined up for blocks. Pretty much closed the town."

"That had to be frustrating, all that waiting."

"Nope. It's just part of it. Besides we all know everybody so we just visited and waited for the line to move."

Now the tractor turned back to the south, dragging the gang of chisels behind it. The gloved hand swept in the direction of a farm, silhouetted in the still-rising sun, surrounded by trees and history. "Over there," the glove directed, and pushed aside a long pause in the conversation.

"I used to play with the kid that lived over there. Our house was that one." The glove pointed east without moving further around the compass..

"But my friend's house is empty now. There are a lot of empty houses. It just doesn't take so many of us as it used to. When the land was farmed by horse, there was a limit to what a family could farm. Of course, at night, they could take the horse back to the barn while now we just turn on the headlights and keep plowing or harvesting." (The implication that modern equipment may balance less need for brute force with the increased demands of a faster pace. This is progress? Go figure!)

Machine does more work so man can work longer.

"We're only about three percent of the population but we can feed the world with a little rain and enough warm days."

We see an occasional ear of corn that had been missed by the equipment. Not many, though.

Once in a while we'd lift the gang of disks and chisel to skip an unworked patch that was left for better drainage. Did Tony decide where to leave room for water?

"Naw, that's been here ever since I can remember. You can see where the water might run away from the barn and out into this field. 'Guess it just made good sense to leave a little room for it to drain. 'Guess it also makes sense not to mess with a good thing."

'Funny to think that a decision made perhaps decades ago by some unremembered farmer would go unquestioned today, literally shaping the way of the land and the way it is farmed today.

We chiseled, disked and talked of life on the land, an idea that involves more heart than head but takes more brain-power than ever to hold onto a lifestyle that for many has already slipped away.

We backed the big rig into the equipment shed and brushed away the corn stalk parts that had been sucked against the air intake on the hood. Tony walked around the back, an inspection born of habit.

"Here!" He reached low to kick one of the chisels still caked with the rich, dark earth of the corn field. "Want some luck?"

He handed me a horseshoe. A big one.

"You'd be surprised how much metal we turn up in fields we've worked for year. Someone is always leaving us a little surprise. The horse that wore this shoe had to have been a pretty big fellow. Well, it's my field now." said Tony, accepting not just the fruit of his labor but the responsibility of leaving something, something worth having to the next farmer to turn the soil here in Newell, Iowa.

We pile into the pickup. With the crops in, this is the time devoted to getting ready for the long dark of winter and for planning the work of a spring that will come none too soon and then all too soon. I remind Tony of the country song about who is the real cowboy when there are three people in a pickup.

"The one in the middle," he beats me to the punch line affirming what I already knew. Country-western music isn't just a Texas thing. "'Cause he doesn't have to drive and he doesn't have to mess with the gate!"

To the west we stopped just for a moment to watch two huge hog sheds under construction. Nine hundred and more hogs per shed and there are two, side-by-side, the production owned by a corporation located light years from the smell that will inevitably result. And the waste? By the ton! Where will it go? Into the water? Spread on the fields? Where?

At least the farmer with his own capital at risk was building near his house. If anyone was at risk of blowing up a lifestyle, this guy was it. The smell of hog feces is like nothing else. It can cause the value of adjacent property to plummet. The run off can contaminate the groundwater. This is a serious environmental matter.

Anger? Are the neighbors angry?

No. Concerned.

No one could predict the long-term consequences. The farmer leading the way was not being ostracized. He had to earn a living too. But farmers from miles around were watching. They watched the thick, smelly manure being spread on the fields surrounding the houses where farmers with mega-sized operations lived. They drove slowly by the new construction, curious and maybe just a bit fearful. And they would talk when they met down at the grain elevator or after church or when playing cards with the neighbors. Not criticizing but wondering, as quiet and reserved in their opinions as the lives they lead.

They are all curious to know what works. This experiment could easily alter patterns that have held the local economy and social fabric in place for generations. It is a form of technology that is here and potentially devastating to those who are unable to adapt.

On the farm, there are several ways to get paid...or not.

You can farm your own land. You can own a farm in partnership. You can work as a sharecropper and take your half of the crop as payment for using land that belongs to someone else. Or you can work for hire and get paid on a per job basis; so much for plowing a field, so much for a fertilizer application.

Truth is, most of the farmers in this part of the world work a combination of agreements. Tony owns some land, partners with Dale on some others, even does the occasional fee for cash work. In the slow months, Dale and Tony load the pickup with homemade gear and pick up extra cash by sharpening disk blades, which is dirty, difficult, deafening work.

Working with old but still solid equipment made years ago by a local blacksmith, the partners attach small, electrically powered motors to the disk shafts and spin the disks. Then they muscle heavy grinders against the disks, grinding the old disk edges to a new and sharp edge, (imagine the noise!) gaining another season from disks that otherwise would have been too far gone.

In the winter months, they add a heavy black oil to keep the blades from turning to rust before the season and work begins anew. In the spring, there's no need to add oil as the disks won't sit long enough to rust.

Stopping at Dale and Judy's place, we climb aboard the combine, a used number that looks and runs factory-fresh when we stoke the giant diesel engine just for the exercise. Leave an engine sitting and the moisture that is in the oil condenses on the cylinder walls, leaving rust and wearing an engine out long before its natural time.

A combine gets used for 30 days of harvest and sits for the remaining 11 months. I couldn't help thinking about the men and women I had met at John Deere and wondered if they realized that they were building machines that could and would last a lifetime of harvests.

Another few miles of "so and so lives here," "that guy's a carpenter," "the fellow that lives here goes to our church," we found ourselves in the tiny town of Newell staring straight up at the white skin of the grain elevators. Pressed against a sky as blue as blue ever gets, the elevators are the life of this town and the farm families for miles around.

Inside there is the usual friendly reception.

"Scott's a writer. He's writing a book about tough jobs and is working with us."

"Nice to meet you," was all that was said but we knew good and well that Tony's next visit would likely result in a more thorough questioning.

"Where did you say they were from? What kind of book is it that they're writing? Were those guys brothers? 'You gonna be in the book? Are we gonna be in it?"

It just happened that we visited on a day when the stock market would take a huge dive, following the Japanese market that had closed just a few hours earlier. Attention is drawn to the computer sitting on the counter, listing commodity prices, speaking in tongues that only brokers and farmers could really understand. Up a point here, down a half point there and the savvy observer would be able to tell within a handful how many new cars would be sold in nearby Storm Lake.

Farmers haul their work to the elevator where they pay a monthly premium for storage. It's all based on bushels and bushels are based on pounds, 56 to be exact.

The farmer can sell whenever he wants or not...or pay storage for another month in hopes that the market will climb. But if not, pay the price and sell or continue to gamble. Tough decisions, these farmers make and all in an economy where a hiccup in the Far East can drop grain prices in the Midwest or send them to the moon...your guess.

When there is enough grain to fill 25 train cars, the elevator manager calls the railroad and orders the car. Sometimes the cars arrive before the grain is sold. Then the manager must call a broker at Quaker or ADM and hope that someone is in the market to buy and that too many some-ones are not in the market to sell.

In twenty-four hours the cars must be loaded and ready to roll. Otherwise there is a penalty, demurrage, a fee that escalates by the day.

We stood at the counter and watched the future unfold on the same computer that gives the weather. Weather, commodity prices, each a gamble, and the stakes are huge. I was drawn to the screen, hypnotized by the numbers and the consequences when Tony broke the trance. "We've got to get home. If we're late, we'll have a hot wife and a cold dinner."

At the dinner table we talked about 'the business' and laughed at my tape recorder sitting next to the butter. Dale would tease about the IRS and say, "'Better turn that thing off!' Then we'd all laugh and the storytelling would begin again.

(When I slipped into the office late one night to pull a few notes from the tape, I noticed that Stu had labeled the tapes 'farm friends' and I smiled in agreement.)

We talked about Lori's job working with the kids at school, helping teach English as a Second Language. The complexion of the town was changing, had changed, and probably would change some more. If the markets were more global, the little town of Newell was also becoming more worldly.

No, you still couldn't get a jalapeno on your baked potato but there were lots of Mexicans and Somalians, Hmoung Tribespeople, Vietnamese and other Asians moving to Storm Lake and bringing their ways to the hinterland.

Yes, there is more crime in town but folks in the country had still not learned to lock their doors although Lori admitted to locking up at night or at least most nights when she thought about it or perhaps was reminded by the evening news.

And nearly everyone was on the Internet talking to the world, making it feel welcome here in northwestern Iowa.

There is a huge packing plant that belches white smoke in Storm Lake. It went through tough times not too many years back. A highly unionized workforce had made competition difficult so money traded hands, the name changed, and along with it a good many jobs. New management brought in the foreigner who would work and be happy making considerably fewer dollars. Compared to their homelands and expectations, Storm Lake, even at minimum wage, seemed pretty close to heaven.

If you don't quite get the significance of one packing plant to a town the size of Storm Lake, then consider what happened, or didn't, in nearby Spencer, Iowa, once considered by most in these parts to be Storm Lake's sister city.

Not too many years after Storm Lake had weathered a tidal wave of foreign faces, an outside corporation filed intentions to start up operations in an abandoned plant bringing with it 350 new jobs, no small deal for a town of less than 10,000. But what do you know? The townspeople, including the business community, said not just "no" but "hell, no."

Citing the problems still not fully solved in nearby Storm Lake, the folks of Spencer decided to pass.

In Storm Lake, what had been a mostly white, middle-

America, homogenous community for more than a century now faced crime, illiteracy, cultural dislocation, and falling real estate values of what seemed to be of epic proportions.

Storm Lake, to me, looks like white bread America but to some of the locals, it seems as if the sky were falling.

Immigrants are building their version of the American dream while the 'natives' are only hanging on to it. It's only natural that immigrants would be willing to work for lower wages, cram two or more families into a small apartment, and generally do whatever it takes to live in a land of possibility. Beautiful when you think about it or write about it but from the vantage of right next door, the issue starts to get personal.

Back at the table we were working on less global issues.

The big question?

"How do you decide when to plant?"

"We argue!" And the laughter erupts.

"You get a feel for it," was Tony's offering.

"We pay a lot of attention to soil temperature," came the more clinical answer from Judy.

Dale: "Somehow you get a feeling that spring is here. The first thing isn't planting, it's working the ground. That could be as early as March if it's dry."

Judy: "They see a couple of tractors in the field and that's a hint. No one wants to be first or last."

The seed is ordered and paid for in December. The salesmen are themselves farmers so there is lots of discussion about which seed will perform best in which field. Sometime in early spring it will arrive, bagged on pallets. And rarely do the Bodholdts plant a single brand of seed. Plant genetics is pure science so long as you don't count luck. But if you count luck, then you don't take too many unnecessary chances in a business where life itself is a gamble.

"We usually lose a crop four or five times before we harvest it," says Judy referring to the anxiety of simply watching The Weather Channel. Too much rain, or too little. A big wind too late in the season or hail too early and a year of hard labor, a ton of cash, and any hope for a decent harvest can vanish in a heartbeat.

"When it storms at your house, I bet it doesn't bother you."

After the planting, the rest just sort of follows. The corn and beans grow, God willing, until one day, you know.

Harvest is determined by moisture content. Too much moisture and the crop will ruin without costly drying accomplished by huge gas heaters. Too little moisture and the weight per unit volume, call it a bushel, is so low that the price won't justify the work.

At the elevator the charge is three cents per bushel per percentage point of moisture that must be dried off. Harvest too early and you pay for it in drying fees; too late and you just don't get paid. Wait really late and an early snowfall may make your decision for you by laying the crop right on the ground where it cannot be recovered.

On the farm there are always neighbors who stop by, timing their visit when they know the kitchen table will be full of lunch and conversation. To the city dweller, life on the farm must look awfully isolated and empty but that couldn't be further from town or truth.

"In the old days we would work together. We might help a neighbor unload straw or run cement or bale or thresh."

"Today with all the equipment, we don't get as much chance to work together but there is plenty of time to visit."

"If it was rainy, there might be four or five guys here."

Funny to hear this from four adults each armed with a two-way radio. And I'm willing to bet that there are more farmers with internet accounts than city folks. Tony has plenty of book-marked sites on the world wide web where he watches the weather, grain prices, and keeps up with the latest news in agriculture. Lori keeps the family books on the computer.

On the farm who you are is what you do. On the farm your work is your lifestyle.

"I couldn't stand working at the bank," sighed Lori obviously glad to be free of the clock. "At the bank everything was tied to the clock. Here, life is tied to the weather and the animals and maybe that's less predictable but you sure don't feel so trapped. And I don't think I could ever live in the city. Those people don't know how to sit down! My nieces were here last summer and they said, "Aunt Lori, can we go to your mall?" Well, we were just at Wal-Mart three days earlier and I couldn't imagine why they would want to go again so soon!"

"But don't you sometimes feel tied to the hogs?"

"If we're gone, they look after our hogs. When they go off, we take care of their hogs."

I drifted from the conversation to think about a time just after we had moved from the city to the country. I was in Park City , Utah on a speaking engagement when I called home at our traditional time of eight o'clock. Melanie was beside herself as she breathlessly told of spying a small herd of longhorn cattle just outside our dining room window. To hear her tell it, the horns were at least eight feet long which, as a Texan, I have to admit is a possibility.

It seems the cattle had wandered over from a nearby ranch.

Melanie called the neighbors in search of the owner and finally had to threaten to have the beasts 'towed' if they were not promptly removed from our property!

Tony: "And even though it sounds like there's no flexibility, there is. I have to feed the hogs but it's totally my decision when. I can start out in the morning with a plan for the whole day. By noon I may have a completely different plan but it's my plan. So you are flexible...and you aren't. How you treat your animals every day is how they treat you when you take them to town."

Lori chimes in saying, "And we do have a schedule, at least during harvest. I see to it that they get breakfast early so they can get to the fields. Dinner is the big meal. I make them come in at noon. They need the break. Then lunch is about three thirty and that's served in the field. Supper is late, around seven."

After dinner we head back to work, backing the huge John Deere into the equipment shed and wrestling a wide contraption made of ganged soil chisels onto the hitch, then around to the silo where we pick up a homemade floating blade that would level the soil as we chisel. It takes some doing. Wrenches and bolts, a house jack and ingenuity. We finally made the connection enjoying the fact that farm toys are big toys.

On the farm, the only subtlety is in the thinking not the doing. Work on the farm is more brawn than brain. It is only in deciding what to do that a clear head is required.

Two words. Two words that tell why work, and life, on the farm is special—independence and variety. No successful farmer needs someone to set his schedule and dictate priority. Only self-starters need apply. And if you need a guarantee, then farming is not for you. The weather can literally bring feast or famine.

Unlike corporate life, there is no one to pick you up and say, "Too bad. Here's your paycheck for showing up."

Showing up on the farm doesn't get you squat. Production does.

And variety? The worst jobs on the planet are those where man is machine, where there would be no job if they could invent a machine to do it. We've plenty of them. They are sad, depressing places where men are reduced to pieces of equipment. It is true that there are times on the farm when man is little more than a common beast of burden. But, at least he is a thinking, deciding beast and that makes all the difference.

If there is criticism of unions, it is that in so many instances, in the interest of job security, they have created job descriptions that keep people from doing a variety of things, that keep their people from thinking...ever.

It is the natural order of things for man to be his own boss, to decide, to hold his own destiny in his own mortal hands. It is the natural order of things, maybe a root of happiness, for work to be full of change, variety, and challenge.

And nowhere have I seen work that so fits the natural order of things as on the farm, where seasons and self, a gamble on God and farmer makes all the difference.

By 4:30, the ever curious Jason finds his way home from school. He has 32 cats and one weary, black Lab to feed. Jason, the font of knowledge about tractors and pigs, about plowing and computers. When our day is over, his day will come.

When we could stay no longer, Stu was reluctant to stow the video gear. It seemed that everywhere we looked, we were faced with yet another Kodak moment. Through the tall grass at the side of the road, the light straw waving in the wind, reaching effortlessly across and under the barbed wire fence. And framed by the fence, the John Deere marched north then south turning the gray soil black as it chiseled up and back. In the distance stood an abandoned farmhouse that now was filled only with dust and memories.

The homestead stood crisp and white, guarded by that phalanx of leafless trees.

On the horizon the grain elevators in Newell were holding up a blue, blue winter sky. Blue and gold, gray and black, the colors were perfect, needing no adjustment just appreciation. A silver-topped silo, a green John Deere, a rusty red Ford, and the rosy cheeks of children, innocent and waiting for company or snow or a new puppy.

Tony would be off to the Lions Club. He was a new member and didn't want to miss a meeting. Lori extended the supper invitation for another day. Tony invited us to join him at Lions. He insisted that we would be welcome and I knew he was right. But I didn't want to be Show and Tell, particularly not with latent pig stuff clinging to my boots.

Stu and I headed to town still chilled in spite of coats, boots, hats, gloves, and long johns. Stu is easy to travel with. He doesn't ask much. A television with a remote control and a sleep timer, a box of Cheez-its and a big bottle of cheap soda. Oh, and a copy of *USA Today*. And it doesn't even have to be all that recent, just news of any kind.

As is our habit, we were up before dawn cranking up the rental car in air nearly frozen solid. It was twenty-five bucks for each day. No paperwork at all. No insurance. No shuttle bus. Just a pretty good car for a pretty good price.

"Leave it like you found it. We'll pick it up."

We followed the green and white beacon right to the airport, stashed the car keys behind the gas filler door and began scraping a heavy layer of frost off the Mooney.

I ran through one battery attempting to start an airplane that was cold to the core. The second battery barely did the job but after what must have been a dozen close starts, the big Continental engine caught fire and stayed running.

We back-taxied to the end of three-six, announced our departure to no one and pointed the Little Girl in the right direction.

And the right direction is any direction that takes us home.

11

Flatland Memories

Storm Lake put me in a Midwestern mood, whatever that is. I just know that as we flew south to the next adventure, my thoughts were in Ohio of all places. I couldn't help thinking those there-but-for-the-grace-of-God-go-I kind of thoughts.

I grew up in Kentucky, south of Cincinnati, sitting on my grandfather's knee, perched on a bar stool at the Silver Leaf Cafe. My grandfather really was grand. We called him Boom but I never knew why.

You could argue that a little guy had no business sitting on a bar stool with or without his grandfather. You could also argue that half of the TV your kids see, they shouldn't. And every time you say damn, hell or worse in front of your kids, maybe you shouldn't.

The crowd at the Silver Leaf was outfitted in work pants, sweatshirts, white socks and brogans. For Lent they would give up beer and instead drink shots. It was that kind of crowd. They were rough but good-hearted, living in a neighborhood where, as they would say, "nobody had nothing."

Once in a blue moon, I'd slip onto a stool at the Silver Leaf and try not to look conspicuous. But my starched shirts and laundered jeans nearly always gave me away. I rarely mentioned that I am from the old neighborhood. I just looked at the guys, my age, who are sitting on the same stools where their grandfathers and fathers sat, where their kids sometimes climbed up and whispered that they'd like a Coke, where Mom says it's time to come home.

And I wonder what it is that makes some folks choose to stay while others go. And who is to say who is the happier?

I think these things while flying. Especially at night when the world turns dark and the lights of the instruments invite thinking.

At night, from the air, you understand. Light is all that holds the world in place. Almost the instant the sun disappears, the world begins to lose its form, expanding to the stars. In that same instant, man begins to shrink, drawing close to his fire, even the fire of the electric lights that seem to know when it is time.

You can't catch them, those lights, try as you may. One moment they are invisibly cold, the next they are twinkling from houses and barns, ball fields and airports. The lights from airports are the best, the friendliest if you are a pilot. Especially if you are flying VFR (visual flight rules), and need the reassuring flash-flash of white, then green, then white and green again from the beacon to let you know that you are not far from enough asphalt or concrete to slip again to the confining safety of the earth.

If you are flying on instruments, there is less of a hurry to find the field. The instrument panel glows as soft as the lights below as if it knows the way. And it does. Once the sun has ceded the day, the horizon spills into space and the lights of man leave great dark gaps in the night.

Big city lights are beautiful but small town lights tell warmer stories. In small towns, there is church and there is school; sometimes not much else. In May or early June, I imagine as I fly quietly by, moms and dads, relatives and neighbors are gathering to watch the ritual of graduation. Graduation is the biggest event of the year. For some, the biggest of a lifetime. Sometimes it's bigger than the Lions' Club wild game dinner. Bigger than the sheriff's race.

In small town schools, graduation looks different, warmer than what city folks know because the school itself is not much bigger than a family. There is something to be said about organizations of any kind where it is possible to know everyone.

From five or seven or nine thousand feet, I like to slip quietly by and think about how it might be to live in this house or that. How would it be to live among these lights, the ones right off the wingtip?

In the rural communities that dot the darkness below, life is slower and closer. You know your neighbor. Heck, you depend on your neighbor. So your neighbor's pain becomes your pain, and joy is likewise freely shared. You wouldn't dream of missing their kid's big moment just as they will be and have been there to cheer in turn.

Tonight the engine noise is crowded out by an imaginary graduation a mile and a half plus a million years below.

In small towns, formal attire means find the tie, dust the boots. No one will notice that you are wearing the same suit your brother wore to the wedding last June. Their work boots will stick just as unfashionably from their trousers. Besides, no one came to notice, just to support and to see the extended family that brings pride when the team wins or the state tests prove once again that our children are doing just fine, thank you.

Or formal could be the bright yellow vest with purple piping that tells the world you are a member of Lions' International and that there is important business at hand. It could be the constable in his wide hat, metal star, and .38 that has never been fired. It could be just a clean pair of jeans and the Garth Brooks T-shirt you've been saving for something special and this is it.

Sophomore boys with slicked-back hair and shit-eating grins flank the stage steps, there to assist piano-legged matrons in chunky shoes and dirndl skits sailing across the gym to mount the steps and deliver this year's scholarship from the Eastern Star or the American Legion Auxiliary.

The graduates will wiggle in their folding chairs. The State Representative on hand to deliver the obligatory commencement address won't notice that the introduction being stammered out by the superintendent is too long, too self-serving for the occasion. And the sweat will just begin to run down the backs of the school board members, the plumbers and farmers, small business people who have agreed to serve, preserving community values, whatever they are.

Tonight the agendas have been folded accordian style to become make-shift fans reminding us all of the Baptist tradition. Tomorrow they will be tucked in a drawer. Next year, if they survive at all, it will be in attics and closets where they will wait to become a born-again memory sometime after the first baby, or first husband, or when Grandpa dies and the box is opened to receive a program of another kind.

The boys will offer a hand to the Salutatorian, wobbly on Momma's borrowed heels, and she too, will ascend to the center of attention, find her speech with its universal reference to Webster, "who defines commencement as a beginning," as if we didn't expect it. From the side, the bored, which includes damned near everyone, will notice that she is standing on tip toe, her heels slipping out of her shoes as she stretches to the microphone. And what a microphone! The usual dollar-two-ninety-eight affair, purchased with pride by the Key Club at a discount from the Radio Shack in the nearest town of consequence.

Tomorrow, sons and daughters will feel empty and homesick, no longer a Fighting Cougar, or whatever fierce animal, pirate or Indian that serves as both mascot and rallying cry in this school, this shining part of the world.

There is a time in everyone's life when it is time to trade from one team to another, when the goal is reached or when the player is ready for a greater challenge. The team is there to do as the Army challenges, to help you "be all that you can be," and when you and the team have gone, "all the way to state," it's time to move on. Time to trade teams.

And this is true for all group endeavors be they as commercial as a sports' franchise or as personal as a marriage. Sometimes we do not, cannot, all grow together. Then it is time to say your good-byes, proclaim that Webster defines commencement as "a beginning", and wait sadly but confidently for the Greyhound to take you to tomorrow.

I love flying over Ohio. The patchwork of small towns looks like a plan for a model train set. From 5,000 feet, and that's plenty high to fly over Ohio, I can almost hear my Uncle Gene hollering to Aunt Nora to "find these kids something to eat!" We would drive up in an oil-burning Nash Rambler and Dad would toot the horn in crazy excitement as if he truly believed that Uncle Gene and Aunt Nora had nothing to do but wait around in hope that relatives would surprise them for a weekend visit.

Uncle Gene had a voice like gravel shaken in an oak barrel, but light him up with a couple of beers and, lying on his bubba belly, head draped into the cistern, he could sing like the Three Tenors...together!

The cistern was a huge, concrete cavern sunk into the backyard, fed by the down spout. It was there to collect rainwater for drinking which Aunt Nora pumped cool and clear with a hand pump mounted in the kitchen sink. But as good as the cistern was for water, it was even better for singing. I learned to sing four part harmony by laying on top of the cistern with my dad, Uncle Gene, and Uncles Jack and Jed and sometimes J.E. Gross also known as Grandpa. Okay, so that's more than enough for four part harmony.

Well, like I said, fire up that crew with a beer or two, usually more, and who counts parts? Just swell up, lean into the echo-chamber of the cistern and let her rip!

When You Wore a Tulip, My Wild Irish Rose, and my favorite, *Floating Down the River* with several verses and multiple endings limited in number only by imagination and Aunt Nora's patience!

In the cellar was a player piano nearly covered over with what seemed like thousands of odd-looking, hole-punched rolls of oiled paper. Inserted into the mechanism, those rolls held the secrets to a million songs that piped from the open body of the piano whenever a cousin pumped furiously on the pedals. There were always plenty of cousins to pump the piano. Sometimes one of the cousins was me.

The sound was always too loud. It was huge, almost comedic. Janet would shriek her Ohio shriek and the neighbors would undoubtedly agree that the town had fallen under the spell of gypsies.

Uncle Gene and Aunt Nora lived on George Street in Van Wert, Ohio. The middle of the west, the middle of America, the center of the Universe. And now, somewhere some 5,000 feet below, lives another Aunt Nora and Uncle Gene. And I hope the kids are there having just driven in from Cincinnati. I hope that they will love their cousins and maybe learn to sing four part harmony.

There are teams of all kinds. Of course, there is the sports team and the new team at work created by the consultant who him- or herself is now a solo act having been downsized, forced by necessity to declare him- or herself an expert on these things.

There are other teams, too. And it is the other teams that are the most important. These are the teams that we know as family and neighborhood. These are the teams that we know as friends. And these are the teams that, in the end, make us who and what we are.

You can see these things from 5,000 feet.

12

Double Time

Mario said it.

We were walking along the beach in Jamaica when we noticed ants carrying a leaf. There must have been fifty or a million ants. No matter, the leaf was huge compared to the little creatures ceremoniously hauling it to who knows where. But they were doing it, no matter the size, or heat, that any second a wave might wash them back to the beginning.

Mario looked at the ants and then asked the wind, "I wonder which ant is responsible for saying, 'Okay, guys. On three!'"

Fast forward six months and 3,000 miles.

There I was in the basement of the Doubletree Lincoln Center in Dallas, working in the laundry and thinking about ants.

Lorena, the Mexican woman on the other side of the long, low, laundry gondola, was my partner, my teammate. Our job was to reach into the cotton tangle, select a single bed sheet, choose a hem, gently laying the edge onto the dozens of endless canvas belts rolling quietly into and out of a wide green machine. Once the belts caught the hem, we fed the remainder of the sheet into the machine where it would be pressed flat and dry. Inside, the sheet would be digested by more mechanical magic until it was deposited into the waiting hands of Eva, a smiling woman with a face as round as the sun, as dark as fine chocolate and as friendly as the cherub she resembled.

We could hear Eva laughing on the other side of the machine which was hot and dark and seemed to never stop. On our side we just kept sorting sheets, laying them one after the other so that at times it seemed that they were from a continuous cloth as long as the afternoon. Me and Lorena and the ants.

(I haven't forgotten the ants.)

The gondola must have held 300 freshly washed sheets. The laundry's huge washing machines do such a thorough job of extracting water that the sheets are barely damp by the time they make it to the long, low gondolas that line up in front of the big green machine.

Once out of the washer, the work waits for someone to remove each sheet individually from the pile, shake it out and gather one hemmed end.

Let's see if I can describe this exactly. You are holding the gathered end of a damp sheet. Still holding the gathered end, grab back a foot or so farther so that now you have enough mass to matter and, in a motion similar to fly casting, hold one end and toss the gathered end of the sheet onto the pile of sheets already waiting on the gondola. The effect is that you are shaking the sheets and then gathering them so they can be thrown lengthwise into the gondola. ('Probably more than you wanted to know.)

In front of the green monster, two operators stand on either end of the gondola and hand the sheets onto the rollers, one sheet after another until forever or four o'clock, whichever comes first.

Lorena and I handled sheets and sheets and more sheets. So much laundry in a parade that didn't end. Time didn't stand still, it oozed in great lengths of boredom. But what was amazing were those ants. I couldn't stop thinking about the ants.

We stood at either end of the gondola, barely talking. My Spanish doesn't lend itself to conversation and Lorena's English was, well, about as good as my Spanish. You would think that we wouldn't have much to say. But we did.

It was as if our fingers could talk. How could they know, looking at a gondola of same colored sheets, which one to pick up next?

As we fed one sheet into the monster with one hand, the other hand would begin sifting through the gondola looking for the same sheet as the hand at the other end. It was as if our two sets of hands had been rearranged, no longer one set at each end of the gondola but one set on each task. Her right, my left, fed the green machine. My right, her left worked together, talked to one another without words to select the next sheet.

Like the ants, something was happening. Maybe boredom, maybe magic.

I asked about kids, and family and years in the laundry until my Spanish ran out. We talked and gestured, a matter not easy without available hands.

The hands got smarter.

It was as if talking about things, common, ordinary, tell-me-about-your-kids kind of things, made the hands smarter, gave them ownership in a body not really shared.

Our hands flew. Like the ants, they knew which sheet would be next, exactly when to lay the ends onto the moving bands. Exactly. How in the world could two people know within a millisecond when to place a sheet on the canvas belts? It is teamwork, a form of communication not easily described by the scientist but the daily trade of the supervisor.

When two people want to work together, they can do far more than two working separately. With a common goal as the language, hands and feet, even perhaps, hearts and minds, can work together. Flawlessly.

We ran nearly 600 sheets through the hot, green monster in a couple of hours.

The laundry had been quiet at six o'clock the night before. There were a few tired faces waiting for me in the small office. Tired, gracious faces.

"So you want to write about us? We are honored to have you in our hotel. Sammie is waiting to get his hands on you tomorrow!" And on and on, a chorus of welcomes that couldn't quite figure why one of the 'suits' would actually volunteer to work the laundry. They fitted me for a uniform and promised to have it hemmed and delivered to my room.

Talk about feeling awkward. These folks still had an hour or so of a bus ride, yet there they were, waiting for me, and I only had to take an elevator to a suite on the twelfth floor. That would all clear up in the early morning. In green shirt and black pants, I would look like the laundry employee I intended to be.

Sammie, a veteran of 12 years in the rather dark office of a laundry room, was waiting when I arrived at 7:30 A.M. Broad smile, lots of flashy gold in the teeth, muscles where all I had was shirt.

We started to work. First we loaded washers. Actually, we didn't load them. We crammed them. Pushing and shoving, we stuffed a couple of hundred pounds of dirty laundry into machines large enough to wash a Volkswagen.

Some kid must have designed the laundry delivery system. It's a tube that runs 20 stories along the spine of the building until it and the dirty laundry it carries falls out of the ceiling in the laundry room.

"If you feel a whoosh of air, better move away from the chute," Sammie warned. "That stuff can hurt you!"

It could and it does. You don't have to be hit by laundry to be hurt by it. It gets your back and legs, your arms and feet. Laundry, when it falls out of the concrete sky by the ton, gets to you one way or the other!

Some laundry is contaminated by blood or whatever. That stuff comes down separately. Contaminated laundry gets special attention, treated like the hazardous material it is. It is disinfected before being thrown away. Yuck!

The really gross stuff comes from the kitchen. Soured stuff. Greasy stuff. Anything cold and slimy you-can-imagine stuff.

"Here. We gotta bag from the kitchen. 'You want to help?"

"Sure!"

"You want gloves?"

Now, the head housekeeper was watching from across the room. She saw what was happening and must have been horrified that a 'suit' might encounter a little goo. She raced to get gloves even without hearing...

"...do you wear gloves?"

"Naw, I just wash my hands. But some people wear gloves."

"Is there any safety reason?"

"Nope. Just nasty."

"If you don't need 'em, I don't."

At this moment, the head housekeeper arrived, snapping a new pair of bright yellow gloves from a box and holding them high.

"Mr. Scott! Mr. Scott! I have gloves for you!"

Too late. I was elbow deep in yuck.

"He don't need no gloves," Sammie explained to the horrified woman. "He don't need no gloves 'cause he's just like us."

Sammie smiled and realized that the day would not be as long as he had imagined.

I smiled inwardly because I knew that I had just joined the team.

It was nasty. We sorted slop from more slop while mentally I sang the refrain, "Great green globs of greasy, grimy gopher guts, mutilated monkey meat, dirty little..."

"So what gets you out of bed and brings you to this laundry every day?"

"These people are my friends. I like to work with them."

"Yes, but this isn't really what you would call a glamorous job. No windows. It's hot. The work is tough."

"You get used to it. Besides, here I've learned a lot. I can repair the machines. I understand plenty about the chemicals. And, like I said, I like the people. They're my friends."

Sammie was separating and washing, shaking and folding right along with the rest of the crew. "I never ask people to do anything that I'm not willing to do. They know that. They can see that!"

And they could. Take your fancy theory and...press it! If you have good people, leaders have little to do. Sammie is right there with the best of them. The entire operation seemed to work without direction. Work got done. Everyone, except the new kid, seemed to know exactly what needed to be done next and how to do it. Teams formed, completed a task, and then reformed to tackle the next task.

You could learn a lot in a laundry.

Like the ants, there was little apparent leadership, yet somehow, things were getting done.

The theory, if you need one, revolves around the notion that teams practice collective reasoning. Similar to parallel processing where many computers are linked together to quickly solve problems that an individual computer might never solve. Parallel processing, better call it team intelligence, happens when individual team members solve a little piece of the problem, seemingly without connection, but mysteriously working with others on the team.

The weirdest thing happened. Just before lunch a few suits appeared in the laundry room door and asked if they could take me to lunch. I don't think that they believed how serious I was about working with the team.

"Sammie, what time do we go to lunch?"

"You can go anytime!" Sammie eyed the suits hanging at the door to his department. "Anytime."

The folks at Doubletree are about as egalitarian as you get, but be honest. There is something intimidating about dress clothes and titles. At least for me. It has taken me years to finally get that if I'm wearing jeans and boots and you are wearing Gucci...well, I'm sorry.

"Sammie, says it's okay." I nodded to the suits without looking up from folding towels.

"Sammie! What is the official lunchtime and where do we eat?"

"Eleven-thirty in the breakroom but you can eat wherever you want."

"How about eleven-thirty in the break room?" I asked the suits.

"We thought you might enjoy eating in the cafe."

"Well, there are four of us," I said, nodding towards my team as I continued shaking sheets into a fresh gondola.

Heads turned and looks exchanged before someone said, "Sure! We'll be down to get you at 11:30."

At 11:30, we had managed to have completed the tasks of the moment, washed our hands and were waiting for our escort to the 'other world.'

Now, I eat in fine restaurants all the time. I know which fork to use first. I can select the appropriate wine and even know how to swirl the first taste and look pensive before informing the somelier, "This will do." But marching into the cafe, full of suits and ties, while we wore our polo shirts from the laundry room, I felt a tad out of place. To say that my team felt the same way is by far understating the case.

I couldn't wait to get back to my spot, my place in the laundry where it was warm and comfortable.

After lunch, the big guy put me on folding. Actually, I put myself on the job after checking with Sammie to be sure there wasn't something more urgent that needed attention. I folded and folded and folded, dragging towels and bath mats from a bottomless plastic cart. I must have folded a million pieces. Yeah, that's right, a million. And I could prove it, too, if that short woman hadn't kept hauling it away.

Now, here's a point. People like to be able to see a job from beginning to end. There are unknown ways to measure, to keep score, the simplest of which must be to count. How big is the pile of sawdust? How many days have you been in that cell? How many towels are folded neatly on the table?

But that short woman kept hauling them off! I couldn't get a decent count. The pile would grow. Then it would disappear.

How do you count? How do your employees count? Do you haul away the towels before they get a good measure?

At one point Sammie walked over to our gondola and calculated, somehow, that we had managed to feed 679 towels into the press in one hour. It was, he thought, some kind of record. While Sammie praised, I puffed, thinking, 'Writer Boy strikes again!' And later I would think about how anyone might find joy or at least satisfaction in a job, any job, well done. First, they must have a way of keeping score.

Five, four, three, two, one. I folded towels right up to the minute. Four o'clock. Another hour and a bed of nails would have looked inviting.

At the witching hour, the PR folks materialized and took pictures. Every conceivable combination of guest worker, manager, supervisor, and worker bee. I smiled and posed, smiled and posed. They gave me a plaque. I wanted a nap.

So, Writer Boy, what did you learn in the laundry?

I learned that working with people that you like makes the day sail by even if the work itself isn't much to talk about. I learned that there really is such a thing as team intelligence. I learned that once you get to know someone, if only a little, you can work better together. And I learned that working in a hotel laundry is tough work for tough people, made worse when the guests are cheerleaders. (They inconsiderately use too many towels and smear them with makeup.) Some of the prettiest people I know work in the laundry, no makeup required!

At shift's end, I dragged myself to my room and immediately felt out of place.

I had promised the marketing guy that I would fly him to Waco for ribs. He was a student pilot and fascinated by the prospect. I thought it was the least I could do to return the favor of allowing me to wash several tons of dirty laundry.

The promise was a good idea when I made it, but now, tired to the bone, it didn't seem like such a brilliant plan.

I shed shoes, socks and uniform in pieces as I shuffled across the room to wash up. In the bathroom I splashed a haggard-looking face with cold water and lathered tired hands, then, reaching for a towel to dry, I froze.

Nah! I shook the water from my hands. No point in dirtying another towel!

13

I Am . . . the Cookie Man

The operator lied when she said, "Good morning! It's four o'clock."

I wanted to say, "Listen lady, it's either a good morning or it's four o'clock. I don't see how it could be both."

But I didn't. Instead I tried to find my eyes, shove in the contacts and blink my way down to the hotel bakery.

In the bakery I found Antonio Romo, a bright-eyed, Mexican-now-American. Antonio had been in the bakery since 2:30, just an hour or so after he had punched out of his other job at another hotel. And he looked brighter than me by a long shot.

The 4:30 start time had been a gift. I was late!

Tony found a hat, a tall chef's hat. I adjusted it to size, (fat) and put it on. You gotta admit, I was born to cook. Chef pants and coat. Ta da! That's me!

There was little time for conversation. Tony accepted without question that I would be able to pull my weight and immediately began giving orders, you'd call them 'instructions'. Kitchens are noisy and warm, sometimes loud and hot depending on how you feel about it. We were an instant team, not because I was good but because Tony was a master of getting the most out of an extra pair of hands.

With each recipe, Tony would slide a thick notebook full of plastic-covered pages across the prep table and point around the kitchen as he called out the first few ingredients I would need.

"So Antonio, what is there about this job that gets you here at such an ungodly hour?"

"When I was small," Tony began after a short apology for his English, "I lived with my family in Mexico. One day, my father built an oven, the kind made of stone. It was outside.

"Everyday I would carry the wood and build the fire," said Tony, his eyes and heart now in Mexico. He spoke with that beautiful accent that is independent of language, more a matter of sincerity. "The oven was very hot, maybe...five hundred degrees. My father would bake the bread. All kinds. Wheat, Italian, even cactus. I remember always how it smelled. So, maybe I have always wanted to bake the bread. And cakes. And cookies. Whatever. I just like to bake."

And bake we did. Tony had already made the dough for Danish and formed it into individual swirls. The proofed swirls had risen beautifully. My job was to use a pastry bag to add the cream cheese on some, then a large spoon to add apple, cherry or lemon to others. I imagined watching the customers as they attempted to pick out the one with the most filling and worked a little harder to make them all the same!

Then they went into the oven and I, on to the next task.

I love the kitchen. It is clean and bright and always smells good. There are tools everywhere with machinery of all sizes. The kitchen is a man's place, better than a garage because you can lick your fingers.

We used two regular forks held like chopsticks and dipped them into sugar icing to drizzle across the tops of the giant sweet loaves. Then Antonio showed how the fingers worked better so I tried that, a little here, a little there. There's nothing like playing with food and calling it art!

It was hard to watch what I was doing and still go about the work of learning about my host. Several hours into the shift, and still well before sunrise, all I knew for sure was that he was born in Mexico and lived, I guessed, in poverty. (I'd call scavenging for wood to bake bread some kind of sign.)

I knew that he loved to bake and was called to the profession by the haunting smell of rising dough and the romance of working in the wee hours of the day.

I knew that he was living and working the American dream. Twice, in fact, as he had two jobs.

But how did he make that leap from gathering firewood to master of the pastry kitchen?

I thought about the day I made it across the kitchen, exchanging my dishwasher's mop for a cook's apron and spatula.

Drafted. That's what happened. I was drafted. I was eleven and my dad, the manager of a Frisch's Big Boy coffee shop in Cincinnati, needed a dishwasher and I was elected. It was a unanimous vote of only one voter, my dad.

So everyday I hustled to work. Hot, sweaty, nasty work. Hard work in un-air conditioned kitchens. I got paid,too, about seventy-five cents an hour. (Dad was trying to keep payroll costs down and figured that a kid didn't need money. Thanks!) Oh, yeah, I loved it!

Once in a while, Charlie Collins, the moonshiner/fry cook from Tennessee would yell, "Heads up, kid!" I'd turn around to see that Charlie had launched a dirty dish or bowl milli-seconds before calling my name. The darned thing would always be mid-flight before the warning came, so the kid learned to think pretty quick and, in the process, earned the respect of a chronic bar brawler, good 'ole boy who, despite a ton of shortcomings, was as gentle as they come.

Once in a while Charlie would be on duty alone and find

himself snowed, the kitchen term for too busy to handle things gracefully. We also use the terms, 'buried' or 'in the weeds.' On those occasions Charlie would sometimes ask for my help. I did little things like toasting buns, maybe dropping fries, and later, after he figured I could handle it, I loaded the grill.

Eventually I could just step in and find a comfortable rhythm alongside Charlie. By the end of a long summer, Charlie had gained a helper, I had gained a friend and mentor.

One day I went to work early so that I could pick up my paycheck and saw my dad getting clobbered at the grill. It seems he was short a cook and had stepped in to cover.

"Not now!" was all he could manage to say when he saw me come into the kitchen.

"Can I help?"

"No!" And he went right on living in deep snow.

The phone rang. It was the main office, announced a waitress.

"Damn!" my dad hissed through clenched teeth. I can see this as if it were yesterday.

He wiped his hands on a side towel and tromped to the phone.

I strapped on an apron, folding over the top and taking the strings for an extra turn around my skinny middle.

When my dad returned, all the orders were out, the grill was clean, and I was in the process of restocking the block.

That was the last time I was scheduled to wash dishes although I have since washed many and probably will again.

I wondered how it was for Tony. Did his dad let him bake the bread or did he have to learn on the sly? Was it the baking that turned Tony on or the idea that becoming a baker was in some way forbidden or exclusive?

"So, Tony, how did you get to be a baker? Did you just apply for the job?"

"Oh, no, sir! When I come to Texas, I work as dishwasher at the Fairmont Hotel. But I always like the bakery and I always want to be the baker. I liked to see the cakes especially.

"One night shift I was alone cleaning up and I saw a cake. I thought that it needed more decorations so I find some almonds and toast them and put them on the cake to look pretty. When cakes look good, they taste good.

"In the morning, the pastry chef, he sees that someone has put the almonds on his cake. He was a German man and sometimes could be tough. So when he asks who puts the almonds, I didn't want to tell him. But I did.

"So he says, 'Well, Antonio if you think you know more about how a cake should look than the chef, I think we gonna have to make a change here.'

"I thought he gonna fire me for putting the almonds on the cake!

"Antonio, you gonna have to change your apron because you not gonna wash my dishes no more. No, Antonio, you are gonna be a baker and put almonds on all the cakes!

"So, I am the baker! I am the Cookie Man!"

When it was cookie time, I was in rare form. Tony slid a recipe book across the stainless table, pointed to the scales and weights and left me pretty much on my own. No problem. I was a great cook in Organic Chemistry. Why should this be any different?

First the flour. I zeroed the scale and added the counter balances. Flour and flour and more flour. It seemed about a million pounds total. Then there was the baking soda, a pinch, followed by cinnamon, two big pinches because the cook likes cinnamon!

Somewhere along the way, we added fifteen pounds of walnuts, three quarts of fresh eggs and a whopping twenty-two pounds of chocolate chips. And, oh, yes! Sugar. White sugar, brown sugar, lots of sugar. And oatmeal. A couple of pounds of oatmeal.

I slipped into a sugar high merely from being in the room!

All of this plus a few other ingredients went into a mixer

the size of a house. It took both of us to roll the huge mixing bowl into place and winch it onto the mixer. Then, poof! Before you knew it, cookie dough! Lots of it.

Antonio and I began to scoop. I forget but it seems that we got about 400 cookies from one batch. We're talking mega amounts of cookies. And this on a holiday weekend when the hotel was not particularly busy!

About seven o'clock, the pastry kitchen took on new energy in the form of Pastry Chef Tu Van, a Vietnamese dynamo of energy and bravado. Tu Van was the vanguard of a phalanx of Italians and Germans, Americans and who knows what that eventually showed up, an army of white chef toques and tall hats to transform the entire kitchen into a bustling den of art and magic.

"Bellisimo!" the Italians would yell to no one in particular. Letting the rest of the crew know that art was in the air seemed de riguer.

"Beautiful, Bubba!" That's the refrain that was Tu Van's signature. "Beautiful, Bubba!" he would shout as he passed by, a short tornado in checked pants and white coat. "Beautiful, Bubba! Beautiful! " Tu Van would toss in a handful of flour or pinch of who knows what as he inspected your work.

Antonio and I whipped out a batch of rolls that were delicious. Unfortunately, they did not meet Chef's standards. "Make again!" said Chef in a Vietnamese accent that seemed to explode from his lips. "More flour! Too flat! Make again!"

And we did. Mixing, proofing and kneading until the wooden-topped work table was laden with gorgeous round balls of puffy dough. Then it was into the forming machine and onto parchment lined trays. More proofing until at last we heard those magic words, "Beautiful, Bubba! Beautiful!"

While the cookies were baking, we made more yeast rolls. While the yeast rolls were rising, we made raspberry sauce by the gallon. It really was beautiful.

When the first batch of cookies came out, I checked the clock. It was right at nine A.M. I'm thinking breakfast;

Antonio is thinking home. So at 9:30, we said "Adios" and prepared to hit the bricks. Tony had a family to see; I had a flight plan to file.

In not so good Spanish, I thanked Antonio for allowing me to work with him. I wished him a Merry Christmas and a Happy New Year.

In not so good English, he invited me to work with him anytime. I felt complimented but Chef Tu Van looked as if he felt left out.

"Don't worry, Tu Van. I speak your language, too!"

"You speak Vietnamese?" He looked incredulous and rightfully so.

"Not exactly Vietnamese but your language. Beautiful, Bubba! Beautiful!"

When I walked into my room to change, I looked into the mirror. Cookie man. Yep, that's me all right. The DoubleTree Cookie Man. I wanted to go stand by the cookies and wait to hear, "You make the best cookies. They're the reason I love to stay at DoubleTree. 'Makes me feel like I'm coming home."

But instead I hoisted my bag for the umpteenth time, stepped under my favorite hat, felt in my pocket for keys to the Little Girl, and headed off for another adventure. I was tired. Dog tired. No problem. I had a pocketful of cookies!

14

Sunrise at the Charray Inn

Me and the Little Girl, this time with Melanie in the right seat, gave up on adventure long enough to earn a living doing what I do best, speaking. About a hundred times a year, we get invited to keynote at one conference or another. I love being first. I hate the after dinner slot.

Every audience, like every team, has a group personality. No matter who are the customers, it is the job of the server to love them unconditionally. To be honest, some audiences are pretty tough to love.

Through the busy season we flew from one end of the country to the other and back again, stopping home sometimes for no longer than it took to refuel the baby Mooney and reload the suitcases.

Since my real job is to observe and learn so that I can

share, the adventures never really end. Always there is something to discover.

Some of my favorite places have to include restaurants. Okay, I can be more specific: coffee shops and diners, truck stops and local dives and, more specific yet, for breakfast.

In these places where the real people hide, breakfast is intended for the early risers. For them the grill gets hot sometime after five thirty. The coffee is freshly brewed and the hash browns are just starting to crisp. In the south, the cook, dressed in white, may whip up the first of several batches of grits. (Don't ask me what are grits. All I can tell you is that they are perfect with over-easy eggs and they taste like whatever you put on them.)

Put butter on grits and they taste like butter. Put garlic on grits and, well, you get the picture. (And, by the way, pronounced properly "grits" is a three syllable word.)

The other breakfast run, the one that begins right after the bars close, belongs to the street people, the after bar drunks, the police who attempt to nail them as they drive from beer bar to breakfast bar, and the ambulance guys who haul them off if the police, (pronounced pō-leese), don't get to them in time.

Inside, sitting at the counter, there is a truce. Drunks ignore the cops, cops ignore their radios, and the tired graveyard shift waitresses often ignore everybody.

Too much smoke. Too much grease. Just enough hint of coffee to set the scene.

At the moment, I am straining to look beyond our left wing tip hoping to catch a glimpse of a favorite such breakfast place, the Charray Inn, a pin-neat place that fits. Not too fancy, not too earthy. Just clean and pleasant.

Around the side of the building, someone remembered to add a little diner. It couldn't seat more than a couple of dozen, even then you'd have to be real friendly. And friendly is just the way to describe the Charray which was named after Charlotte and, have you guessed? Ray. Okay, not so original but it does the job.

Inside the place is as warm as the grits that bubble on the two-eye burner. The fan on the hood serves up enough white noise to make reading the paper possible against the clink of dishes and the soft southern accents that drift from waitress to cook, cook to customer and customer to newcomer, all family once inside the glass door. Two regulars are squeaking, left then right on the bar stools at the counter. Leatherette covers, chrome side rims, lifted straight from the fifties made more comfortable by the memories they evoke.

The counter is just long enough to define the kitchen and become a catchplace for 'stuff.' The stools look to be an afterthought. "We've got room. Why not add a couple of stools?"

To the outsider, perhaps a refugee from the office trying to look country by wearing too-new denim, the place is a step back in time, a southern study of how things used to be and probably never will be again.

"That didn't sound very good," the young waitress said into the dish sink when she pulled the stopper. Gray, soapy sludge slurrped through a stack of egg-stained dishes, coffee cups and glassware. Someone had gotten ahead on dish clearing and behind on dishwashing. Now there would be a greasy starting over, a disappearing to the elbows to set things right.

She was obviously the cook's daughter. Blonde hair just like Momma with a matching Tennessee accent. (That's Ten...asee not Tenna...see. It's subtle but you know it when you hear it.) They were a perfect mother/daughter pair. It could have been an Ivory Soap commercial. Maybe not.

The daughter didn't really want to be up so early on a Saturday or any morning and it was obvious. Mom had to have someone and at fourteen (I guessed!), it was time for the kiddo to be up, slinging hash and pulling her borderline chunky weight.

"Lou!" Momma yelled over her shoulder as she deftly flipped a set of eggs. Up and over. I've done it a million times and I still marvel to watch those cackleberries sliding over the edge of the pan, yolks lined up side by side, rolling back over the edge over so easy. "Did you say one patty of sausage?"

Lou didn't answer but Momma knew and slipped another patty from the grill to the plate. Customers breezed in, shouted "Good morning!" or sometimes just "morning!", seated themselves, waited for their 'usual' to appear and turned through the embarrassingly thin newspaper until they were out of news and coffee. Then they stacked up their dishes, tucked the paper between the napkin holder and the wall for the next guy, and sauntered to the sink in a friendly gesture of helping out, like being at home, only at home, they probably wouldn't do it.

Someone said, 'gree-its' and it made me smile. Gree-its. You can't write it just right but say it and notice how good it feels to relax your mouth. Gree-its and you cain't hardly sit up straight. (Southern kinda gits to me!)

"Let me have that rag and I'll wipe that table off."

In the south, in the real places where the 'regulars' go, there is this sense of home that's almost better than home. It's a cozy feeling that wraps around you, a blanket of hot coffee and people who would miss you if you didn't show.

"Bah-y, Gene. 'See ya tomorraw." And they will, regular as rain. You will be able to set your watch by Gene or any of the others that drink too much coffee and probably could tip a little better than they do but don't because they are family.

From the sink just behind the counter, "Sit anywhere that feels good. We'll have you some coffee as soon as we wash some cups." Then, into the once again murky water, "Ever thing in the were-ald musta been in that water! These dishes are kudzu dishes. They just keep agrowin' and agrowin'."

A gimme-capped trucker at the counter fished into his pocket and landed a plastic eyeball in a drinking straw. (You have to have been there to truly get the picture.) He made a show of planting it in his coffee and, once he had sufficient attention, he smiled, slurped a swallow of brown through the clear plastic and smiled, saying, "'gotta do somethin' when you stop in here. Lord knows the food's not no good."

Momma sailed a rag past his ear. Daughter yelled, "I'll be raht with ya soon as I wrench these dishes."

We slipped a couple of bucks under the plate, said our good-byes and hoped we would pass this way again.

So the spring slowly unwound. There was a lot of speaking in fancy hotels and resorts, plenty of fine meals and vintage wine. But the best stuff, the real stuff, came in unexpected moments spent lovingly in unexpected places.

15

Cold, Green Water

There was no flying into Valdez yesterday. Alaska was closed. A big rain-soaked sign tacked on the gate invited no one. Not even the locals were getting home, and for certain, these two adventurers would have to wait. Maybe until the morning, maybe longer. The Alaskans we met at the airport seemed resigned to the fact that nature will have the final say, no argument allowed.

Valdez. I haven't been there but already I know that it has an LDA. (What those initials stand for escapes me but they mean something to the effect of 'don't fly this unless you really, really know what you are doing or unless you really, really want to get to Valdez and are stupid enough to risk your neck to do it.')

An LDA gives pilots left and right guidance only. No vertical navigation, just left and right. So you can follow the electronic beam into the murk, sightless, as it progressively narrows. For altitude guidance, you're on your own. You could be dead on the LDA and still allow the plane to descend too low too soon. (Then you'd be dead on the mountain.)

Left and right guidance would be all you need if you were flying in a two-dimensional world. It's fine for driving a ship or car but airplanes need up and down in addition to left and right. Master but one and you could easily nail yourself to the side of a mountain.

With an LDA, when it comes to flying the proper altitude, you are left to follow charts and a stopwatch in the hope that when you run out of beam, you will be correctly positioned to land. Oh, yes! One more small detail. The LDA is not lined up with the runway.

Unlike the more common localizer approach that funnels you to the end of the runway, on an LDA, when you pop out at a few hundred feet, the runway will be somewhere left or right. Go fish!

LDAs are used when God decides that a mountain is the best thing to put at the end of the runway. There is no straight-in approach. Instead, you fly through the goo, eyes glued to the altimeter and stopwatch and, assuming you get out of the murk in time, you jog left or right and set her down. Simple as that.

Yesterday was an especially good day for waiting.

We found a hotel, sort of. It was one of those over-priced places where the guests seem to come and go most of the night. One set arrives, takes their turn playing the television too loud and then settles in just in time for the next set. It was one of those places where everyone talks too loudly in the hall, where a toilet flush sounds like a fire drill.

So I'm up, cross-legged and naked. Sitting, computer on lap. And why not? I had been writing in my head since four A.M. and the wake-up call should come at five. 'Won't need it.

Last night we ate at Hogg Brothers Cafe. Well-named.

The food was passable and quick, perfect if you weren't too picky. We sat at the bar and charmed a chubby waitress into handing us the clicker so we could surf the bar TV until we found CNN. CNN and The Weather Channel. Find those and you've got civilization.

The decor was pigs. There were pigs everywhere. Stuffed pigs and photoed pigs. Pig drawings and pig cartoons.

I ordered jalapenos for the baked potato, 'baker' in restaurant terms, and she brought an entire bowl. So I slapped a fistful onto the hot potato as a reward for having to sit and wait while I unconsciously counted one tacky pig after another. At Hogg Brothers, they had turned pig into art. Not good art but art.

Before I finished my salad, I was thoroughly pigged out.

Outside the rain came a little harder. The cloud base looked to be about 200 feet, maybe lower. No, there would be no more flying today. Maybe not even tomorrow.

Last night I dreamed of Melanie. It was a soft and delicious, sexy dream. After 22 years, I'm still dreaming of the girl I was lucky enough to marry. I hope to still be dreaming those dreams for another 20, make that 40 or forever.

Melanie had cried yesterday when we kissed good-bye, again. She is not good about being left at home. I am not good about leaving her. She made me promise that this would be the last long adventure. I said yes and probably told the truth.

If the clock is right and the hotel clerk was paying attention, in three minutes, the phone should ring. In an hour we should have the weather and an idea as to whether we will be flying or driving to meet the Arco Juneau, a 40-million gallon tanker that will be home and classroom when she sails with the tide Saturday morning. We'll see.

The phone never rang. Cheap hotels!

No matter, I was awake and working. And, since I had the nerve to run the shower and flush the toilet, no doubt the rest of my floor was awake as well.

I was brushing my teeth and thinking about the day. Maybe I am excited. For certain my aim was off. I rinsed and absent-mindedly spit into my shaving kit!

I left a few bucks on the bed for the housekeeper. One, a

tip for cleaning the room; the rest as consolation for having to work this dump.

In the lobby, I chided the night auditor for missing my wake-up call and, simultaneously noticed that the clock over the desk read 4:30. I was an hour ahead of myself! That made me want to go back to the room and un-tip the housekeeper for not getting the clock right. Oh, well. I'm up.

The clerk is a bright, young man who is studying computer science. I already know that his e-mail handle is 'salmon.' It's perfect for an Alaskan and a miracle that no one had beat him to it!

He asked what I was doing in Alaska and when I told him, he did what everyone does. He began to suggest jobs and titles.

"Have you ever watched the show *The Pretender*?"

"Sure."

"Well, that's what you are doing. Maybe there's a title."

He also suggested, "America's Toughest Jobs From the Inside."

"Nice. But it's not exactly a cross-over title."

"Why should it matter? The people who will read this book watch *20/20* and *Dateline* so you might as well have a title that they will understand."

Good point.

There are no words to describe the flight from Anchorage to Valdez but spectacular might be close. As I write, my eyes see the soft white clouds, not too bright, just cotton soft, a movie-like, special effect framing a view of snow-capped mountains. Those magic mountains were several thousands of feet below, perhaps four or five miles in the distance, literally sparkling in the sun as if Disney had returned Matterhorn Mountain to its rightful owner.

For the longest time, the engines whined, holding us carefully aloft. We floated into the cloud deck with flaps extended, wallowing at high power and low speed along a slalom of jagged mountains. Everywhere there was snow and ice. The blue sea looked oddly cloudy with islands of floating ice.

There is not much to Valdez. History maybe. And then only if you went looking for it. Town? There is none. Just the Totem Inn with its friendly waitresses and regulars who offer to refill your coffee when they get up to refill their own. Gimme caps and steel toed boots are the uniform du jour.

The hairy smoker at the next table admired our camera and inquired if we were using the new smart Lithium batteries. Huh? Smart Lithium? I caught myself thinking that this guy wouldn't know 'smart' if it fell on him and quickly realized that I was getting a taste of my own medicine, a dig left over from a previous adventure.

Somewhere in the conversation that followed, we learned that 'Hairy' was an engineer. Still, looking at the crowd, I got the feeling that a hot date would barely require dressing in the good boots and a clean pair of jeans...for both of them!

The food and coffee were hot and ample. The place smelled of winter even on this last day of August. Rain had followed us from Anchorage and threatened to paint the entire day gray. And it did.

We enjoyed just hanging out until a mountain of a man with a smile as broad as the day sauntered up to our table, offered a massive paw, and introduced himself as Wayne, the local Arco rep. Wayne was in no particular hurry. Make us comfortable, get us to the ship.

On the way to the Valdez oil terminal, Wayne insisted that we stop to watch the salmon spawn. It is an eerie dance, this spawning. The French refer to an orgasm as 'un petite morte', a little death, but salmon put the French to shame as they swim upstream, mate, and die.

Fish. Great, beautiful fish. Swimming by the thousands, perhaps millions, until they find their mate, do their wiggle dance and then, rolling onto their sides, die what seems to be a slow, uncomfortable death. Sometimes the bears come ahead of death. Sometimes the eagles, and if they are not really hungry, they may lazily peck out the eyes of the hapless water creature.

Still, to die beneath mountains of such beauty, to lie

down in the very waters of life, well, perhaps that is some reward. Alaska seems to be all about life and death held in the same instant, wrapped in the same thought.

At the terminal entrance we were subjected to elaborate but largely useless security. We were searched and wanded with the hand-held metal detector and then allowed to go back outside to bring in our luggage. Duh!

The Arco Juneau, the first ship to move oil from Valdez waited unseen, anchored around the point at Berth Five. At the very end of an already isolated complex, Berth Five is, without the presence of a tanker, not all that impressive. New looking metal bridgeworks jut into the Sound just to the east of a small island on loan from James Bond's *Dr. No.*

You couldn't dream this island. It pokes out of the water, round and sudden, straight out of the Sound like a granite whale coming up for air. It has no beach. The island is a perch for dense fir trees clinging tightly to its huge, gray granite slabs. The blue water, a funny sort of blue, laps quietly at the edges.

Look from the north and the water is the water of ages, melted from the ancient ice flows. Look from the other direction and the blue water is noiseless against the behemoth hulk of the Arco Juneau.

The Juneau, all 883 feet of her, all 942,772 barrels to be, was riding high in the water when we shuffle-scraped the long walk to the gangway, two heavy bags banging our legs with each awkward step.

Now here's a bit of engineering that hasn't quite worked out. The Chief Mate, (did I get that right?) was standing on deck at nearly eye level to us. A cheerful-looking fellow, he tossed us a line and offered to haul over our gear, across a gap of about 15 feet. All I could think about was our equipment or my glasses or, worse yet, my computer falling into that blue-gray water.

Besides, I thought maybe it was some kind of newcomer's joke, like sending the new kid for a left-handed monkey wrench or, as we often did at Denny's, telling them to go to the cooler and bring back a quart of pink goat's milk.

"No, thanks," I smiled. "We'll just haul it up and over."

"You sure?" He looked concerned, a good actor I assumed.

The gangway was a challenge. By the time we climbed to the top, we were looking through the stair treads nearly 60 feet down to the water. At the top, the contraption leveled out, arched forward, and finally ended in a set of steep stairs on the deck of the Arco Juneau.

For the planning and ingenuity it took to bring oil across 865 frozen miles from Prudhoe Bay to Valdez, it seemed that there was not an original thought left when it came to deciding how to walk a man and his possessions straight across from the dock to the boat.

Later, when the ship was loaded and nearly squatting in the blue water, the odd construction of the gangway would make sense. It had to be built to work for ships of, and at, various heights. No wonder it's one size fits all...just not well!

The ship consists of a long, flat-topped hull, little more than a streamlined container for oil that just happens to float. At the stern end of this barge-like affair sits a five-story structure affectionately called 'the house.' It's tall, it's flat faced, it's plain and it's home.

The house inside is hospital green or boring beige depending on which level you are on. It was clearly built for function with only the occasional nod to comfort. When we stepped into the house, we were met by the Captain, at age 34 sailing his first tour as The Old Man, The Boss, The Man...The Captain. And, although you could sense that he was a natural when it came to being in command, it was immediately clear that we were interlopers, welcome but not really.

It turned out that we were not supposed to be boarding the Juneau! Someone had oopsed and here we were boarding a ship that was already well-stocked with visitors. The Captain's father was sailing for the first time for a close-up look at his son at work. Arco had also embarked on a program to enhance crew team work, something called TeamView 360, and had managed to board two consultants who the crew referred to as "The Shrinks."

If that wasn't enough, apparently some goof from a west coast newspaper had boarded a few years ago and turned a friendly invitation to experience a tanker firsthand into a searing expose, a shrill piece founded on truth, built more on exaggeration and supposition.

If the Captain, Todd Barr, was less than thrilled to see us, his crew seemed to be of the same opinion.

The Captain made his feelings abundantly clear. He wasn't sure why we were on his vessel and he would reserve final judgement about the extent of our welcome. He directed us to our cabins suggesting that once we were settled, he would be available in his office. (We correctly interpreted his suggestion as the command it was.)

Our cabins were all the way aft on the port side. I got the last one, a fairly spacious though sparsely furnished cube about nine feet to a side. Metal locker, metal dresser, metal I-don't-know-what-it-is. (It looks like a baby changing station or something that belongs to one side of a hospital bed.) Everything done in the same lovely institutional green. Boy, if you are prone to motion sickness, this is the place to be. Everywhere you look would remind you of how you feel!

We had seen chunks of ice floating in the sound on our descent into Valdez and now, sitting in front of Captain Barr's nailed-to-the-floor desk, we had a pretty good idea about why more than just the climate were so cold in Alaska.

Over the next few days we would come to learn how the past actions of one rather intoxicated tanker captain and the inaction of his able but slightly inattentive crew could and would affect the lives and livelihood of millions. Hazelwood is on everyone's mind in Alaskan oil. Not in a villainous sort of way. They haven't got time to revile the guy. They are too busy covering their own frozen asses.

This sounds a lot worse than it is. Todd is a nice guy. No

doubt a competent guy, just one who wants to be in total control of his environment. Hey, that's what captains do! And the fact that he was driving a monster of an oil tanker only added to the situation.

Oil, especially in Alaska, especially to Arco, especially to Captain Todd Barr, is serious business and there is precious little effort to spare on a couple of boat riders from Texas.

No surprise. We had encountered similar levels of reserved hospitality and knew, make that expected, that this Writer Boy would have to overcome the issue through performance not charm.

"Captain, first let me tell you that we understand; we are visitors subject to the limits of your hospitality. In the worst case we simply will not get in the way. In the best case we may actually be able to make a contribution. But in any case, we understand that this is your ship and we expect to follow the rules. No problem."

The Captain told us about the other PACs (persons in addition to crew), and gently mentioned his dislike of reporters, especially ones who write exposes about a company and industry that he clearly loves.

"There probably is a place for expose journalism," I said. "It's just not what I do. I'm here to learn about how and why work gets done on your ship. I'd like to be able to learn about it by doing it rather than watching it."

The edge softened slightly but the guard never dropped. We were invited to begin by watching the loading process. The Captain hinted that we could work our way into other activities. Perhaps the Chief would find something for me to do once we were underway.

Dismissed.

Ha! I love this job! Always a challenge. Besides, I had a secret weapon, Stuart. In a matter of hours, he would know half the crew and be kin to the other half.

There are only three things to do on an oil tanker: Make the ship go, keep the people going, and load and unload the cargo. Simple—just not easy.

Simple.

Water on the outside; oil on the inside. A mantra we heard in one form or another a million times over.

In port almost all the action is in the Cargo Control Room, a fairly spacious chamber at the forward base of the house made considerably less spacious by the friendly presence of the pumpman, a hulk of a fellow named Randy.

In short order we figured that Randy needed a large frame to house his equally large heart. His good nature never flagged as his fingers walked across a control panel that was the centerpiece to the cargo loading room.

Working under fluorescent light with the crackle of walkie talkies accenting the atmosphere, Randy delivered a non-stop, running commentary about how to unload several hundred-thousand barrels of ballast and replace it with some 862,000 barrels of Alaskan crude. If we had to earn our way into this guy's good graces, the toll certainly wasn't high.

Before any real work could be done, two small boats, the color of the graying sky, pulled long trains of oil containment booms into place, encircling the ship with a floating rubber dam that would, God forbid, capture any oil that attempted to escape the dozens of watchful eyes.

The deck wasn't a beehive of activity. It just wasn't. But that's only because the activity was spread across a deck nearly an eighth of mile in length. A walk to the bow takes several minutes. Turn around and you've got your exercise for the day. Somewhere, spread across acres of flat deck liberally interrupted by miles of pipe, line and cable was a squad of busy and largely self-directed deckhands, lost in a forest of pipe and pump, shadows moving in shadow.

An oil tanker is not a huge vat of oil with an engine but a complex network of individual tanks carefully sized and arranged to safely transit great expanses of sometimes treacherous waters. The big goal on everyone's mind is to do this without spilling so much as a single drop. Water on the outside; oil on the inside. Simple—not easy.

I had decided that I would not make one mention of

Joseph Hazelwood and the infamous Exxon Valdez but the fact is, Hazelwood et al cannot be escaped. The Exxon Valdez incident did far more than impact the environment of the Sound. It dramatically changed the environment of the entire industry. Hazelwood turned out to be in every move we made.

Today oil spills larger than one half tablespoon must be reported to an army of environmental agencies. The average motorist, changing oil in the driveway, probably contributes more direct pollution to the environment than a modern oil tanker. I know. I've seen it. And I'm here to tell you an amazing story!

The Juneau had arrived at berth about the same time Stu and I were being frisked by terminal security. By the time we clamored across the tall, aluminum gangway, the ship was tied nose west to the pier.

As the pumpman explained, the Juneau was empty of cargo but quite full of ballast which explains why the Juneau was riding low in the water as she snuggled up to the dock. Keeping an oil tanker in trim is both science and art as fluids of one kind or another must be carefully positioned in the tanks to supply enough counterbalance to keep the structure stable in the water.

Oil off, ballast on.

Ballast off, oil on.

It is a complex and carefully managed ballet that begins at the bow and slowly works itself aft.

Working intently at the cargo control panel and in constant radio communication with the deckhands, the pumpman begins unloading ballast. Carefully.

Some ballast, the seawater that has been pumped into segregated tanks, can be pumped directly into the bay. That which is from the sea returns to the sea. This water exits the way it entered, pumped through huge, grate-covered openings on either side of the ship called appropriately, sea chests.

Other seawater ballast had to be pumped into the main cargo tanks. This ballast is also off-loaded to make room for the Alaskan crude. It is pumped ashore to special treatment plants where the waste is reclaimed and the now-clean water returned to the bay.

Off-loading starts from the bow and proceeds aft. The great ship, all 883 feet of it, begins to tilt upward, lifting the bow high above the pier and dropping the stern until it looks as if the ship is about to sink into the harbor.

Throughout the process, deck hands unroll long metallic tapes into the various tanks to double check the LED displays in the control. Check and counter-check. The tape ends contain transducers that sense the change in conductivity and emit an audio signal that delivers the news."We've got oil," or maybe just an inch or so lower, "we've got water."

The unloading proceeds slowly. Daylight slides away and the air turns cold. The pumpman waits and the deckhands shiver in the darkness. The measure of the moment is in terms of "ullage," the amount of room left in the top of the tank. "Innage" is the measure of cargo in the tank and, not surprisingly, "thievage" is the measurement of free water in the oil.

Huge, stork-like contraptions called chicksans have been maneuvered to stretch their ungainly legs from pier to ship where they are attached to the manifold, a network of serious-looking, gray pipes that wrap across the parade of pipe running lengthwise along the deck. The manifold pipes are uncapped. The chicksans extend, literally beamed aboard by dockside technicians wearing wireless control gear, a child's game in giant proportions and even greater consequence.

Once attached, the cargo moves on and off via the chicksans, monitored constantly by the ship crew, dock controllers and curiously unseen observers high on the hill above the bay.

Ballast that is pumped out is partially replaced by inert gas generated by the ship's powerplant. This is critical to reducing the risk of explosion. Oil floating on the dirty ballast water releases vapor into the tanks. Add air, a spark and...

The trick for the crew in the engine room is to run the powerplant at just the right mixture of air and fuel. Too much air or too little fuel, and the oxygen content of the exhaust will exceed 8% and be useless in suppressing a potential explosion. Run too rich (too little air, too much fuel) and the exhaust smoke will belch black. And when a tanker belches, environmentalists have a stroke!

The stack police sit high on the hill watching the Juneau's tall stack through powerful binoculars. If the smoke turns black, the radio erupts instantly.

"Arco Juneau! This is Berth Five. Your smoke is black!"

And with that, the magic timer starts, ticking away the seconds before there is the possibility of a fine. The pumpman calls the engine room and within a matter of seconds, the adjustment is complete.

"Arco Juneau! That's better, thank you."

An hour goes by. The ship rises higher against the pier. Ballast off.

"Arco Juneau! Berth Five. Your smoke is black!"

The pumpman dutifully signals the engineers who, this time, are perplexed. Their readings show a near perfect air/fuel balance. But the three minute clock has started.

Two minutes and change.

"Arco Juneau! Berth Five. Your smoke is still black! Please advise."

"Can you help us out? Our equipment is showing right on the money. Are you sure it's black?"

"Well, it looks white from here but we got a call saying it was black. Maybe it was the ship that just passed behind you."

Finally the last tank was ready. Time to call for loading.

The warning horn sounded, signalling that fueling was about to begin. Now the potential for danger begins to multiply.

The vent stack poking above the maze of pipe on deck will soon spew heavier than air inert gas. The inert gas is forced out of the tanks by incoming oil, becoming a potential source of poisoning, even possibly death, to the crew working the tapes and policing the valves on the vast, now dark expanse of metal deck. All on-deckhands don respirators. Inside crew members double check that exterior hatches are dogged tight. Cargo control begins counting ullage in reverse.

Pumpman tossed me a respirator and suggested I check out the deck. I covered the respirator inlets with the palms of my hands and pushed the mask tight against my face, then breathed in to suck the rubber close and make a good seal. Quietly, I slipped across the hatch, turned and dogged it shut behind me.

Outside, the inert gas could be seen against the sky, oozing silently from the stack and drifting south in a light wind. On a calm night it would have settled, looking for the slow, the forgetful, or the foolish in hopes of dropping them silently to the deck. But not tonight. Tonight in the light breeze, we could safely sneak an unmasked breath or two, hurry a bit of uncovered conversation, all the while keeping one eye on the vent stack.

In the darkness I met Butch, an ex-paratrooper who loves Harleys. Closer to the bow, there was Kelly who once dreamed of a career in marine biology but now, standing on the solid steel of the tanker deck, she figured she had gotten about as close as she would get. And Joe, a licensed officer who tomorrow would man the con, now walked the decks, flashlight in hand, reading the tapes, verifying valve positions and taking time to talk with the new guy.

At five there was a quick break for a hearty dinner. Good, plenty, hot and friendly. All the things a dinner should be. Good, if hurried, conversation and then out to the deck or down to the control room.

I stole a nap. Just a couple of winks, long enough to get a second wind and catch part of another watch. About one A.M., I called it quits, bid Wayne, the shoreside loadmaster, good night, and hung up my vest and respirator for a short three hours.

By now the count was near 450,000 barrels, little more than half.

I didn't sleep. I died.

At four A.M., the ship was about to stretch itself awake. I was up first or nearly so. The control room watch had new faces and new numbers winking from the panel. A new voice called from the deck, "Seven feet, ten inches" (the space remaining in a tank being filled with dark, precious cargo.)

"Four starboard is looking at six feet, three and a half. Almost," called another.

A cruise ship, about a mile to starboard slipped by as quietly as a shadow. Ducking under the low fog that laced along the opposite shore, the great, lighted boat blocked the few yellow lights that dared to call themselves a town. In an hour or two, the sun would lift over the mountains and wake the awe-filled tourists to a day in always sleepy Valdez.

I raced up two decks, yanked against a hatch at the rear of the house, and rattled the knob on Stuart's door. "Wake up!" I half whispered, half shouted. "Starboard for the picture of your life!"

And it was. Quiet as a promise, the lights and sleeping souls sailed past.

About six, a horn blew. Stuart, standing on the bridge wing, nearly exploded at the suddenness, spilling hot coffee on his vest and staining his pride. (I'd tell you what he said. We could hear it forty feet below on the deck. But you get the picture. Stu isn't crazy about surprises.)

The tapes and LEDs inched closer until finally the topping off was complete. The cargo control folks had called for a gradual slowing of crude until a trickle was all that was left to handle.

For 16 hours I had been constantly reminded that there would be no oil spilled. None. Zero. Nada. So far, we were right on target but far from finished. There were still chicsans to swing away, great oil-filled pipes and valves to isolate, hardly a cinch.

Kelly invited me to put my ear against the giant straws of

the chicsans that had sucked ballast and then, reversed, spitting oil by the millions of gallons into waiting tanks from the ship. I wondered if this was a 'new kid' prank but listened anyway. Number five, nothing. Number four, a lazy hiss. Number three, nada. The same for chicksan two and we had not used number one.

Now the complex job of disconnecting the chicksans.

Chicksans are remarkable examples of ingenuity and creative engineering. Huge, articulated pipes that swing across the dock and clamp to the manifold on deck, they are maneuvered by remote control until positioned so that clever hydraulics can grip the flat surface of the manifold, holding it in a death grip until the master commands otherwise.

Kelly removed brass stopcocks and we listened to the hiss of retreating oil as it slithered back along the snake-pipe it had come, almost but not quite making the leap to the ship. When the hissing stopped, the chicksans were sneaked back across the chasm of peculiar blue water.

The huge manifold valves had been closed and smaller valves opened to allow the last of the renegade oil still lurking in the dark pipes to finally slide into the deep recesses of the cargo hold. One by one, Joe slammed the great black covers shut. I slid a few quick bolts into place to hold the covers in position while Joe slapped in an o-ring that had to measure two feet across. Then more bolts and yet more. A few quick turns of the two inch nuts and the cover was secure.

Air gun at the ready, J.F. followed up. Done. Buttoned up. Masks off. We can breathe again.

Kelly was at work emptying the drip pans. Over 800,000 barrels, 36 million gallons and less than a quart managed to escape. And that, only for a moment.

In all, not one drop. Not one single, innocent drop made it to the water. None on the deck. None to be found. None. None. None. The average shade tree mechanic spills more. I've had breakfasts with more oil than we had wiped from the pipe end. Done. And I felt good!

Water on the outside; oil on the inside.

By seven o'clock the command came to rock the ship 'forward and aft.' This is an odd maneuver designed to warm the turbines before shooting all the juice and slipping free of the pier.

The deck crew worked in symphony, paying out lines thicker than my arm. Each was winched onto the deck and stretched against the drum, secure in the event that they might be needed in a hurry.

The deck secure, it was time to sail.

And sail we did. A majestic ten knots under a yellow Alaskan sun just starting to reach over snowy mountains. A sun that would compete with earthly splendor like eagles and whales, white-capped ocean and snow-capped mountains. And in the end, when the sun slips ahead of the ship to rest in the deep, blue waters, we will all be richer yet sad to see that such a spectacular day has come and gone.

We slid over blue, blue water in the shadow, and sometimes reflection, of tall white mountains. We dodged ice chunks as big as a station wagon above the water, larger than a small house below. Kelly, one of the A/Bs (Able Bodied Seaman) called them bergie bits. They were blue-green like the edges of cut glass on a shattered windshield, only beautiful, beautiful.

Mid-morning a pod of pilot whales and their offspring danced off the bow, spouting white water, giving up not a care for us or the rest of the golden world above.

I made a few notes to help me remember what we had seen and done so far:

"I got a little dirty bolting up the manifold. That was fun. 'Got a little winded helping with the lines up on the forecastle (fo'c'sle). That was interesting. (I met the bosun doing that.) Mostly I'm tired from watching and enjoying the people. They are all interesting, all coming to the sea for different reasons, most staying for reasons unexpected.

Andrew the steward assistant is working in preparation for a new baby. He misses home but Arco pays more than he could dream of making doing a similar job at home in Long Beach. Bill the steward loves the business but, unlike most of us who love foodservice, is smart enough not to fantasize about owning a restaurant. His room on ship looks like a model home complete with a computer workstation and stereo.

I still haven't checked out the life preserver and survival suit stuffed behind the chair in my room. 'Better get to that as we are now well into open sea. Hell, why bother? We've passed the rocky stuff!

Saturday, August 24

The sail board had listed six as our sailing time. After the folks at Berth Five started a long test routine to check out their new systems, no one believed that we would actually get underway anywhere near six o'clock. Whoever does such things, changed the sail time to seven and no one believed that either.

Before sailing, two strangers boarded the ship. One was the pilot who would guide our vessel through the Sound. The other was a uniformed officer who would give the captain a breath-a-lyzer test before the lines could be cast off!

Surprise, surprise! We sailed promptly at seven.

Sailing out of Valdez was not a simple matter of firing up the engines and blowing the horn. We had a tug on the bow, one tied firmly to the stern with lines as big as my leg and another, a curious looking tug, following along as if the idea of a parade seemed too good to pass up.

Once clear of the dock we lost the tug at the bow but the other two were with us for the long haul. The tug tied to our stern, all red and black, looked almost angry; not like the happy little tugboat you see in children's stories. This one stood tall in the water and sent great clouds of hot, black smoke swirling in the cold morning air. What do the environmentalists think about that?

The bow tug was designed not to push us into position but to serve as emergency steering and control in the event that we lost either power or rudder control. This was one of the many, call them improvement reforms that resulted from the Exxon Valdez disaster.

The other vessel, also a tug although blue and a bit weathered, was present for an entirely different purpose, to monitor our navigation and speed, making certain that we did not stray from the channel or exceed the very modest speed limit of five knots in the inner bay and ten in the Sound.

In theory if we were to make a mistake, they would notify us and stand by to assist. In reality a stray from course meant not much more than a warning via radio and an immediate report to the Coast Guard who would then investigate and assess the appropriate penalty.

18:20 02:20 Zulu

I called Melanie on the satellite cell phone and owe Captain Barr six dollars. (Stu wasn't so lucky when he called his wife, Debbie. He'll try again later.) The first thing Buns said was, "You sound tired." Boy, did she nail that!

It's not like I've been doing much, I haven't. There has been too much to see and learn to let sleep interfere. It's a good thing she wasn't standing downwind of me. I didn't get much beyond shaving today. By the way, on the Juneau, it is a rule that you must shave daily. Who'da thought?

For seven incredibly, beautiful hours we sailed slowly, barely fast enough for effective steering control, until Captain Barr released our outboard company and allowed the Arco Juneau to show her stuff.

Beyond danger and federal regulations, the pilot stepped to the ladder and climbed overboard into a launch. The launch would rendezvous with a 70 foot boat known as a sleepover. Several Valdez pilots shared the fully-staffed vessel using it as a convenient home away from home while waiting to pick up inbound tankers. Our pilot would wait until 1700 hours (5 P.M.) for the scheduled arrival of his meal ticket home.

The quiet sea queen finally awoke, the gentle hum of the engines replaced by the rattle and hum of my locker. There is almost no perceptible rock or roll. This girl is flying south and I'm enjoying the ride!

At 1300 the entire crew was invited to the non-smoking lounge to meet with the two passengers I had yet to see, the ones referred to as 'the shrinks.'

Get this. On this tanker there is a writer, a videographer, the Captain's father, and two psychologists. Does this sound like a bad movie or what?

Eleven mates crowded into the lounge and were greeted by a tall man in his fifties, wearing jeans, glasses, and a T-shirt, who looked like a psychologist trying to look like a sailor. His sidekick was in her early forties, short and kinda saucey with a full head of dark, electric-frizzed hair. She wore a plain, blue sweater, and jeans and was otherwise unremarkable except for an indeterminate accent, just enough to make her seem exotic. Mike and Addy. Mr. and Ms. Shrink.

In spite of that intro, they really were delightful, just a mile or two beyond the audience. Mike was selling and trying to be soft about it. Still he lost his audience when he suggested that soon they would be able to tell an 'integrative-flexible' mate from those who are "hierarchic-decisive.' Hoo-boy!

Good stuff they had but gee whiz! Could we put that in layman's terms? Maybe charge an extra buck or two for leaving the clouds?

Addy offered the group the anonymity of "slipping your forms under our door," and then closed in on the morbidly curious by adding, "We've had individual meetings that have lasted two hours and we've had some that lasted as long as five."

I know I was sold! If I had been at sea long enough, maybe five hours alone with her would begin to look good.

In the crew mess I heard of a shorter path to happiness that totally bypassed the consultant du jour.

"Get us a satellite TV so we can watch football and I'll be happy!"

Let's see. Breakfast was hash, eggs and the sweetest home fries I have ever tasted. Lunch was a Philly cheese sandwich. Dinner was prime rib, (delicious!), a baked potato with lots of Tabasco, the sweet taste of the homemade rolls and pecan pie.

I'm tired, I'm full. But it's not yet time to close up shop.

8/25 0600 local

The rhythm of the ship changed just enough to wake me. Three thirty. The four-to-eight watch would be reporting for duty in half an hour. Not me. I was still bushed from a late night trying to keep my notes fresh studying for EMT training. I would need the EMT certification for two later adventures and, even though there is a ton of course material to learn, I hated taking my focus away from one adventure to study for another. But when time is short, you do what must be done.

Was it Pareto that said, "Time expands so that what must be done gets done?" Or maybe he is the guy who said, "The job expands to fit the time allowed." Whoever. All I know is that this job takes all my time and that it gets done!

This is the kind of crap that I was thinking, lying in my bunk, waiting for sleep to come, and realizing that I needed to get up.

A ship never sleeps and I knew that elsewhere folks were rolling out of bed getting ready for the watch change.

Joe and Butch had worked the midnight to four A.M. watch and were surprised to see Writer Boy grace the bridge at such an ungodly hour.

"What are you doing up?"

"Can't learn much lying in bed. How's it going?"

Joe showed me the weather printout and course plot. He was working under the red glow of the chart table light but since the weather printout was, for some reason, half its normal size, we ruined our night vision and removed the red filter. It looked like rain and felt like rough seas. Six feet. Just enough to break over the port bow.

Light extinguished, I felt my way across the bridge, hating to be over 40 when the eyes adjust but not so quickly. I nearly broke my neck with a graceless exit to the starboard wing where J.F. was huddled behind the dodger, a glass screen under a tiny roof. The dodger offers little protection from the elements but little is better than none and J.F. didn't mind me squeezing in far enough to avoid the steady drip of rain that ran off the edge of the Arco Juneau name plate hanging just above my head.

The sky was dark and full of rain. If there was a moon, it was hiding. No stars, of course. Only the light from the mast on the fo'c'sle more than 200 yards away.

Standing watch is about the most accurate job description on the planet. You stand. You watch. For a long time. Longer it seems when it is cold. The idea behind standing watch outside the relative comfort of the bridge is that you can hear better. (Maybe they should call it 'standing listen.')

There was precious little to hear other than the constant moan of the wind. Step around the dodger and the moan became a howl. Something straight from the movies. Something that a foley artist would add to the soundtrack, our impression of life at sea, only this time, amazingly accurate.

The sea was not content to play in swell following swell. This sea wanted to climb onboard. Again and again it did just that, breaching the gunwale at the port bow, reaching in great fans of white spray over the bow, running along the deck plate, looking for an escape that it always found through chock or scupper. Like a child touting another, "you can't catch me," the water rose close to the top of the deck, pushing the ship to her side, letting her roll upright before doing it again.

"Ever been scared?" We were standing in this dark morning, seven or eight stories above the sea where every movement of the ship is magnified by our distance from the center of gravity.

"No." There was a pause broken by, "Well, maybe once."

"Do you see the kingposts?"

I could. They were maybe 300 feet from the house, each with a dim light at the top. About 30 feet tall, I'd guess. Squinting, I could make them out in the dark.

"One night we had a storm. I was standing watch. The Captain even let us come inside, it was so rough. We took a huge wave on the bow. The wave broke about halfway up the kingpost."

"So you were pretty scared?"

"Maybe a little. The wind was 70 knots. We were actually moving backwards."

From below, the constant throb of the engines never so much as stuttered even when the ship plowed into another tall swell and was pushed back ever so slightly.

At five-thirty, the mate called the deckhouse watch and ordered the deck secured. No one was to venture onto the deck and risk leaving the ship without a plan.

Dawn came almost un-noticed. As quiet as the night, this sun rose timidly behind the clouds never managing so much a glimpse at the day of its own making. By six, when the cofffee was brewing fresh in the galley, the sun had given up, brushed over by thicker, grayer clouds.

On the horizon, just off the bow, gray clouds turned black, a sign of a low pressure area spinning more wind and water over a region that needs neither. We sailed right through.

When I left the bridge, the hooded radar showed nothing. Not so much as a fishing boat within reach of the unseen beacon. Nothing but empty and plenty of it. The bright GPS display counted our progress, marking the miles in knots, the hours in local and Zulu time, and the sea in a pale blue that in no way resembled the sea I watched below. This one was nothing like pale blue. This one was dark and angry with wind that blew the tops off the tallest waves, a sea of flags of white spray that fell on the deck before running away to do it again.

At eight I reported to the bosun for duty assignment, tired but willing.

The eight o'clock muster was a bust. With the deck secured, no one can leave the house. This left only make-work (janitorial duties) and there weren't enough of them to go around. Who'da thought I'd be disappointed to miss an opportunity to scrub floors and paint stairs?

Tom, the bosun, sent me below deck to search out the chief engineer, a nice enough fellow named Bob. Unfortunately there was precious little, make that nothing, that an inexperienced hand can do in the engine room.

Now there's a misnomer, engine room. More like engine city, engine cavern, engine the-biggest-goddawful-place-you-have-ever-seen.

I turned the handle on the door, gave a gentle shove, and nothing happened. I tried it again, then again, and finally put my shoulder to it. The air pressure welling out of the depths of the engine room was incredible. Your guess, as good as mine, there must have been a dozen levels all connected by a rat's maze of red ship's ladders. Indiana Jones would have been stumped and perhaps a little frightened.

The heart of the engine room is heat, and noise seems to be its number two by-product. A few quiet people lost in themselves populated the various levels, each seeming to follow some master plan, none connected in any way to the others. Their ear plugs and the low frequency hum pushed them even deeper into themselves. Two monster-sized steam boilers created super-heated steam at a cool temperature of 905 degrees. The steam spins the turbine 6,000 times per minute. The turbine catches the reduction gear which in turn speeds the propeller shaft a lazy yet powerful 100 revolutions per minute.

The prop must weigh 40 tons and there's an extra prop lashed to the deck. The shaft must weigh another 20 tons, its backup bolted in place in the engine room. Still, it's not like you and a couple of the boys could swap one out in a few hours after a six-pack and a little creative use of a come-along. Nope, these puppies are massive with a capital 'M.'

I am told that the change out involves pumping cargo or ballast out of the stern so that the entire ship kneels in the water, raising the prop and shaft above the waterline. There's even a special wrench! The wrench is under a million coats of paint somewhere on the side of the stack. How you could maneuver it is yours to imagine.

Upstairs the steward caught my disappointment and offered a tour of his freezer. Thirty days supply of everything but perishables, with plenty of beef, chicken and fish. All top quality, what you would expect in the finest restaurants. And, surprisingly, there is plenty of choice at every meal. I wouldn't want to ship out with a skinny cook and I haven't!

15:37 Atlantic, 00:37 Zulu, (6:37 P.M. Buns' time)

Captain Barr invited me to his office to complete a few forms. He found us on the bridge and suggested that we 'stop by' on our way to the mess deck. After two, or is it three days into the ride, the Captain is ready to talk.

I enjoyed his company. A bright and thoughtful man, Captain Barr is on his first tour as captain. His is no small responsibility. Millions of gallons of crude oil, enough to pollute the sea from here to kingdom come. Twenty-five or so souls aboard, the fate of an entire company in his hands.

We talked about leadership.

Captain Barr says there are three things that send a man to stand watch duty in a blizzard at night, three things that keep ships floating when they get in trouble and three things that have to happen for the good people to have the oil they need to heat their homes and start their cars.

Communication, mutual respect, and discipline.

Barr says everyone deserves to know what is happening. People thrive on information. They want to know what is going on with their jobs. Top management at Arco has been shooting really straight. The people understand that the industry is moving towards automation. They expect it. And because they have been given the truth, they accept that there will be change. They don't like it but, because they have the facts, they understand it.

"Respect" was all Captain Barr said when I asked what was the 'second thing.' In the conversation that followed, I found that he meant mutual respect. "I respect my crew, and, I'll never nickel and dime them."

It's too easy to justify not paying overtime or getting cheap with the food. But, Barr says, the crew is out here for 60 days or more and they have to feel good about what they do and who they are working for. To take a short cut in how the crew is treated, invites the crew to take shortcuts in their work and in Valdez or the harbor at Cherry Point, shortcuts aren't acceptable. There is too much at stake.

Barr recalled a mentor, a stern no-nonsense captain that impressed a young Seaman Barr, not with his tight-fisted control but with his method of sorting through the crew in search of trustworthy individuals. This captain had a habit of asking loaded questions. If you were a genius and knew more than the old man, so much the better. But if you didn't know the right answer, heaven help you if you served up a portion of BS.

"It's knowing that I have a crew that feels comfortable saying 'I don't know,' that lets me sleep at night. How could you sleep if you suspected that your crew would try to BS their way through if they got into trouble? They can handle it if they know and they can call if they aren't sure. It is knowing that they know the difference that keeps me from being pinned to the bridge."

And finally there is this idea of discipline. Not the rigid no questions asked, aye, aye, sir and a salute stuff, but discipline borne of necessity not ego.

With the deck being secured for the entire day, this Person In Addition to Crew was going stir crazy. I needed out and decided to take the outside ship's ladder up to the bridge. My hat blew off. My favorite hat, the one that Melanie had made for me with N95MK on the front. It was right there, right there on the main deck! Why, I could open the aft hatch, reach around and retrieve it without breaking the letter of the ruling. Spirit maybe, letter no.

On the way down to the main deck floor in the house, I ran into Butch who was on watch.

"Yo! Butch! I lost my hat. It's right out the aft hatch. Can I reach out and get it?"

"Sure! Right after I call the bridge and get the okay."

Point: This wasn't mindless rule following. It was respect for crew discipline, the same discipline that meant little or nothing when it came to fetching a hat would mean everything if and when the chips were really down. And therein lies the lesson: Discipline of the I-told-you variety is cheap and worthless but discipline borne of respect is priceless.

Captain Barr is a talented kind of guy, just the sort that would feel as comfortable and confident maneuvering in a traditional corporate environment yet here he is walking 120,000 tons of steel and cargo in and out of Valdez. Ask him why he chose the conn over the executive suite and he gives the answer you are glad to hear. "I like it. I watched my dad work a nine-to-five job. I watched him commute to the same office every day and I decided I wanted something else. This is what I wanted and I got it."

Sunday (I think): 19:07 Alaskan

Somehow this turned out to be the best day. It was long. I started before four A.M. standing watch. Boring. I got kicked off the deck team due to weather, and I ate too much. Dinner was another hit, broiled chicken, mashed potatoes, and, in honor of Mom, steamed broccoli.

Worst of all, in spite of numerous tries, the satellite phone system refused to connect us to home. I can't think of a day that I have not called my Boogie Buns.

But I think I may have turned a corner.

The Captain invited me to chat and I learned a lot.

Randy, the pumpman, stopped by after dinner and took me to his favorite place, the pump room.

Joe let me manipulate the nav system. It works about like the one on 95MK, just bigger.

Harry offered up an impromptu lesson on cargo loading.

I was looking for Stu when Randy rounded the passageway. "Do you want to go to the pump room with me?"

"Sure! Is it okay?"

"No problem."

The big guy un-dogged the starboard hatch and started to step through. Now, I knew the deck was secured and had just about swallowed my tongue when he whipped out a radio and called the bridge.

"Bridge! Pumpman calling."

"Go ahead." It was Harry, a nice guy for sure but also a pretty tough cookie when it comes to following policy, especially his! And he was the guy who had ordered the main deck secured.

"I need to go to the pump room to put away some tools. I'm taking one of our riders with me."

Oh, geez! Harry is going to say 'no' the instant he digests the word 'riders.'

Harry's reply of "Go ahead" was less permission than a vote of confidence in Randy.

We stepped out into the wind which was nearly 30 knots. This was no place to be goofing off. Randy walked close to the house, then up and over a set of stairs to clear a quartet of pipes without so much as losing a beat. Not bad for a big guy. The pump room hatch was at the base of the house. Randy used a dog pipe to free the hatch and invited me to step inside.

In about a hundred years I could learn to like the pump room.

Walk out onto a steel grate landing. Place your feet at shoulder's width apart. Look straight down seven floors. Start climbing. On the way down watch the shadows, notice how steep the steps angle, and listen to the clanging of pipes as if some lost soul were banging on a dungeon wall begging to be let out.

Like a deep metal tomb made all the more pleasant by the wall fixtures, the alarms for oxygen, sulfide alarm, and methane. Add in colorful stations offering escape apparatus and you've got a pretty good picture of the place. Oh, yeh! It was dark. Bare bulbs every now and again. Swell!

Randy wanted me to really get the idea of the pump system so we stopped some 60 feet from the bottom for a lesson. Pointing right to left, he recited the names of the huge pipes climbing vertically along the wall: segregated ballast, tank number one, number two, crude oil wash, stripper, tank three and tank four.

"What are these?" Randy beamed at his ever so reluctant student.

I made an effort heightened by the thought that I may never leave the platform until I managed a passing grade. I repeated the menu, caught my breath and waited for the big guy to say, "Hey! That's pretty good! I had one trainee for 90 days and she never did get that right!"

"And maybe she didn't mind standing here with her butt hanging 60 feet over the keel," I thought and simultanously headed down the ship's ladders, one after the other, all the way to the ladder and grate maze at the bottom of the vessel.

Randy had a mess of tools to put away and I helped, scooping them as fast as I could while keeping my eye on the ladder out. The ship groaned and the prisoner banged again. Let me out of here!

Back in the semi-real world, Randy called the bridge to let them know that we were clear and the pump room was secure. In the cargo control room, Kelly had her feet propped on the panel, hiding with a good book. Randy offered a review lesson and, what do you know? His star pupil pointed out that, based on the pump room lesson, the wall chart was wrong. Well, nah, nah, nah nah nah!

We tried to call home and were again unsucccessful.

Harry was at the conn; J.F. on the starboard wing,

standing watch. I paced a bit, worrying that Melanie was worrying. I have pretty much a perfect record when it comes to calling home.

The spray was shooting up over the bow. Then, looking as if it were choreographed, the dancing water followed the airflow like dolphin mist, landing lightly on the foredeck.

I asked Harry about the displacement of the ship, dead weight versus cargo weight. All of it moving through the sea at nearly 18 miles an hour. The engine room had sent up their own assessment of progress based on fuel used and turns of the screw. Six thousand rpms on the turbine became 75 turns of the 24 foot prop. Each nautical mile cost us a half barrel of fuel, 21 gallons. Not much for mileage on the old pickup but then a pickup doesn't drag 56 feet of its body beneath the road.

Imagine that! Fifty six feet of this ship is below the water. Talk about icebergs!

Lesson over, curiosity satisfied, disappointed at not talking to my sweetie, I left the bridge only to be replaced by another student, Andrew, the young father-to-be.

"Hey, Andrew! What would you like to learn today? 'Wanna take the helm?"

I turned and saw two faces. One brown and young, and one with rosy cheeks you would expect of the Irish, were bent over the wheel sharing and learning, seadog to seapup. 'Guess Harry's not so gruff after all.

My Mates

Over and over I heard the phrase, 'my shipmates' used as if there was some sort of unspoken bond. It turns out that there is.

Familiarity breeds...commitment.

Over and over when it comes to great teams, and I am just recognizing this, the fact that you are my shipmate means something special.

The Captain said it yesterday when he mentioned that he rarely socializes with people inside the organization. There are only a few, he said, that he would call if he were passing through their town on vacation. And yet, these are his shipmates and, at least while at sea, there is little that he would not do to help out when needed.

Randy mentioned it as well when we talked about the drill for handling an onboard fire. Once the alarm is sounded all hands are expected to report to their fire stations for muster.

"I know," said the big guy, "that if I don't report, I'll be missed. And I also know that they won't let me down. I can flood the engine room with foam in a matter of seconds and that's the technical side of it. But if I know you are there, if you can hang on in some small corner, you know we'll be there to get you. That's because we're shipmates."

Just like riding the rails, when we're 'out there,' we're 'out there' together.

Michelle

She has that curly mouth that reminds me of an actress, I couldn't tell you who. Dirty blonde hair pulled back so that it flops on the collar of the Arco Marine jumpsuit. She's Bitsy Beekman, Rosie the Riveter, and the Girl Next Door all rolled into one fast-talkin' package. A woman in the engine room. If you want to talk to her, you can wait in the crew mess and take your chances because she rarely sits still for long. Or, you might catch her nine stories below the mess desk up to her elbows in the machinery that makes this monster move.

Not long ago she would have been an oddity but today she is nothing more than a competent, licensed power plant specialist doing her part to keep the lights burning in Seattle. Ask her what it's like to work in what not long ago was an unquestioned man's world and she just smiles. After a pause, you might hear, "You have to be competent or at least eager to learn. At first, the guys just sort of ignore you. With all this sexual harassment stuff, they're afraid to say much of anything. You just try to blend in and once they understand that you're just trying to do a good job, you know, with nothing else on the agenda, everything is just fine.

"I heard you talking yesterday to the guys about whether or not there is an 'engine room personality.' They said no but that's not right. I started as a messman when we had two on duty and you were waited on; not cafeteria-style like we do it today. Well, if you had two tables, the engine crew would be at one table and the deck hands at the other. The engine guys would just eat in silence while the deckhands would be talking a mile a minute.

"Working here gives you a chance to have two personalities. Here, a lot of us are kind of loners. I'm very independent. But shoreside, things are different although working out here does change the way you think. This isn't what you'd call a glamorous job. Look at these hands, not exactly what you'd call pretty. When I'm at home, my best friend and I go out. She takes three hours to get ready. I just wash my face and I'm ready to roll!

"The engine room is different. The deck guys have a boss. In the engine room, your boss is your partner. That's a different relationship. We depend on each other and there is a lot of mutual respect. That's the best way to learn, when the boss has to teach you so you can pull your weight as his partner.

"Every time I come back to work, I can see myself grow. It's amazing to look back five years and think about how much I've grown. Then I was interested in knowing how things worked so that I could get through the shift. Now, I'm at a different stage. Now I want to know why things work."

"So, what's your dream job?" I ask.

"This is it!"

18:26 Arco Juneau 02:26 Zulu (8:30, Buns' Las Vegas time)

I joined the deckhands and was assigned to chip paint with something called a needle gun. Plenty of air hose, ear and eye protection. Even a mask.

My job? Paint the number "3-2p COW" which stands for

crude oil wash, a mushroom of rusting gray metal growing in a sea of gray mushrooms somewhere on the port side, just north of the spaghetti manifold that straps the ship from gunnel to gunnel.

The sun poured itself across the deck and then into the sea against the sky. The entire world, or at least my slice of it, was brilliant with color and the crisp sound of the sea. My air gun blended in, muffled behind yellow ear plugs, warm in my hands and heavy in my arms. This is the kind of work for which a day is made.

Once in a while, just once in a while, man needs hard, mindless work. And this was it on both accounts. There is plenty of time to think when you are chipping paint. But you don't think. You just watch the paint peel layer by layer until there is shiny metal where there had been red, red rust.

Then you paint. This time with a long handled brush that looks like it has a broken wrist. Thick, gooey, gray paint that slathers on and sucks its way into the rusty crevices that were beyond the reach of the needle gun and patience. And try to stay upwind!

The 20 or so knots on the bow add to the 15 knots of our speed for a pretty brisk air, whipping at my shirt and flinging paint toward the house some 500 lonesome feet away.

Once in a while the Juneau puts her nose down just to be playful. Then the dancing water reappears, jumping over the fo'c'sle and turning to salty mist before it sails over my head. Not exactly heavy weather but pretty exciting stuff for this landlubber!

It seemed everyone on deck stopped to share the myth of a classified ad that supposedly read, "Painters wanted. Sailors need not apply!"

I liked being part of the team. I liked being teased when the chipping and painting was done. When they discovered that I already had the long, used-to-be-red hoses rolled and stowed in the house, there was more teasing. "Hey! Slow it down! You'll make us look bad!"

Someday very soon they will be selling this ship to another master who will get a bargain. One great ship with two elegantly painted COWs!

The news came just in time to spoil lunch. Several of the crew were being R-O-B'd. And, if that sounds like robbed then so be it. It seems that the company is short of seamen, for the moment. If a replacement cannot be found, the message is faxed that someone is to Remain On Board. Folks who live life working 75 days straight may suddenly find their plans shattered, their stir-craziness turned up a notch when word comes that families or friends, children or wives will have to wait. One more week, maybe two. One more trip to Alaska, maybe one. Maybe.

Michelle had been counting the days, as had Kelly. And I forget but it seems that it is only the females who just happened to have been ROB'd this trip. There are a few long faces though most of the rest are counting the hours until the big white and gray ship nudges up against the dock at Port Angeles.

Stuart will be leading the pack and I don't blame him. Ruth, the cook/baker, is counting on her vacation. She told Stu that if he was too slow leaving the ship, and I don't think that's possible, she will, "Run over your fat ass 'cause I'm going home!" (Ruth has a way with words.)

Life on this ship revolves around the crew's mess, a cheery, yellow place with placemats picked out by someone's grandmother and wooded restraints to hold drinks in place in rough weather. Everyone checks the bulletin and chalkboards religiously for what little news sneaks its way over the rails.

The watch posts current conditions and standing orders on the chalkboard. 'Mon. Aug. 25th 0700 60 degrees 25kt l/o port partly cloudy.' (Monday at seven in the morning, it is 60 degrees with a 25 knot wind. The lookout is on the left side,which tells you that the wind is blowing on the right side of the ship. It's partly cloudy.)

There are other postings that announce that the shrinks are holding a session at 1300 hours, the deck is secure and there are five openings left in the pilot pool. (Three dollars gets you in to guess at what time the pilot will come on board to guide the ship into Port Angeles.)

Another sign, a wooden ship silhouette hanging from the clock, reminds us to advance our clocks when we slip from Alaska to Pacific time late tonight.

If you are up, feel free to raid the fridge which is always stocked with Dove bars. You can find hot coffee and a Crock Pot full of soup or stew at any hour. And there is plenty of fruit and snacks on the table.

All the comforts of home except home.

Tuesday

The eight-to-four crew of A/Bs mustered as usual on the main deck level giving an all new meaning to the term 'motley crew.' Tom, the bosun, was near the port hatch which I had undogged earlier when I stepped out to feel the morning. The bosun wore his omnipresent English driving cap, looking about seven feet tall which must be close to the truth. He cleans up pretty good but today in honor of the deck work that needs to be done to prepare the ship for port, he wore his baggy, light blue jump suit which makes him look even taller. The man has no butt at all, a walrus mustache, and a personality bigger than the ship.

Kelly leaned into the doorway of the stair leading to the A deck. She looked whupped. A big girl with a pretty smile and pleasant disposition, she could be your cousin from Wisconsin. You know, the one you don't get to see very often but who feels like family just the same.

Joe was there in his Arco Marine jumpsuit. Dark hair and eyes, a medium-sized guy who is always neatly dressed even given that we are on an oil tanker not working in an office. Going off watch, not on, thinking about breakfast, not deck work. Joe has his finger on the pulse of the ship. Joe is easy to get to know, always has a friendly word and is interesting to talk to. Joe will be equally comfortable with officers or crew as will J.F.

J.F. stood near the cook's locker looking fresh. A yuppie. Articulate and cheerful, J.F. will 'sail up,' as they say, so long as the industry survives the bean counters.

Butch rounded out the crew, sauntering in from nowhere just in time to catch the First Mate's briefing. Oh, yeh! I almost forgot Andy who is easy to forget. Probably the hardest working member of the crew and definitely the quietest. If I sailed with him for a few years, I might figure him out but probably not.

Helen may have been there somewhere but I think not. Helen is picture pretty but around me for some strange reason, she is as silent as paint. She tends to wear work clothes that, although clean, have so much accumulated paint, oil and who knows what that she has the aura of PigPen from the Peanuts comic strip.

Exactly at eight, Harry came down the stairs and proceeded with the briefing. Harry is the God of Safety. He walks and talks safety with all the zeal of a convert. We got the message about hearing protection, a demonstration on lifting modeled by Joe, and a good cop's closing warning of "Be careful out there."

The entire time, and I was watching, not once did Harry look my way.

On deck we set to work getting things ready for port. There were life rings to put out, some with emergency floating strobe lights. There were foam applicator nozzles to place, handy in the unlikely event of a fire.

Tom and I worked on laying fire hose and positioning back-up reels in key places on the deck. Just before break, Tom asked me to handle the last of the reels, dragging it up the starboard ship's ladder and installing it center fo'c'sle.

Off our bow a squall was taking aim. The seas seemed to roughen just a bit and the spray across the bow that looks so beautiful from the comfort of the bridge began to take on an entirely different personality as I dragged the rolled fire hose up the ladder.

Into the rack, untie the roll, attach to the hydrant and

then, hose end between legs, screw on the heavy brass nozzle. By now, the spray was creeping closer, encouraged by the rain racing toward the ship. Like a roper who has just made the last turn around a calf's leg, I raised my arms and turned to the ladder, wondering if someone knew that I was working alone at the bow.

Over my shoulder the rain was gaining. I thought about running and realized that a slip might be worse than just getting wet. Worse, if green water decided to jump over the gunwale, I'd be wise to stay on sure footing.

I walked faster looking over my shoulder every few steps, certain that I could not make the house in time and I was more than right. By the time I made cover, I didn't need it. Besides, the day was bright and beautiful, the sea was fast and as blue as blue ever gets. Even the rain felt good now, running in small rivulets down the small of my back. I had dry clothes in the cabin. No problem.

Earlier, Tom and I had assisted the pump room crew checking the COW system. They radioed for us to open a COW machine on the starboard fore deck. We did and waited until we could hear the oil coursing through the lines. Then the machine was closed and we waited until the system came up to pressure. Kelly, a licensed operator who has yet to sail as a third mate, was at the controls under the watchful eye of Harry, Mr. Safety. We were in doubly good hands.

Now it was our turn. A quick walk the length of the deck to check for leaks, scuttles in place just in case the twisting and bending that stresses a long, heavy tanker at sea had opened one of the stiff joints in the thousands of feet of deck piping.

No leaks.

As we walked past the kingposts, those two tall metal masts midships that hold cargo booms and give the ship a sense of style, Tom told me a funny story.

A ship is a constant contest between metal and rust. Ships aren't painted; they are coated. Read the label on the can and see for yourself. But not everything can take paint.

The guy wires running in four directions from the kingposts are a case in point. Several cruises ago an A/B was suspended in a bosun's chair from the kingpost, assigned to coat the guy wires with pinion grease as he was lowered to the deck.

Upon reaching the top, the A/B spooked and dropped the can of grease. Pinion grease at room temperature has the consistancy of a stick of butter. The bucket dropped, hit the deck right side up, and the pinion grease popped straight up in one big glob. Remarkably, the grease came straight down, falling back into the bucket, spilling not a single, impossible-to-clean drop! The seaman was so excited that he nearly rapelled down the kingpost, slipped into the bucket, and managed to smear pinion grease clear to Kingdom come!

We were wet again.

By the time I reached the after deck, the rest of the crew was involved in paying out lines in anticipation of our docking some seventeen hours later. I pitched in and we winched and pulled until the thick, eight inch line snaked lazily to the starboard rail.

At 10:20, the huge air horn began to blow itself hoarse from the bridge.

"To your fire stations. This is a drill. This is a drill."

From the house, orange-jacketed bodies spilled east and west, parading towards one of two 48-passenger life boats hanging solidly one deck above main deck. We watched from the bridge, stuck in our bumblebee costumes, forced to watch rather than participate as heads were counted and boat engines started. With the boat drill over, the orange miniatures below us headed toward fire stations where, one by one, the bright yellow foam monitors were forced to spew forth a test of first rust red then clear water, beating back imaginary flames. And all I could do was watch.

Game over, our little world began to turn again. Cooks cooking, enginemen checking, and able bodied seamen—and women—hauling things across the wide deck of gray and steel. Long fire wires of thickly braided steel were wound in figure eights on bits fore and aft. Each end was looped back upon itself forming a long cable with ends just right for hooking over a bit. (The fire wires hang over the side for tug boats to grap to when we are alongside the dock to pull us clear of the dock in case of a catastrophe.)

The bits are nearly four feet tall, maybe 18 inches in diameter and probably weigh a ton or more each. The fire wire is a couple hundred pounds of wrist-thick, braided, stainless cable. We're talking toys of giant proportion.

16:00 hours

Off the bow, the sky was black as night, sucking in the light of late afternoon, hiding what I knew would be rain by the bucketsful. Elbows resting on the porthole sill in the crew mess, I was prepared to spend the afternoon studying while my work clothes hung all over my cabin, not really drying but at least wicking the wet evenly from sleeve to sleeve. If you can't be dry, then uniformly wet is the next best thing.

Pumps came wandering in, a man with a mission. "I have a header that needs a little look. 'Wanna help?'"

"Sure! Is it the one at the manifold? I saw the third mate struggling with it this morning."

"Uh-huh. And we need it for discharge tomorrow so if it's going to get fixed, it's now."

"Gonna rain, Pumps. That's a squall right on the bow."

"We'll have to hurry."

We didn't take much, just a five-gallon pickle bucket filled with a handful of tools. A hammer for knocking the paint away from the bolts, a screwdriver, a couple of wrenches, and the obligatory shop rags. Pumps dressed me in a jazzy blue garbage bag that was, if you believe the label, a rain pancho. (Yeh, right! It was a garbage bag with factory installed arm holes.)

I chipped off the paint, a skill I have elevated to an art form since boarding. Pumps lifted off the indicator stem and attacked the bolts. By the third bolt, and there must have been a dozen, the squall that had been threatening turned threat into promise. The sea began to well up, higher and higher with each rolling swell until it began to look like we'd soon be taking green water over the side.

"Better hurry."

"Yeh, I can see."

We finished the job after digging through a couple of pounds of rust brown grease. Everything on a ship that you can't see is rust brown. Water dripped then ran down my back for the second time today. Elegant work this is not, but I love it!

Before I left home Melanie caught me packing my second favorite pair of work gloves. Dirty, greasy, worn and torn. Manly sort of gloves.

"You're not taking those! You'll look like a poor boy from the country. I can't send you out looking like that."

"Is this the same as changing your underwear in case of an accident?"

"Humor me, please."

So we packed the second favorite pair, a brand new pair of calf skin gloves. They smelled like new, almost as good as smelling like old. (The first time I wore them I was cleaning Alaskan crude off the chicksans.Yesterday they chipped paint and today they hauled lines.And now they are full of grease. My new favorite pair of gloves.)

What little daylight there was has slipped into the ocean, dragging life from passageways to cabins.

The ship seems deserted. Only the First Mate and the look-out are on the bridge. When I padded by, the galley door was closed and, peeking in, Ruth was inside, alone, hosing down the floor as if rinsing off an entire voyage. The floor was clean but she continued to scrub, looking well beyond the worn tiles.

It was Ruth who told us that on her first voyage, she cried every night for a week feeling like the loneliest person in a dark and formless world. She still feels that way every time she returns to sea, cook/baker her title. Ruth, her name. 'Nice lady', an apt description.

I will miss her hoarse cry, "Stuart! Scott!" sounding for all the world like our old neighbor Mrs. Gallagher who would call her Catholic-sized brood for dinner. I would respond, wanting to be Smitty Gallagher at least until after dinner.

Ruth called an entire ship to breakfast, lunch and dinner, remembering your name and whether or not you liked onions after a single brief introduction.

Pumps has gone off for a nap. He too will be called out at 2:30 in the morning. None of us will really need a call. Once the engines slow to pick up the pilot, we'll all know that morning and Cherry Point are near.

Stuart has showered and packed. He plans to sleep in his clothes, camera loaded and ready to shoot.

In the morning, well before we'll see the sun, we'll see the long, lighted dock at Cherry Point. More tugs, more lines. First the light heaving line followed by the messenger line which will be pulled back to the ship. Finally the messenger line will lead the huge mooring lines to the tugs where they will be wrapped and winched until they are taut, pulled over the rail through the chocks until only the slightest warp can be sighted along their length.

Tom had mentioned he would be glad to see Cherry Point although I was surprised at this since he would not be leaving the ship. In the morning, I would hear him say, "It smells like oil which sure beats the hell out of how it usually smells, like cow shit. This whole valley is full of dairies (expletive deleted) up the environment!"

Who'da thought!

The whole ship is not sleeping. A few stand watch at half effort, preserving their energy for what they know will be a long tomorrow. Those who were ROB'd have unpacked and are waiting for yet another day like all of the 60, 70 or 80 before. They took the news in good humor but I know it hurts and I've only been on board for a few days. A few wait to rush home. They are homesick but to hear them talk, many are homesick for home as they dream it, not for the home that is.

Tomorrow a few of those who live locally will choose to remain onboard even though home, the address, is but a few miles from the dock, a silent acknowledgement that home, where the heart is, is in the house, on the sea and with this odd assortment of mates.

And me? I sit here one last time on an up-ended camera case. This time with pen in hand, writing like writers have done for ages. The computer, that new writing machine, is packed and waiting. In a minute I'll fire up the cell phone, (we're close enough now,) and wait for the voice that makes me hungry for more. Home, as it is, is sweet enough for me.

Tomorrow we will go ashore and it will feel only a little bit like leaving home and a whole lot like going home.

The rest of the crew has a call-out for 3:30 in the morning. Even after working with me for three days, they were still surprised to see me add our names to the sail board. But to me, it seems that to stay warm in my bunk while my mates are tending the ship would make fun of the rest of the experience. So we will be up. We'll sleep on the plane ride home. After all, this is a sea we probably won't sail again.

'Can't speak for the girls but what small boy has not floated a boat in the bar ditch or built a raft to sail forever down the creek and thought about going to the sea in real ships? All of us, I suppose. For me the Juneau was a dream I am glad to have borrowed.

A few hours ago I walked in on Stuart and found him sifting through the hours of video that he brought back.

"I could show this tape to Debbie (his wife.) And she would say, 'That's really beautiful.' And she would be right. But she wouldn't feel the wind or the way the boat rocks in the swells. And she couldn't smell the fresh air or feel how cool it was in the morning. She just couldn't understand without having been here."

"Would you do it again?"

"Not on a ship!"

So there are some dreams worth dreaming and others just

worth borrowing. We'll have other adventures. Some to dream after, some to borrow, all to make us different for having dared.

16

Sniffing for Asphalt

Sniffing for asphalt. What an outrageously accurate description of an instrument approach!

When the ceiling lowers faster than the temperature, begging the clouds to cling to the wing and stabilizer, this is when sniffing for asphalt is more than a catch phrase. To pilots on instruments, there is always that moment of doubt when the nose of the plane pushes against the softness of a cloud deck, probing at a couple of hundred miles an hour, hoping once again to find nothing more substantial than the frozen air. Granite clouds are only funny when mentioned from the safety of the hangar. At altitude there is nothing remotely funny about granite or antennae towers for that matter.

A giant of aviation, Jan Lopresti is rumored to have said, "Life is short...fly fast!" Well, it's possible that flying fast is the very reason why life is short! Still, some of us cannot, do not, resist the urge to strap a few thousand pounds of low tech metal and high tech avionics to our butts and race along at a few thousand feet hoping to once again commit a crime against gravity and pull ourselves behind three-bladed props into the province of God and angels.

At 15,000 feet there isn't much to see and even less to do. The autopilot holds the plane, silently adding a bit of trim here, adjusting the course just a bit there as the plane slices softly through whatever puffiness might reach out to brush against the flawless sweep of wing.

At 3,000 feet, now here is something to see. Railroads and swimming pools, plowed fields and picnics all come into crisp inspection at a level where the colors of the earth translate into thermals, columns of unevenly heated air that rise up to bump against the belly and make back seat passengers grab for the armrest as if holding tight to a falling plane makes it fall less or softer or who knows what?

At a thousand feet, the warning horn sounds, a reminder that a landing is little more than a controlled crash. The idea is to make the wings lose their ability to support the plane at precisely the moment the plane has given up all but a few inches of altitude.

No more altitude, no more lift. Perfect! Set her down gently, bleed off a little excess speed and turn triumphantly onto the next taxiway! A crash with a happy ending!

The perfect analogy...life as a controlled crash. That is the way I want to go. Out of altitude and life at precisely the same moment. Think of the lost souls who never coax a single foot of altitude out of their lives or, if they do, find themselves so frightened by heights that they climb no further, dying full of lift unrealized. A waste.

A friend, Holly Stiel, made a clever quote saying that dead people do the same thing all the time. People who are alive constantly do different things. I want to live all the way to the hangar and then, looking out for the last time, runway and infield framed in dark contrast of that cool, dark place where airplanes wait to fly again, I want to say that I did different things and used me all up, the purest form of stewardship of a life freely given, gladly taken, fully spent, nothing left but memories of deeds done, laughs laughed and love loved.

Flying was supposed to be a hobby, something pleasant to keep a middle-aged guy out of trouble. I like to call it the perfect answer to midlife crises when so many men think about fooling around (and a few do.) Flying is better than sinking into the couch, beer mug and beer belly to death by monotony.

I hit mid-life and thought about fooling around.

Then I thought about buying an airplane. Too expensive.

But not nearly as expensive as fooling around! So I bought the plane!!

(I love to tell it that way but the truth told is I never once thought about fooling around.) I love everything about Melanie. Everything. Growing up together is even better than flying and not much different. Fear and promise, moments of unbounded joy, disappointment. Different things every day when you do it right.

I think about flying and I think about work. And I wonder why more work isn't like flying...or being married to Melanie. Most of the folks we have met on our adventures are doing what turns them on and fills them up. But there is no avoiding the thought of how many people are in a rut so deep they can't see the top, so deep they have no awareness of the rut they are in, that life could be so much better for the choosing.

Maybe it's the fear of failure that leads to so much failure. Surely as there is failure in the doing, there is, perhaps, a greater failure in not even trying.

Robin Williams, that great dead poet, turned my head with carpe diem...seize the day. Seize it? Hell! Choke it! Shake it until the very life is wrung out of it, so that history is left with a day completely spent.

Today is New Year's Eve and we should be watching football. Even though there is chardonnay chilling, we're following a dream bigger than a bowl game. Carpe diem!

Landing with the airport in sight, with the runway nicely lined up beyond the nose is a trick. Landing when you must sniff for the asphalt, now that's another story. You know it's there somewhere. The non-directional beacon is sounding in your headset. You're right over it. Just hope that your altimeter is telling you exactly how far over it you really are. The ground is there somewhere and if you are crossing that puppy in the right direction, that asphalt you are seeking is right in front of you...sucker!!

Nose up, gear down, flaps out, power off...sniff, sniff, sniff. It should be just ahead. Another hundred feet, then another. 'Shouldn't need to go much lower before the runway lights float into view. Sniff, sniff...not yet. Sniff, sniff. The palms do sweat.

There! No, I guess not yet. Now, there! That's it. Sweet smell of asphalt, 5,000 feet long and calling softly through wisps of cloud or fog or whatever you call this muck that threatens to wash over the runway and hide it again.

Sniff, sniff. There it is. Check the gear again. Strobes on, landing lights. Like a cook carefully creating, add the remainder of the flaps, taste the airspeed, feel the control wheel. No buffet of stall, plenty of airspeed.

Sniff, sniff becomes chirp, chirp. First the mains settle, then the nose.

"Steer with your feet," your instructor's voice never leaves your head. Flaps up to transfer weight to the tires for better braking. Then clear at the first taxiway and tell the tower the obvious.

"Mooney niner-five-mike-kilo is clear of the active."

Or maybe we should simply say, "Mooney niner-five-mike-kilo has found her way through the cloud and murk and we are here to tell about it. And, Tower, now that we have that behind us, can we go again?"

The greatest joy is doing what turns you on and fills you up. The second greatest joy is finding it!

17

An Adventure is Born

I took a deep breath to measure the air the patient would need against my own desire to suck in life-giving oxygen. Thirty seconds, max. If the job wasn't complete in that time, I would retreat and continue CPR while the brain spun another option or summoned the courage to try again.

The patient was as lifeless as lifeless gets, staring open-eyed from the hard table. I worked quickly, sweating, wishing that the patient would sweat or swallow or somehow signal that I was making progress. The chest didn't move, hadn't moved since I first bent over the gaping mouth to feel for a sign of breathing. There was none and I was not surprised.

The contents of the jump kit from the ambulance were spread in half-spill on the floor at my feet. I selected a blade for the laryngoscope, snapped it on, flipped it up to turn on the light in its tip and then in a sweeping motion pushed past the tongue, probing beyond the larynx, looking for the vocal cords. Target acquired. Hold. Steady. Now, fish the long plastic tube along the blade. There. Blade out. Scope tossed carelessly onto the table. Feel for the syringe to inflate the bulb at the base of the tube, toss the syringe and grab for the bag-valve mask and...breathe! Both of us!

Except the patient didn't...exactly.

And if he had, I would have needed medical attention myself.

This patient was a dummy, a real dummy. Plastic. Lifelike in every way except that unlike the real patients who would benefit from my new found knowledge, this patient would never breathe. But he would endure one clumsy stab after another until this student, like the hundreds before, learned how to flawlessly slide a life-saving plastic breather tube into the throat.

This one would never complain, never sue, never tell how many attempts it took to finally figure that the secret is to lift, hard, and pry upward until the tube could slip into the lungs rather than uselessly into the stomach.

From the very moment when the idea of exploring work in America started to wart on me, I knew that I wanted to look from the inside. We had played in Arizona, spent a long night on the Mexican border, traveled the shining east coast rails with Amtrak and been launched from bed in the wee hours of the morning in Dallas. Now, all that were left were the final two adventures and, as luck would have it, both involved pre-hospital emergency care.

One, the med-evac unit in Kansas City came as a result of a fortunate meeting with its director, Mark Holcomb. Mark, in addition to being a first-class trauma doc, is also a pilot. So it was a given that he would invite me to look in on his world of gunshots and knife fights, heart attacks and unexpected deliveries.

The other adventure, working with the Phoenix Fire Department, came as a result of an engagement to speak at the California Fire Instructor's Workshop. Always looking for ways to relate to the audience, I mentioned this project to Walt Lihuin, the conference's business manager. Walt wasted no time in introducing me to the good folks in Phoenix.

Easy, except for one small detail. There was no way that I could participate. And participation was the founding premise of the project.

What to do? The logical thing was to drop these adventures in favor of something I could handle without special training. But Sally O'Malley in our office had once commented, "No guts, no story," and I figured that she had a point.

It turns out that the minimum training required for either of the two adventures was to become certified as an EMT (Emergency Medical Technician.) Simple just not easy. (There's a concept I keep running into!) Earning the EMT certification required over 100 hours of classroom instruction plus a long list of special classes and experiences.

With a little help from the state of Texas, I contacted two extraordinary EMT/Paramedic instructors at Scott & White Hospital in Temple, Texas. Scott & White is world-renowned as a center for emergency medicine training. They were more than willing to accept another student.

Unfortunately, the course is given over a period of months on a schedule that would wipe out my ability to earn an income through speaking. When you add that Temple is about 175 miles distant by car, you have a problem. Unless, of course, you have a Mooney. Ta da! Just the solution a flyboy would love!

With the benefit of one-on-one instruction on a schedule tailored to mine, throw in the opportunity to fly to work, and magic! No shortcuts, no slack. All I asked for was flexibility in scheduling. Otherwise I did everything any other student would do. I worked in the emergency room, rode the ambulances, learned to use special tools to extricate the injured from wreckage, and covered all the classroom materials in spades.

And I've gotta tell you, I had the time of my life.

Am I an expert on emergency care? Not even.

Imagine a grain of sand on a mile long beach. Divide that

grain in half and divide it again. That's how much I know about medicine.

But can you trust me to perform within the scope of my training? You bet! I know it and know it cold.

I'll tell you one thing more. I learned more getting ready for the final two adventures than in all the others combined. More data, of course, but also more about how humans learn and how they behave under the stress of an emergency. And I learned that if I didn't already have the best job on the planet, this is where I belong!

It was hot. Oppressively hot and the uniform felt like it weighed a ton. James had moved the hose truck to an open space behind the station where a local auto salvage service had parked a wreck of a sedan. White once upon a time. Bald tires, no interior. A real junker.

It was also to be my classroom for the evening.

The rules were simple. Tear off the doors and peel back the top. Oh, yeah, and stand by in case the tones come floating over the radio and we have to respond to a real call.

James had the floodlights aimed at the wreck, portable air compressors running, and a James Bond assortment of tools that made Dr. No look like a beginner. Laid out with pants already tucked into tall boots, the bunker gear waited for teacher and student. Bunker gear...the coat, pants, helmet and boots keep firefighters from being burned in a fire while simultaneously cooking them from the inside.

Tonight was no exception and I was grateful to see the sun slip behind the station. Still, the temperature hovered in the nineties. In a matter of seconds after pulling up the red suspenders of the pants and flapping the velcro of the coat across my chest, I began not to sweat but to drip. The boots were too tight. (My feet are the only part of my body that is macho-size. The rest of me qualifies for the 98 pound weakling award.)

Now, until I opened the car like a tin of tuna, I would

have to drag this get up around like a sweaty yellow anchor.

The first job was to pull out the windshield. Not break it out; pull it out. In the real world of roadside wrecking, there is a patient just beyond the glass. So no more violence. Cover the patient to protect and use a fire ax to chop around the windshield edge, then with gloved hand, tear neatly along the dotted line and poof! Instant access!

Before I could get too enthralled with my handiwork, Bruce handed me the Jaws of Life and shouted that I should lower the shield of the helmet. Swell. Is it not hot enough for you, Bruce?

I took the giant tool and nearly fell over. (Bruce has biceps. I push a pencil for a living!) I cradled the tool in my arms, not out of love but self-defense, and shoved the huge, metal pincers against the support where Bruce was pointing. It's simple, really. Aim and squeeze. Turn the dial behind the jaws and standby to be amazed. Turn to the right and the jaws close; to the left and the jaws slowly open. Either way, the jaws move with awesome power.

The jaws spread slowly taking the lower driver's door with it. Then to the top hinge which popped off, dropping the door instantly.

Now to the roof support nearest the driver's seat. Squeeze. Snip. Pop.

Around the car, one post, one snip at a time until the roof sits unsupported except for the last, the left rear support. I ran out of steam and had to hoist the tool so that it could rest on my shoulder. Weak arms gave way. Only the body, full of sweat and drained of energy, was left to guide the jaws. Squeeze, snip, pop and the last post surrendered.

And so went the one-student class on emergency extrication. One down and a score to go.

Pre-hospital emergency care is not the clean, genteel choreograpghy of surgery. It is rough but disciplined. It is dirty and dangerous, dull at times and occasionally disgusting but, it is never without order and thought. It moves fast but is rarely hurried. Sometimes, unlike what happens in surgery, you have to go after your customers. You may have to crawl under or climb over. You may have to talk them down or cut them out.

It is the most exciting form of medicine, maybe the most exciting job on the planet.

Attempting to accelerate the training is like trying to run in water. The spirit may be willing, the instructors may be the best, but there is simply too much material that must be covered, make that mastered. You can hurry but it does little good.

If there was one move that made things go faster, it was the serendipitous fact that when Bruce first fired up the slide projector to begin feeding me massive amounts of slide-borne guts and gore, I was sitting in front of the machine. Naturally, I reached for the advance button and never let go. You can't begin to know how this influenced my training. Because I was in control, I could fast forward through material that I knew well from reading the book. A slide would pop up and if it was material that I already owned, I would immediately dive into a mini-briefing as I cited the important details and moved on to the next slide.

If the material was confusing, no one moved until I felt comfortable enough to push the button.

What I learned was this: Learning is more effective when the learner is in control. Before this project I knew that, theoretically. Now I understand it and never again will I attempt to feed adults information. I will present and allow them to drink.

I read the book, a huge textbook, twice. Cover to cover, word for word. I read while flying Little Girl. I read while flying commercial airlines. I read at home. I read everywhere. I even read while racing in an ambulance to the next call. Siren blaring, equipment jostling, I read and read and read.

My first day of ride-outs was in Williamson County, Texas. At the crack of dawn, I was wheels up from Kerrville, punching a Mooney-sized hole in a thin layer of clouds and pointing the nose eastward. At Georgetown Municipal, I left the Mooney and called the only cab in town, a bright, red Toyota driven by a polite, young man who was the owner, dispatcher and driver. He lives with his mom so she manned the phone while he quickly dressed and headed in to pick me up. Fifteen minutes, three miles and seven dollars later, I was deposited in the hands of Jeff Jarvis and Scott Parker to work the eight-to-ten shift.

Scott immediately hustled me outside for a look at the ambulance, my first. Scott offered an impromptu lecture, call it 'Stretcher 101.' Thirty minutes or more.

I thought the subject was stretcher but it turns out that Scott was doing what emergency response personnel call 'scene size-up'...on me. Scott wanted to know up front if he was dealing with a serious student. Who could know if or when the radio would call us out? Scott wanted to know what he had riding in the captain's chair behind the driver's seat.

The day went slowly.

About three o'clock, the pager on my belt began to squawk. A disembodied voice called out unit eight-o-nine followed by what is called a chief complaint, then an address. By the time the dispatcher was ready to repeat the information, we had loaded ourselves into the unit and were ready to roll, strobe lights flashing, siren at the ready.

She was sitting in her car, door open, with the heat at a stifling temperature. The local volunteers had beat us to the punch and had the situation in hand. Seventy-plus, she was somebody's grandmother. The volunteers had quickly figured that she was diabetic and were administering one of nature's fastest acting drugs, cold orange juice.

By the time Jeff reached her door, she was already responding. Still a tad confused. Still a little dizzy but much better.

Jeff dropped to his knees so as to be less intimidating and commenced taking her SAMPLE. Ask the average Joe for a sample and he is likely to whiz in a bottle. But SAMPLE is nothing more than an acronym to help you get the facts, Signs & Symptoms, Allergies, Medications, Pertinent medical history, Last oral intake or menstrual period, and Events leading to the distress.

Diabetic and sporting a recent heart bypass, our roadside granny was feeling better but, to be certain, we obtained her permission to transport. The new kid helped load her into the wagon. I took vital signs and shamelessly practiced my medical specialty...bedside manner.

The next call was a simple transport. Nineteen and frightened. Eight months pregnant. Her water had broken the day before and now she needed a medical lift to the hospital in Austin. We were there 'just in case.'

On the way to Austin, I took her vital signs, held her hand and did my "Dad" thing, talking about how little ones need to be loved, asking her if she had been good about prenatal care, not smoking, no alcohol. The answers made me smile. 'Seemed like another healthy one on the way. No ring, but, she said Dad is a chef at a Chinese joint.

"Uh-oh!" She grimaced and the blood pressure shot up—mine, not hers!

"What are you feeling?"

The ambulance was bouncing along I-35 on the outskirts of Austin and I was mentally reviewing the module on gynecology.

"It feels kinda leaky down there."

"Kinda leaky?"

"Yeh, like it did when the water broke. Like I'm running out onto the mattress."

"Okay, I'll get a pad and we'll take a look. If it's just more water, the pad will help until we get to the hospital."

"What if it's not?"

"Then you get off the stretcher and I'll get on!"

Later that night the boys loaded me in the ambulance and hauled me to the airport. I think they were impressed by the little Mooney. Scott turned on the load lights, two huge exterior lights that are just right for working an accident scene on a dark and stormy night. It turns out that they are pretty good for pre-flighting a Mooney on a pitch black ramp, too.

I fired up the engine, turned on a few lights of my own and called Austin approach, 121.1, then 119.0 for clearance and permission to poke a hole in their airspace.

The night was as clear as black crystal. White runway lights flashed past as the Mooney picked up speed, then lifted her cute little nose to say "good night' to the guys from Georgetown.

When I finally leveled out, a short 6,000 feet, I began to think about what I had learned while riding under that fat Texas moon. 'Semper Gumby,' was Scott's motto. He says he got that from someone else but wherever it comes from, it is right on target for this, and any other business. Semper gumby, always flexible.

You don't expect to find philosophy in the back of an ambulance. You don't expect that ordinary guys, the kind who might buy you a beer or invite you to go hunting, would take their work so seriously. But if there is one word to describe this crew, it has to be 'serious.' We talked EMS at lunch, on break, while waiting for the next call. They taught me and grilled me and spent an entire shift attempting to share wisdom with a trainee barely prepared to absorb simple facts.

Scott said that, above all, the service should do no further harm. No surprise. That sounds remarkably familiar to the Hippocratic Oath that admonishes the healer to 'do no harm.' But Scott says that in emergency healthcare, the warning extends much, much further.

How far? Well, here's Scott's list:

Do no further harm to...

  ...the patient's family.
  ...the patient's beliefs.
  ...ourselves.
  ...other emergency personnel.
  ...our beliefs.

...society.
...the patient's friends.
...bystanders.
...our partners.
...our families.
...our profession.
...our service.

A pretty tall order for people who often train on their own time and at their own expense. A tall order for folks who often are volunteers, willing to be called out in the middle of the night, to walk into the face of danger to do the good deed. All for nothing except the feeling that the world may be a little less painful to someone who cried for help.

Semper fi. Semper Gumby!

Oh, there was one more important lesson. Jeff said that you can be the best medic on the planet, have the smoothest bedside manner, respond to the call before they hang up the phone but, by golly, if you park the ambulance on the roses, that's the one thing that gets remembered!

"Mooney niner-five-mike-kilo, cleared to 350." That's 35,000 feet. Ain't no way. This little puppy is good to 20,000, tops.

"Approach, Mooney nine-five-mike-kilo cleared to flight level three-five-o. I'll try!"

"Sorry."

———————

The plan was to troll the waiting room for customers. Maybe pat a shoulder, reassure a loved one, even find a new someone in need of assistance. You know, make myself busy. As I drifted through triage, Jerry, the nurse who had drawn the short stick, commandeered my services to help with a momentary backlog.

I was busy taking vital signs and practicing getting a SAMPLE when a woman, a huge woman, gave an all new meaning to the phrase 'darken the door.' She was wearing the huge woman uniform, stretch pants and a T-shirt dotted with beads and baubles.

"Can you help me with my mother? She fell this morning and can't get out of the car."

Good lord, I hope it doesn't run in the family.

Emergency personnel don't retire so much from old age as they do from bad backs. I didn't want to prematurely add my name to the list.

It was a Geo, naturally. Nope, it couldn't have been a pickup. A van would never do. It had to be a compact, fit more for a circus act.

I rolled a wheelchair into position while the helpless woman struggled to free her foot from the door frame.

"Ma'am? Is it your left or your right?"

"My left but the right leg is stuck. I need help."

"Okay. So long as it's the left, we can probably do this. Miss, you pull the right leg out. Ma'am, just step out on your right foot and pivot into the wheel chair."

The struggle continued while I waited to scoop up my catch in a wheelchair positioned against the car.

Right leg out, pivot, bottom in motion.Uh-oh! Her bottom looks like it may not fit...fooop! Bottom wedged in; EMT student pinned against the car!

I attempted to pull the chair backward up the slight incline and only managed to pull the plastic grips off the handles. From the front, I grabbed the chair and sat back, using my weight to wrench the chair up the ramp, wedged my foot behind one wheel until I could maneuver to the back and, leaning nearly horizontally, pushed my charge across the waiting room.

"Ma'am, tell me what happened."

"My knee gave out on me and I fell in the kitchen. It was an accident."

An accident?

"Any chance you might have been a little dizzy just before you fell?" This was an even money guess. Very few people are actually attacked by their carpet.

"I was a little dizzy. I've been dizzy on and off for a week."

"Any chance you might happen to be diabetic?" Another even money guess.

"Yes."

"Got any idea what is your blood sugar?"

Pause. "No."

"Well, we're going to take a quick look." I could have, should have, asked when she ate last but this one hadn't strayed too far from the kitchen.

I pricked her finger, milked out a drop of go juice and fired up the machine. Nearly 600 points. Fine if you were playing gin rummy but about six times what is healthy. No surprise. This woman wouldn't know healthy if it bit her.

"I notice you smoke. Anything else you want to tell me about your health?"

By this time, the knee was secondary. I had a time bomb ticking and who could predict if and when it might explode.

I grabbed for the blood pressure cuff, stretched it around her arm and hit the auto pump switch. The cuff puffed, stretched and groaned before it popped off her arm. I tried again and then once more before going in search of the thigh cuff which I put on her arm. Blood pressure was over 200 on the systolic.

"I don't want to wait."

"Pardon me?"

"My knee hurts and I don't want to spend the afternoon waiting."

Let's see if I have this right. You eat yourself to near explosion, you smoke with both hands even though you are diabetic, and to top it off, you have totally ignored your blood sugar and now you want me to bust my chops to roll your backside right past everyone else?

That's what I thought.

"Yes, ma'am. We'll get you right in. No-o-o problem," I said with a smile.

This woman thought of herself as a victim. It couldn't be her fault that she was 200 pounds overweight, that she smoked like a chimney and that someone had failed to check her blood sugar for over a week. Well, victim, my ass. This woman should be charged with felony assult, against herself.

That's the problem with the emergency room—lots of sick and injured people who need their sense of personal responsibility surgically re-installed!

Jerry and I hustled her into a room where I took her vitals again just to confirm the first round.

When the nurse came in, I recited the signs and symptoms and continued with the rest of the SAMPLE before adding the vital numbers.

She smiled as if she knew what was coming and said, in her best bedside manner, "Ma'am? I'm your nurse. Let's get you onto the bed so the doctor can look at your knee. First let's see about getting you out of your panty hose."

I backed to the door figuring that I had done all that I could do.

"Excuse me! New guy. Unless you're needed somewhere else, I could use your help."

Oh, brother! I don't mind blood, pee or puke but I sure as hell didn't want to see this woman butt naked. 'Trade you two catheters and a bed pan for this one! Anybody?

"You know, this might be difficult with her knee being hurt and all. I could just cut those suckers off. What do you say?"

Around the corner, a 38-year-old female sat bolt upright in bed, her mouth and teeth as black as the activated charcoal swill that Mike was forcing down her throat. Another victim, no doubt. This one of an overdose. 'Guess the drug dealers have taken to shoving drugs down buyer's throats. Like the lady with the bum knee, this certainly had to be someone else's fault.

Mike was bundled up like a space explorer in latex gloves, protective mask and glasses, and a paper gown that covered what was left. In emergency terms, this is called BSI, body substance isolation. In human terms, it is the practical matter of keeping the ugly goo that tends to leak from everywhere in the emergency room from getting into and onto the folks who are trying to help. This is all further complicated by AIDS, a word that is never far from thought in this business.

There must have been a dozen souls to tell me that they could never work in the gory world of emergency medicine. Nonsense! There is plenty of unpleasant gunk that can leak from the human being. But the least pleasant of all is not blood, nor pee, nor puke. It is the general ugliness that all too often seeps from the human mind. Now, that's ugly.

Mike peeled off one glove and then, like a five-fingered rubber band, shot the remaining glove into the trash. He tossed the glasses aside in a short display of disgust and slamdunked the paper gown into the trash. He was finished detoxifying Ms.-I-Think-I'm-Glamorous-With-Black-Teeth.

I stepped into the room to watch a minute too late; game over, nothing left but the tedium of watching another victim of circumstance.

I took vital signs trying not to make eye contact. Mike stood quietly in the corner either watching the new kid or taking a short breather.

"My name is Mike," I said, enjoying the joke. "If there is anything you need, just ask for me!"

It wasn't two minutes before we heard the raspy bellow that I would hear over and over again. "Mike! I gotta pee!"

Outside the room, the real Mike looked at new Mike and said, "Mike, I think you've got a customer!"

I got Ms. Blackteeth off the stretcher and helped her gather her gown for the trip down the hall. She was a perfect size nine if you don't count the beer belly. Together we waltzed arm in unsteady arm, a staggering duet du john.

I stood guard outside the door.

"Are you all right?"

"Yessh," she moaned.

Then the flush and running water. The door rattled open and we reversed our clumsy dance back to her room. Thank God for latex gloves.

We went again and again with me changing the sheets in

between runs, occasionally checking on other patients, sometimes leaving the watch in the hands of hospital security. My friend was OED, Order of Enforced Detention. Ain't it a bitch? Someone tries to kill themselves and then, once in your care, you are responsible if they are further injured.

So here we had a nurse, a doctor, a med tech, a student, and a security officer all tied up over a doper.

While I waited during her third trip, I hid her cup of water.

After what seemed like a dozen trips to the can with this goof ball, a pretty nurse intercepted me in the hallway and handed me a present saying, "The next time you and your girlfriend make a trip to the john, see if you can collect a sample for the guys in the lab."

"Sure!" I smiled not really knowing exactly how to make the request but absolutely certain that Miss Gottago would present me with an opportunity.

"Miiiiikke!" she bawled from behind the door. "I gotta goah." This was more moan than before.

"Fine. I'll change your bed while you're out. And, do me a favor. Give me a sample in this cup. Do you think you can manage that?"

"You want me to poo in a cup?"

"No, the other thing. No poo. The other thing."

I took a second look at this woman, considered that I was doing this at my expense, and thought of taking one of my own samples to the lab because clearly my behavior was pathological.

I made the whiz trip at least a half dozen times before my dance partner was shipped off to psychiatric.

All the while, two women behind the curtain that made one emergency treatment room into two were in near hysterics. They heard every word and decided that whatever the bill, the entertainment was worth the expense.

I had picked up one of the women and her daughter earlier on an ambulance run to the nearby mall. The patient was a funny, round lady with good hair and better sense of humor. She had nearly fainted and, since she was diabetic and owned a newly installed pacemaker, we scooped her up and hauled her in. I enjoyed joking with her and her look-alike daughter.

I had worked the day shift with the ambulance crews and was surprised when I reported for night shift rounds in the ER to see the mother and daughter still there. But while I was thinking about the names and faces that made for the evening drama, I couldn't resist thinking about what it was that brought us all together.

Me, a volunteer for a job many would not do for pay. Others, professionals, were doing what they loved and it was also their livelihood. It was surprising to learn how many well-paid medical professionals were also volunteers in the their home communities. Nurses that cost the hospital who knows how much would often ride for free to serve their local EMS. Go figure.

(I got it figured. You must be called to emergency medicine. Why else would people work so hard to get a job where they work so hard?)

And go figure why the others were in the ER that night. Some were there strictly by accident; my lady from the mall, the elderly woman that we brought in from the nursing home earlier that afternoon. There was no good reason why some of our patients were spending an evening with us. It was a choice, a strange choice. One that I can't quite figure and probably never will.

We were channel surfing one night when I came across an episode of *Chicago Hope*. Just as I was about to continue the surf, a voice from the TV stopped me cold. The camera zoomed slowly in for a close-up as the screen doctor said these words: "Most of what we do is clean up after bad choices."

He knows.

If ego has anything to do with working in emergency medicine, everyone would want to be a flight medic. They wear the coolest uniforms! At least that is the case at Scott &

White where the uniform is simply killer, tight fitting black with teal trim along the sleeves and legs. Zippered pant legs with instrument pockets near the ankle top off sharp, black flight boots. If I did this for looks, and maybe the opportunity to fly, this would be the spot!

Every med-evac crew has a uniform pin. If they like you, they may give you one. If you are from another med-evac operation, there will surely be a trade.

I wandered by the med-evac office outside the ER and noticed an attractive med-evac nurse holding court, telling the small group about a recent surgery. She was blonde, trim and looking good in the Star Trek uniform that identifies the med-evac elite from a mile away.

I picked up the converation midstream: "...I asked him to give me boobs while he was at it but he seemed to think that would complicate things too much."

"Your boobs are fine. 'You want more?"

"I wake up in the morning and I look down at these guys and say, 'oh, hello.' I wanna look down and say "goo-oo-od morning!' I'd like to be able to bend over and polish these boots without using my hands!"

In the ER, everyone has a uniform that serves to instantly communicate skill level, responsibility, and pecking order. My EMT-Student patch pretty much put me at the bottom.

The tired looking guys in lab coats who hung out in a sorry clique at the end of the counter were doctors-to-be. The most tired looking group were residents.

The administrative staff holed up in the middle of the area, barricaded behind computers, clip boards and rules. In slow periods they seemed to feel obligated to preserve the walls by papering the entire emergency room with notices. "Lidocaine is now stocked in this drawer." Or "Do not lean on this counter." Important stuff.

Clerical support folks couldn't seem to agree on a uniform, which was a surprise seeing how they seemed to love rules. They wore everything from exercise clothes to evening wear.

A blonde ponytail named Amanda was practicing being young and cute and doing a good job of it. A nursing student from nearby Baylor University, Amanda was working her required hours in the emergency room and had partnered with an equally young woman in a slightly different uniform. So I asked, "What's the difference in these uniforms?"

"Hers is unattractive. Mine is simply ugly."

"Oh."

One of my precepts was named Robert, a short, eternally-studying single Dad who loved his work and everything connected with it. Somehow he had gotten on an Elvis kick, a habit that half of the ER folks loved and the other half would have gladly volunteered to break him...either of it or for it! No matter what the situation, Robert would manage to work in the phrase "a hunka, hunka burnin' love."

"The ER," said Robert, "is like this magical island where you see it all and get to do it all. It's a hunka, hunka burnin' love. A hunka, hunka..."

Robert rounded the corner nearly knocking into Della, a rotund cleaning woman who stared out at the world from beneath a handful of dredlocks and a frown that seemed permanently attached. 'Ohhh, Dell-la. You're such a hunka, hunka, burnin' love."

The frown melted in a heartbeat.

Robert, like half of the folks in emergency medicine, was studying for advanced certification. Like the rest of this crew, he spent half his time looking for a chance to practice his skills and the other half talking about them.

"I got a two inch, number sixteen IV in yesterday," he told a breakroom audience one morning. "I threw it in from the door."

What he was saying was that he put in a very difficult IV and was so good, he didn't even have to come into the room to do it. He just tossed it in like a dart. Just a little exaggeration!

A few doors down, another OED (Order of Enforced Detention) was talking with the on-duty shrink. This patient, a young woman with several especially unattractive do-it-yourself prison tattoos, had attempted suicide by hanging while in the county jug. If that wouldn't make me suicidal, I can't think of what would. Screwing up a suicide attempt!

Somewhere under the cloud of tears and poor choices was a pleasant young woman.

A nurse asked me to take her vital signs.

"Should I go in while the shrink is with her?"

"No. This psychiatrist is pretty nice. We have some who are real assholes. Save it for them."

When it was my turn, I knocked on the open door and announced that I needed to take her vital signs. Mike arrived to draw a blood sample. Easy except that she spoke almost no English, a shame for someone who was a native Texan. No wonder the poor kid was down on her luck. No doubt some liberal goofball thought requiring her to learn the language of commerce was an affront to her culture.

Well, do you want to know what is a real affront? Keeping people ignorant for your own self-centered, political goals. How in the world can this girl ever pull herself out of this deep hole when she couldn't find work if she wanted to?

(In Spanish) "Hi! My name is Scott."

Her eyes rolled back, the hurts of a lifetime turning to quiet tears. Imagine how it must feel to watch yourself die and be forced to do it in front of a couple of white guys who obviously wouldn't know pain if they had it.

"What's my name?"

"No se." (I don't know.)

"My name is Scott. What's my name?"

"Escott?"

"Bueno!" Then we learned hers and introduced Mike.

"What's my name?"

"Escott." Only this time with a little more life.

I ran out of Spanish before I could explain that Mike was about to draw a little blood so we used the term Dracula, a name that pretty much explains itself. This time I got a smile and it wasn't a Spanish smile or an English smile. Just a smile that said "Thanks for not hurting me any more."

"What's my name?'

"Escott."

We held hands. I tried to take away the sting of the needle and felt helpless at being unable to. All the while I was trying to think why this child would end up in this room at this moment. Her fingers bore the jagged blue lines of a prison tattoo. L-O-V-E was spelled out below each knuckle on the hand that I held. H-A-T-E dripped off the other hand.

Me and Dracula finished our work and left silently. The guard nodded 'hello' when we opened the door. He poked his head around the corner to see if all was well and it was not.

In the room next door is another young woman. This one is comforting her child, a small boy with small glasses and thick dark hair that stands up straight in a flat top. I take his vital signs and get his chief complaint, then take time to visit.

She is a teacher and feels sorry to be late for school but her son woke with breathing difficulties and she felt it important to get him checked. I agree.

"What do you teach?" It was only small talk while we waited for a doctor. Had there been an emergency, my skills would not have allowed me to do much more than call for help but I stood by for support, thinking of another young woman and her son, one that I had married a couple of decades ago.

"I teach disabled children." My face probably darkened but hers was nothing short of radiant.

"My children are wonderful," she continued, telling me that many of her students carried Do Not Resuscitate cards. We're talking about the severely disabled and I am thinking the hopelessly trainable. Why bother?

She told me with infinite pride how one had spent over an hour to crawl all the way across the room just to see a computer and how another had said a word. Just one word but it was a word. This from students who, if they were to stop breathing on their own, would be left to die. I could see how they would miss such a loving teacher and how perhaps it was not merely the computer that compelled a disabled child to spend an hour crawling across the classroom.

I thought of another young person, her body twisted with cerebral palsy and a list of disabilities. She had been abandoned by her parents, left in an orphanage until her mother and father had a change of heart. Now, 20 years later, her family thinks of her as a beautiful swan, a work of God's art still in the unfolding.

Years ago we had worked with this young girl to produce a video tape on Cerebral Palsy. Christine, our editor, and I worked for hours on the project. We would edit for a while then cry for a while. When we were finished with the work, I said to Christine, "If I were God and could do anything to change Vanessa, do you know what I would do? Nothing. She is perfect. Absolutely perfect."

There is some medicine that is simply not necessary.

In the hallway I watched a gurney roll by, not noticing or thinking until a hand reached out from under the sheet and grabbed for mine. A small smile was mine for the taking. "Hasta luego, Escott. Bye, bye."

Around dinner time the electric doors slid open and a crew from nearby Temple wheeled in a kid that I would get to know as Bullet. Bullet had taken a trip from the back seat of his father's car to the front windshield. Naturally, no seat belt.

Bullet was thoroughly packaged. Strapped to an orange backboard, his head secured in foam blocks, a fistful of 4x4s taped to his right knee.

We lifted him, backboard and all, off the stretcher, onto a gurney. The assessment began all over again, not that the field assessment was suspect but simply to verify it here in the relative calm of the emergency room.

Tender abdomen, possible internal injury. There was the knee problem and, due to the mechanism, strong suspicion of spinal injury. It took five of us to remove the backboard, checking his back as we did.

I snipped off the shirt, a favorite I would come to find out. The pants were pretty much gone already. Emergency medicine is quick but not subtle.

It was decided to insert a nasopharangeal tube to allow his stomach to be suctioned. The idea was that since his head was immobilized, if he were to vomit, it would be easily aspirated into the lungs. We didn't want that. And Bullet didn't want the tube.

The head blocks were still on pending an X-ray. The nurse began inserting the tube and Bullet began to wail. All this was complicated by the fact that Bullet's mom is hearing impaired and nearly beside herself with panic. The fact that she couldn't hear what was going on just added to her fears.

I had worked briefly with the hearing impaired while in college and took it upon myself to keep track of Mom. My sign language is so rusty as to be nearly nonexistent. Thankfully, Mom could read lips so long as someone understood that they had to face her for it to happen. I held hands with Mom while assisting the suction with the other.

"You can help by swallowing when the tube starts to tickle your throat." The nurse was as tender as you could possibly be and still be threading a plastic tube into someone's nose.

Bullet must have missed the communication because the instant the tube hit the back of this throat, he forgot to swallow. Instead we got a close up look at his dinner. In an instant, five sets of hands were turning Bullet to the side while we suctioned and wiped. Mom and Bullet cried. Me, too. Then it was over.

I promised Mom that I would go with Bullet to X-ray and that I would report.

In the waiting room I played host to a raft of relatives, assuring them that Bullet was in capable hands, wanting to throttle someone for not making the kid wear a seat belt. The family was not a wealthy family, just your working class poor. Earlier in the week Mom had made the final payment on the truck. There was no damage insurance. Now, in addition to a whopping bill from the hospital, the family would be without transportation to work. When it rains, it pours. I slipped $20 to an aunt in exchange for a promise that she would remember to replace the favorite shirt (and forget where it came from.)

I showed Mom the hand sign for Scott that had been created for me by the deaf students I had taught to be short order cooks at Denny's more than two decades ago.

She laughed at the sign which is a combination of the letter 's', the sign for 'nice' and the sign for 'cook.' It translates literally to mean, "Scott, the nice cook." With everyone lightened up, I left to check on Bullet and any other strays that may have wandered in.

In one room, a highway patrol officer was reading the rights to a trucker who had had an accident. Nothing serious but it required a blood test. I helped the med-tech and moved on.

In another room I comforted an elderly lady who had been brought in by a local crew. The paramedic looked at my student patch and explained, without me having to ask, that "It's Friday and some of the nursing homes are dumping their more difficult patients." It's called a Gomer tote, a run to a nursing home for nothing in particular.

On the Internet there is a joke that explains, "You know you are in EMS if you believe in aerial spraying of Prozac."

Do you know what is a 'Samsonite?' It's a patient who is waiting for you with their luggage packed." I didn't get it either until I heard paramedic Stu tell about a woman who called for an ambulance anytime she needed to go to the state hospital for tests. She couldn't or wouldn't afford a cab and ambulance runs are paid for under Medicare. (Your tax dollars at work.)

The hours had slipped by. I had been lucky to find a place where there were plenty of customers. When things looked pretty settled, I would head for triage and troll for another customer. There was never an empty waiting room, always someone but not always an emergency. Many treat the emergency room like a family doctor only less waiting. And, if you claim poverty, no paying. I assisted with quite a few cases that were by no means emergencies. Many, had they happened at my home, would have been treated with nothing more than a dab of antiseptic ointment.

One trip to triage netted a screaming woman who needed immediate help with her husband. On the way to the car, I did as best I could to get the chief complaint and begin assessment. In a matter of seconds, I assumed CVA, cardio-vascular accident, a stroke.

The gentleman had become incontinent, paralyzed on one side, and unable to speak although quite capable of understanding.

I rushed him straight to a room where a nurse was waiting. I knew that the treatment was immediate oxygen via non-rebreather mask and was frustrated by the nurse's insistence on getting him into a gown. Gown, my ass! This guy needed O_2, not protocol.

Okay, so I over-reacted. This guy was so far gone that maybe it wasn't all that important that we take things in a different order.

I hooked him to the monitor and recorded heart rate, blood pressure, blood oxygenation, and took his temperature.

From the end of the bed where I was standing, the guy looked like me. Middle-aged, graying hair and mustache, only I was standing and able to talk. He was sitting and being hustled around, unable to communicate. He pointed to his crotch. I got it instantly and reached for a urinal. But the guy had no control and before I could get things lined up, he was all over the place.

Embarrassed.

I felt awful that he would feel awful.

When the doctor entered the room, it was about time for me to exit. I had done what little I could do. The doctor asked him to raise his right hand and the left leg went up.

Raise the left hand and both leg and hand went awkwardly into the air. I knew what a panic this guy must be in. From a captain of business to out of control bed-wetter in one horrible morning.

As I left the room, his knowing eyes followed me out. The mouth moved but no sound came.

"I know," I said, "And you are welcome. I'll check on you later."

When the moon rises up, the loonies come out and this night would be no different. We served them by the dozen. In the hallway, just before shift change Sandy stood shaking. I thought that perhaps she had worked a difficult case but that wasn't it.

"Hey, Kiddo. What's the matter? You look to pieces."

"You're not going to believe this." Her voice was hoarse, conspiritorial.

"Try me. I've been around."

"I was standing in the butt hut smoking a cigarette and talking to this guy in a wheelchair. He had a broken back so I asked him how it happened. You know, just making conversation, that's all.

"He said he broke it jumping from a bridge and I asked him what river he was swimming in and he said he wasn't swimming. He was trying to commit suicide.

"I asked him if that was how he got the cuts around his eyes and he said, 'No, the police did this to me.'

"So I said 'Why did the police do that?' and he said they were trying to beat him up for eating a girl."

"Eating her?" I said.

"Yeh, that's what I thought. But it turned out that he didn't mean in a sexual way. I asked why he was eating her and he just looked at me and said, 'I was hungry so I just started taking bites of her face and ears. And when the bastards caught me, they beat me up."

The next day the sun was out again, standing watch over

a thoroughly bizarre world, holding back at least a few of our foibles. I trolled the waiting room and looked up to see two smiles and hear Bullet shout, "Hi, Scott!" Mom signed from 40 feet away, "Hello, Scott, the Nice Cook."

Bullet was wearing a new favorite shirt.

I passed my pre-test with a nice high score. Bruce brought me a bag of presents that included a blood pressure cuff and stethoscope. The flight home that day was a quick surf at the tops of a layer of white, white clouds beneath the bluest sky you can imagine. The controller at Fort Hood gave me a vector of 2-0-0 saying it was, "to get you clear of the active portion. We've got Stingers (missiles) flying in here today."

No problem. I felt invincible.

A few weeks later we flew to Austin so the State of Texas could add its stamp of approval and I could turn in my student patch for that of an EMT. My patch came from Stu. He said it's a tradition that your first patch should be one that someone before you had worn. Of all the gifts Stu ever gave me, that will remain my favorite.

Now, finally, we were ready for the last two adventures.

At forty-five I became an instrument rated pilot and it changed my life. At forty-seven I earned the EMT and would like to go on to become a paramedic. What would you like to do? Whatever it is, it's not too late to start. Do you want to get to the end of your race and say, "I should have or could have...but didn't?" Not me!

Here's to the folks who, regardless of their situation dare to dream and dream big. To them goes the prize of a life fully lived. Carpe Diem!

18

Angel of the Air

I didn't count them but I must have spent two hundred hours, maybe more, getting ready for this adventure. There were the countless flights to Temple, Tex., to study with the folks at Scott & White Hospital. Beyond the actual classroom time, there were hour after hours of study. Before the first session with Bruce, I read the textbook cover to cover, nearly 800 pages.

In between class sessions, ride-out and rounds in the ER, I read that damned book a second time. Of course, there was study time for the unit tests and, before taking the state final exam, one more time through the text. All to know a whole lot about not too much.

Still, I am very proud of the EMT patch. I wish I could wear it on my business suits. To tell you the truth, it scares me a little. The thought of holding a life in your hands, literally and figuratively, is scary as the devil himself. And here I was, flying from Georgia to Kansas so that I could ride out as the third medic on a helicopter ambulance. You've gotta be kidding!

I was watching a sun the color of molten iron begin to dip into a cool and cloudless horizon. Day to night, just like me. This afternoon, I was in front of an audience of executives from Continental Grain; as a speaker-consultant, decked out in my usual uniform (we call it Docker Casual.) Tomorrow I would be wearing a different uniform, playing to a much different audience. Day to night.

Now, the outside temperature was well below zero. This night would be a cold one. We sailed silently almost, Stu dozing in the right seat; me, wanting to doze in the left. I had already had a very long day. First, the four hour flight to Georgia with a fuel stop in Jackson, Mississippi, then the speaking engagement, and now, another five hours to Kansas. I'll be one pooped puppy by the time I spy the green and white beacon of Brown County Executive Airport.

For a long time we watched cloud remnants and jet contrails dissolve into pink, white, and blue imitations of Chinese writing. I tried to decipher it and decided that it must be a message from home. 'I love you, too, Boogie Buns!' I messaged back.

A month or so ago, Melanie and I had flown almost this exact route and were startled to witness a brilliant shooting star. It lasted only seconds, not nearly long enough to make a wish but we wished anyway. You cannot share wishes or they won't come true but I'm willing to bet that her wish involved me, just as my wish belonged to her.

The sun is gone but the sky is painted pink. The sunset was dramatic, a curtain of blue darkness pulled over the day. The stars started winking, one at a time, as we sailed past choochoo intersection. (Guess what city was off the right wing. Choo Choo.)

We talked to Memphis Center, slid just south of Indianapolis, and finally connected with Kansas City Center as they passed us from one controller to the next, pushing smoothly through clouds that now drooped lower to close around us. Usually you cannot see the strobe lights under the wing tips but, when flying in clouds or rain, the strobes light up the moisture, like throwing dust into flame. Suddenly you see what has been there all along. Tonight we were hypnotized by the stutter-flash of the strobes as we pushed against the cloud deck.

For a long time, we watched larger cities glowing their yellow glow. Now, with the clouds wrapping around us, we would see the occasional soft glow of small towns back-lighting the layer below us. We flew unnoticed by all, save an air traffic controller or two.

Flying low at a conservative 7,000 feet to avoid head-winds, we still managed a quick 175 knots, just over 200 miles an hour. Try doing that in the old Chevy!

About a hundred miles out, clouds began to fall away leaving us with a night as clear as crystal. Without the clouds, what little heat was left in the farmlands below would quickly escape into the atmosphere. Tonight was going to be a cold one.

At exactly a hundred miles out, we picked up the first static-filled, automated weather report. We were right about the temperature. Nine o'clock and already pushing zero.

As always, I began to fiddle with the GPS and paged through the charts. I don't like surprises. The most likely approach looked to be Tyger1. Perfect. (Melanie calls me Tiger!) I'd spent half the day thinking about Buns. (And yes, I call her Buns!)

Melanie had baked brownies just before six this morning. She wanted to send Stu and I off with a reminder of home. Actually, she wanted to go with us. I was saving my brownies for later when I could think about the baker.

Tomorrow would be another first day, the toughest day for most of us. I've faced a lot of first days. When we were kids, our folks seemed to move at the drop of a hat. Sometimes, because the family just kept getting bigger; sometimes, because of my dad's work. There are five boys in our family, each as different as different could be. And yet, put any two of us together and you would know in an instant that we are brothers.

I can tell you this: I love my brothers. But when Paul Stacy came along with the initials PS, I breathed a sigh of relief since I pretty much figured that this was a sign that there would be no more little guys to make me miserable.

Thirteen different schools, probably twenty different houses, a half dozen states from Kentucky to California. My dad always figured that the moving wouldn't hurt us. He said it would make us strong, teach us to adapt and meet new people. I guess he was right. I could never figure why so many parents make such a big deal out of moving if it might cause the kids to change schools. It does build character.

Today I make a living out of first days. Every day brings a new venue and an all-new audience. Will they laugh? Will they love me? It builds character.

So why was I dreading flying air-evac? It certainly wasn't the flying. As the thought passed through my brain, the Little Girl slid into a cloud, forcing me again to watch the instruments. Hell, if I can fly a single engine airplane at night in all kinds of weather, it isn't the flying that was bothering me.

It was the fact that tomorrow I might find myself put on the spot supported only by new and as yet fairly untried skills.

I thought about that as we popped into the crystal clear skies south of Kansas City. I checked with the GPS and, as expected, Little Girl was right on target. Approach invited us to fly a vector to join the ILS to the south runway.

There at ten o'clock were the white rabbit lights that strobe their way from darkness to runway leading all who see and know to the crisp red, blue and white lights that announce the runway and safety, fuel and rest.

"Ground, November niner-five-mike-kilo is clear of the active. Good night."

I'll skip to the end and tell you that this is not a job I would like. Too much waiting and, even though you probably get to see the most complicated trauma cases, it's also true that many of your customers come pre-packaged. By the time you arrive for the pick-up, the interesting work is done. Still, there must be a reason why they reserve the best of the trauma best for med-evac operations.

My hosts were the good folks at LifeNet, a for-profit helicopter ambulance service operated by Rocky Mountain Helicopters. Jim Mitchell, my family physician, thought that I wouldn't like the idea of a for-profit ambulance service but I do. A little competition begets a lot of great customer service. And that's exactly what I saw at LifeNet.

The morning fog was thick enough to slice. Upon landing the night before, we got a hint of things to come. A thin mist was blowing across the tarmac when we taxied to the ramp. The ATIS recorded weather information reported a temperature-dew point spread of only two degrees. Any time the dew point (the temperature at which the atmosphere cannot hold any more moisture) gets within four degrees of the temperature, you can pretty much bet that there will be fog. This is especially true if the wind is calm.

Now, at seven in the morning, we were stepping out of our car, pulling on our blue EMT jackets, wrapping ourselves less in nylon and more in a bone-chilling fog. If this kept up, there would be no flying today.

Inside we introduced ourselves and tried to get acquainted, a process not easy when you are armed with video equipment. There are too many questions. The crew going off duty is groggy from too little sleep. The crew coming on duty is grumpy from insufficient coffee. And the new guy is still off balance, unable to find the men's room and uncertain as to where to begin the conversation.

"Hi! I'm Scott Gross. I'll be riding out with you today." When the pause persisted too long, "You are expecting us, aren't you?"

Once we got over the formalities, we did what emergency medicine people do best. We waited. Someone asked if I knew what EMS stood for. I did. Earn Money Sleeping.

That happens to be simultaneously an accurate description

and totally unfair. There is a lot of waiting and the helicopter ops folks probably do more than their share. Perhaps a better analogy might be the one I often hear used by pilots to describe flying—hours and hours of boredom punctuated by moments of sheer terror.

We couldn't have known it then but our first customer would not call until well into the afternoon. We spent the morning in that state of mind somewhere between 'nap' and 'go.' We chatted until lunch, thinking that we would get a call until, finally, we gave in and two of the guys fired up the outdoor grill and turned the office into home.

We began our day with a few hours of boredom. So I spent the time getting to know the crew.

It takes big bucks and specialized skills to operate a helicopter service. The choppers themselves are multi-million dollar investments. You don't light one up and go for a spin. They say that every hour of air time requires 2 to 3 hours of maintenance. So an ambulance operation by nature includes a maintenance operation.

The wrench turner in charge is called a crew chief, a funny title. The crew chief never goes flying, couldn't put a Band-Aid on a skinned knee and rarely spends time with the crew.

Our chief is named Willy.

"Is that your Mooney with the fancy paint job?" Willy sidled up to join the conversation and, without a formal introduction, jumped in talking about airplanes. I liked him instantly. Willie, it turns out, has flown a Mooney or two himself so we killed a half hour lying about flying while the flight nurse poked and prodded a half dozen marinated chicken breasts that were floating on the grill.

There is something special about working with pros, even when they could use a closer shave like Willie or even if they are doing nothing more than grilling lunch. Pros may be casual but they are never sloppy. They may trade a joke, even invent a story, but a true pro turns dead serious when it's time to do business.

I knew that I was talking to a pro when Willie, the grin now vanquished from his face, said about his job, "If I make a mistake, someone else pays. That's too much responsibility to be sloppy." And I knew that the only smoke blowing was from the grill.

At LifeNet, there are two birds and two full time mechanics.

The main chopper is decked out with more medical equipment than you can say grace over. A stretcher for one, non smoking.

There is an onboard oxygen system, all the cardiac drugs you can imagine. There are splints, and tools for intubation. There is a trauma kit; that means blood to you. There are pediatric supplies, the works. The only thing not onboard was a back-board. They usually are supplied by the first response team, the folks who call for assistance.

The pilot and crew wear headsets and, in spite of the advanced technology on board, I was surprised to discover that the headsets were from another age. These did not have the noise cancellation technology that we have onboard the Mooney so they were loud, making it difficult to talk to the customers. Most of the time the crew wore one ear piece pushed back.

There was talk of changing to helmets with built-in mikes but I couldn't figure that one. Helmets might make it easier to communicate with one another but to hear a patient? I don't think so.

Talking to a crew member required pushing a small switch, wired in-line with the headset jack. On the Mooney the headset microphones are voice-actuated. Talk and the mike turns on. Plus I have the ability to isolate the back two seats for those times when I want a sterile cockpit, free of extraneous conversation during take-off or landing.

Communications needed a little work, so says the amateur.

About the time we got the chicken out of the way, the radio called. First the distinctive warbling tones, then the voice instructions. Emergency crews are usually 'toned out.'

Each station has its own set of tones capable of breaking into a heated conversation or a deep sleep. After the tones, the dispatcher gives the nature of the call, the location, any additional information that might be helpful followed by the time of the call.

The responding crew radioes that they have copied the information and gives their time out.

In a matter of seconds, and this is a business of seconds, we were buckling ourselves into the chopper which was perched on the tiny, dollied pad that chopper ground crews use to move the equipment in and out of the hangar. It's a short, flat, four-wheeled cart that serves as visible testimony to the skills of anyone who can land on one.

In the winter months, an electric heater keeps the interior and its contents of drugs and solutions warm in between runs. It sucks energy from a bright orange extension cord that runs several hundred feet from the hangar. There is high-tech and not. This is not.

By the time the side load doors were closed and locked, the long metal blades had already begun to turn. Slowly at first then faster until the gentle swish had changed to a rapid thumping noise covered only partially by the high-pitched whine of twin jet engines.

Our objective was a rural hospital more than forty minutes by chopper, just under three hours by ambulance, and, in terms of modern medicine, probably about a decade behind the fancy memorials to our north.

The patient-to-be was a sixty-seven-year old male with chest pain. The local doctor wanted to take no chances as his patient had a history of cardiac disease. This wasn't his first trip to visit big city medicine but it was to be his first experience of such high-tech and high-priced transportation.

On the way to the pick up, there was little to do. The interior bay of the chopper is kept in a state of constant readiness; restocked at the beginning of each shift, more often if necessary. We were carrying nearly every drug you could ask for. The bar was open. We could serve Heparin, a commonly used blood thinning anti-coagulant, the perfect aperitif for those suffering with symptoms of stroke or chest pain unrelieved by nitroglycerin which we also carried by the bushel.

There was Epinephrine, call it a quick-start for the heart. If the ticker doesn't, a good shot of Epinephrine will often rekindle the fire.

In the drug box you could even find a jigger or two of morphine, perfect for those nagging pains that just won't seem to go away.

What is missing are thrombolytics, call 'em clot busters. These are the magic potions that can prevent, even reverse damage, from a myocardial infarction, the "Big One" as Fred Sanford used to say. Thrombolytics must be administered within a matter of hours. Since we are dealing with a helicopter service that lasts only minutes, there is plenty of time for designer drugs when you get to the hospital. Clot-busting thrombolytics have a very short shelf life and cost a couple of grand per treatment, so save your bucks. If the chopper ride doesn't break the bank, the pharmacy bill will.

The ride was short and smooth. Most of our Mooney time is spent between eight and twelve thousand feet, which is relatively low by commercial standards but much higher than the fifteen hundred that we were flying today. I carry a small camera in the leg pocket of my turn-out pants. Like a tourist on a big bird, I was soon busily snapping photos.

Looking at the world from the top down invites speculation. What are those people doing right now? Are they cooking dinner? Taking a nap? Are they happy with the way they have chosen their lives? Do they know that they have walked a path in the grass where they short cut between the house and the garage? Do they know that from up here every house in their neighborhood looks like the one next door? Do they know that from down there the same is true?

So we flew and I took pictures of scenes that could have been a closer look at a well done, model train layout.

Along the way, Gary, the pilot gave periodic position

reports. The shorthand for this is 'lat-longs' meaning latitude and longitude. If you took the Earth and overlaid a mesh screen and numbered each intersection, you could precisely identify any place on the planet.

Well, that's what we have, only the screen is invisible. Latitude counts distance north or south from the equator. Longitude counts from an imaginary line that cuts through Great Britain, which, at the time the system was devised, was certainly the center of the world if not the center of the universe.

"North, thirty-eight degrees, fifty-six point four; west, ninety-four degrees, thirty-seven point nine. ETA is twenty-three minutes."

You could translate that to read, "we're right over a white farmhouse near Ottawa, Kansas, and we'll be there in less than a half hour." You could, but who would know which white farmhouse?

We crossed over a small airport with a few toy-like Cessnas parked neatly near the hangar, their noses pointed into the wind. When landing at a small airport without radio service, one quick indicator of which way the wind is blowing is to look down at the ramp. The line guys always park the transients with the noses sniffing into the wind.

The houses began to get larger, the trees reaching higher. Beneath us the flat roof of a country hospital drifted by. Rain soaked grass wrapping around the asphalt parking lot offered one last gasp of pre-winter green. Across the street, cars waiting to turn into McDonald's, marked their positions with the glare of early evening headlights on a wet highway.

The nose rose just a bit. Gary adjusted the pitch of the blades causing the chopper to shudder and rock, settling ever lower. The last few inches disappeared. We felt not even a bump to tell us that we had arrived.

This hospital, like so many rural hospitals, had all the look of the single-story nursing home that economics dictate it will someday become. Behind a few windows was that warm, yellow glow announcing that someone was there.

Perhaps they were watching. Maybe they were praying that the huge metal bird now idling on the lawn had not come to fetch them to someplace scary.

Randy and Jim loaded our stretcher into a waiting ambulance. The ambulance crew wore blue uniforms and patches that said that they were volunteers. Maybe farmers. Maybe the barber. Ordinary people who have given their time and dollars, a gift of themselves offered with little thanks to any neighbor who calls.

The ambulance disappeared around the corner. I took a shortcut through the building, and smiled at the lady at the desk. She didn't question the uniform, just nodded and pointed to her left.

The run report might read like this: Sixty-seven-year old male, chief complaint: severe chest pain unrelieved by nitro; recent MI; cannot tolerate recumbent position; BP 130/60, HR 90, respiration 16; Dr. requests transport for advanced cardiac evaluation.

Even taking a shortcut, the guys in the ambulance beat me to the room. It was Halloween. Really. One of the nurses was dressed like a witch but, forgetting the date and seeing her only from the back, I was fooled into thinking we were at a Catholic Hospital. It was a good thing I didn't call her 'Sister.'

The old man was upright, alert, and in good humor. Work boots, his, stood in the corner, worn and muddy. His jeans carried with them a piece of the land that he must have called home for a lifetime. This is the kind of guy that doesn't go willingly. He must have really been hurting for the little white-haired lady waiting in the hall to get him this far.

There were enough leads attached to his chest to wire a small office phone system. Nearly a dozen adhesive patches, each with a different colored wire attached led to a monitor that beeped from its perch near the bed.

A young doctor was trying hard to be in charge while the chopper pros did their best not to overshadow or undermine. Our guys see this kind of patient everyday. A country doctor may have had the training but only God knows when, and then it was crowded against a tidal wave of other things to remember.

We made the transfer, a pull against the sheets, sliding our customer from one uncomfortable bed to another.

I comforted the Mrs. still anxiously picking at her cuticles. She, in turn, was pacing the hall and comforting what must have been a son. Women are so much stronger than men. They out-live us, they out-work us, they out-love us. They even let us act like the boss and have the good grace not to let us in on the joke.

"We'll have him there zip quick," I promised.

"The family is on the way. They should be there when you get there. Will you watch for them?"

"I promise."

"It'll take me about three hours. They told me not to worry but I'm worried. You know, he's had this before and he's not a young man anymore. I told him not to work so hard. He's had a terrible cough for days but," she shook her head, simultaneously annoyed and proud of his stubbornness, "you can't tell that man anything. Never could. Will you watch for the family? There should be a bunch of them."

"Yes, ma'am."

I had to turn away. This is the difficult stuff.

Blood is easy.

Outside a small crowd had gathered. Big deal, little town.

A veteran had cornered Gary and was reliving a Viet Nam memory. Gary just wanted to fly and kept looking over his shoulder to check our progress.

In minutes we were shaking the tree tops with our downwash. The guys on the ground turned away to protect their eyes, stealing a glimpse then turning away again.

Inside the chopper our world had changed. No more tourists. Just business.

Jim started an IV line, the second. One began a slow drip of saline. The other was there just in case.

"I'm Jim. How do you feel?" All this above the noise of a helicopter at full power.

"OK."

"Do you have any pain?"

"Yes, right in my chest. It hurts worse to lay down."

It was here that the new guy had his second warning. Patients who are uncomfortable lying down often have fluid in their lungs. Needing to sit up is a huge sign. I hadn't missed it. Jim and Randy hadn't missed it. Perhaps the doctor, aware of a previous episode of heart problems had jumped to a conclusion. Had anyone mentioned the terrible cough?

Randy fished the X-rays out of the brown envelope and held them against the window and what was left of daylight.

"On a scale from one to ten, how would you rate the pain?"

"A seven or eight," came the muffled voice from behind the oxygen that I held just over his nose. Wearing the mask had caused a touch of panic so I decided to hold it. His respiration rate was right in the middle of the range although he did seem to be using his stomach muscles which is sometimes a sign of labored breathing.

"I'll give you a little something." Jim reached for the syringe taped to the side of the monitor. Into the unused IV shunt, he pushed a few cc's of morphine.

Seconds later, "how's that pain now, sir?"

"A three. Thank you." There was gray hair just around the edges. His hands were large and rough. I think I saw a tear as he turned to watch his world sailing by. I wonder if he imagined that this must be the view of angels.

"Look at this." Randy had the X-ray plastered against the Plexiglas window. He was running a pointed finger around the lower left lobe of the lung. X-rays aren't my thing but I could see the cloudy image and thought the same thought.

"I think he's got pneumonia," he half-asked.

We flew past field and farm, along the river where the casinos have come to replace useful endeavor. Their lights called, even from the altitude.

By now it was dark, early evening, the time when families

think of dinner, when the night shift is taking their turn.

The white overhead lights in the cabin began to dominate although they were unable to match the beauty that floated below. We could have as easily been on another planet or perhaps from one. Here, on our perch, we were apart. Quiet, in spite of, perhaps because of, the roaring jet engines that burned just inches above us. Quiet and isolated in spite of, perhaps because of, the three graceful steel blades that held us.

The city swam into view and we all strained to watch when someone, Randy, I think, spotted a sea of headlights pushing against a dam of emergency vehicles blocking a freeway.

"Hey! That should have been our scene!" I don't remember who said that but the tone implied an "I'll trade you three cardiac transfers for one of your scenes."

Too bad.

We had a little trouble finding the hospital. It was new at accepting med-evac flights and the landing pad was little more than a few reserved parking spaces hidden in a forest of tall pole lights.

Gary spotted the lights of a waiting ambulance and fire truck that was standing by, just in case, and steered us just a bit further to the south.

Once over the target, Gary took extra time settling the bird. All eyes, including those of the patient, were straining. The people on the ground were watching too, all of us behaving as if a helicopter could be landed by group sight.

The scene belonged to the lights. First the huge and powerful searchlight on the belly of the craft. Then there were the sodium yellow lights that surrounded and menaced the LZ, forty foot torches that both called and threatened.

On the ground there were the red and white lights of the fire truck. And finally the stutter-flash of the white strobes firing from each corner of the ambulance.

In the light of the hospital window nearby, I watched a face press against a window as I pressed my face to return the gaze.

The shadows along the edge of the moment seemed to move.

Then I remembered that it was Halloween and focused to turn moving shadows into miniature ghosts and goblins tripping about their business of extorting candy and treats from all who would answer the door.

They didn't need another hand on the stretcher so I went to find the family and assured them that Dad, Grandpa— whoever—seemed to be in good spirits and that they could see him soon. A pig-tailed muppet asked me about Pawpaw. An ear-ringed, tattooed grandson asked if the 'old man' was okay. Too cool for me. A worried daughter asked if I had come in with Dad and wanted to know if Mom was 'holding up.'

"He's okay, darling"; "He'll make it, pal"; "I think he'll be fine"; "she's a nice lady and seems to be stronger than the rest of us."

I knew they wanted more but that little bit of encouragement is all that I could offer.

"So how does this compare with other medicine?"

Randy struggles and then gives up saying, "You can't compare. This is somewhat of an unstable environment. You're out on a limb, you and your partner. That's all you have."

"You make big decisions, don't you?"

"Huge decisions. In the hospital I could refer to another therapist, a physician up the chain. Here we have medical control at all times but our protocols give us the freedom to make a lot of decisions. And I like that. I believe I'm qualified to do that."

"Do you ever get home and say, 'I wish I'd...'"

"Oh, yeah. No one's perfect. There's days I can't seem to start an IV on a fourteen-year old with veins," as he makes a wave of his hands and finishes the thought, "that big. Everybody has those days. There are days when you can't get someone intubated. Your partner has to do it, or someone else has to do it. There's those days. No one is perfect.

"We had a car versus train and the train won. And it was a twenty minute response time. They called us when they arrived on scene, so it was probably thirty minutes before we arrived on scene. We were in that 'golden hour'...

"So, when we got to the scene, there was a BLS (basic life support) service team. They had an EOA (a device for securing the airway) in the lady; they were attempting to bag her (breathe for her using a squeezable bag.) A paramedic arrived on the scene and chose to leave the airway in, which is fine. They had put MAST (inflatable) pants on her; they had a carotid pulse. That's all they could get, and she had a lot of fractures. She was pretty much unresponsive. The medical crew there wanted us to leave.. they wanted us to get out of there, they didn't want us to sit around there..."

"Because they felt that the golden hour was slipping away?"

(The golden hour is EMS magic, a belief that the human body can survive just about anything for an hour before the condition deteriorates rapidly.)

"It probably would have been appropriate to secure the airway and then go. But we went ahead and loaded the patient. She did not have an IV or anything. We loaded her in there. We were bagging through the EOA. My partner started an IV, went ahead and paralyzed her, sedated her, intubated her (a tricky maneuver to insert a large tube for air into the lungs) in the air while we were making steps to the hospital.

"A lot of people could criticize that or, you could say, did it benefit the patient to do that? (leave immediately)...and I believe it did. Because...sitting there on the scene, that's the one concept that is important. Because they don't call us. I mean, we're required to have a certain skill level here, higher skill levels than regular paramedics. But, we can't actually do a lot more than they can. They call us because we're fast. We can get there and we can get to the hospital faster than they can. And that's how we should work.

"We don't sit there on the scene and redo what they've done. I don't go on scene to criticize. I go on scene to say, 'You guys did a great job. We'll give you a call back when we get back to our quarters.'"

––––––––––––––––––

We kept the room dark in keeping with the time of day. Even though most of us were working a 24 hour shift, there was no need to turn our lives into full-time fluorescent. Jim and Randy completed the run report.

"See this?"

Randy looked up just as Jim pulled the half empty syringe of morphine from his flight bag, which was left over from the cardiac transport.

"I got it."

Jim squirted the remains of the controlled substance into the trash can as Randy served as a willing witness.

Gary had disappeared to update his log book. I worked my notes. Stuart was doubtless recording it all, although how and from where I could not determine. He has become the master of microphones.

Randy had explained the response radius was about 150 miles. Beyond that, even the chopper was not time effective. For a trauma scene the radius was only about 80 miles for pretty much the same reason.

Pilots are always watching the weather. They have an instinct for local conditions and apparently even the flight crews can catch the disease. The Weather Channel hogged a lot of air time in the day. Okay, maybe that was my doing. But I must have a point as Randy remarked that if there is a scene, he likes it to be south.

"Why south?" I asked although I should have guessed the obvious answer.

"Because when they are south, the wind usually means a quick trip back to the hospital. If you need to have an accident near Kansas City, try to have it to the south. It's faster."

I thought about my orientation to the bird earlier. Gary

made me name Richard Bach's second book as the price of entry.

"Before you can get in, you'll have to help me out."

"Huh?"

"What was Richard Bach's second book? I know *Jonathon Livingston Seagull*, I know one. What was the other big one?"

"Easy. *Illusions*."

"Thank you! Step right over here. This is what we call the football. Gary was pointing to an appropriately nicknamed, black, plastic growth clinging to the bottom of the rotor support, aft of the double doors on the rear of the cabin. I recognized it as an antenna housing of sorts.

"The football is our landmark. Don't, under any circumstances, go aft of the football. We'd have trouble finding all the pieces of your head."

What he meant was that the rotor would act as an expensive, out-sized Veg-o-matic. Got it.

"When we get on scene, I put the engines to idle, lock down the controls, and take up a position here at the football. We don't let any of the first responders under here at all except in the rare case when we might be in a field and need extra help with the stretcher."

Inside it was Randy's turn.

The helicopter is capable of carrying two stretchers but it would be a rare occasion when it does. This is because carrying two stretchers would make caring for either patient difficult.

Of all the terms used in emergency medicine, 'triage' is one of the most difficult to consider and understand. Triage means to select or choose. In emergency medicine, it is the decision as to who gets treatment first. Sometimes it is a matter of who gets treated at all.

The first step in emergency response is scene size-up. The responder reviews the scene first for the safety of the responding team. It makes sense if you think about it. Rushing into an unsafe scene doesn't serve anyone.

Once it has been determined that the scene is safe for the

rescuers, the next question is a matter of equipment and personnel. Do we have enough equipment for the situation? Do we need additional or specialized personnel?

And therein lies the idea of triage. If there is a limit to manpower or equipment, who are you going to help first?

The gut says, "Help the one who is most seriously injured."

Wrong.

Sometimes helping the seriously injured first is the wrong decision. If you work a fatally injured but still living patient at the expense of a less seriously injured patient, it is possible that you will end up with two fatalities.

Sometimes you have to decide.

And sometimes you have to do things that are definitely counter-intuitive. RSI is one of those things.

RSI stands for rapid sequence intubation. Intubation is a matter of securing an airway by inserting a plastic tube into the throat and then, usually, directly into the lungs. It is impossible and sometimes dangerous to do this if the patient is conscious enough to have a gag reflex. Paramedics know how to fix that. They use powerful paralytics to disable your gag and breathing mechanism. Then they insert the tube and take over the responsibility of breathing for you.

Once the tube is in, they're going to 'bag' you. It sounds awful. It looks worse. It works perfectly. A hand-operated airbag is attached to the tube and an EMT rhythmically squeezes the bag for the remainder of the trip to the emergency room. If you are the patient and you are conscious, now is not a good time to complain about the service.

The onboard airway bag is full of tubes and tricks for very occasion. Tubes that go down the throat, tubes that are inserted through the nose, tubes for kiddos and tubes big enough to choke a horse. It flies. It's pretty. It's loaded with goodies. If Santa were an EMT, this is what he would drive.

Randy and I talked trauma beginning with a discussion of one of the most controversial items in the emergency kit, MAST pants.

Now, internal bleeding is serious business. A broken leg can result in death if the femoral artery is severed sending the victim into fatal shock. The same is true for a shattered pelvis. MAST pants are designed to fit over the legs and pelvis, then inflated. The pressure holds broken bones in place and, this is the controversial part, slows internal bleeding.

That is if things go perfectly.

It is the unintended results of using MAST pants that scare the bejeebers out of emergency medical personnel.

It is conceivable that if there is no internal bleeding, the application and sudden pressurization of MAST pants could cause a weakened structure to rupture.

More likely is the instance where there is pulmonary edema, fluid collecting on the lungs. Artificially increasing blood pressure by using MAST pants could cause the patient to literally drown in his own juices.

Randy, like every practitioner that I've met, has his own protocol saying, "If the patient even has a blood pressure, I'm happy. Besides, by the time we could get the pants on, (they are very difficult and bulky) we could be at the hospital."

Would he use them?

"Broken pelvis, broken femur only, and then probably only if they were already on when we get there."

Shift change.

New pilot, Mike. New paramedic, Tune.

The clock ticked and we were hard at work doing what emergency people do best, waiting. About the moment I had decided that we had seen the last flight of the day, the tones began to sound.

"That's us!" (I still haven't figured out how they could tell.)

The entire crew started to move. It seemed slow at first, as if the entire scene had been trapped in Jell-O. Then either my perspective changed or things really did speed up. It was a gradual change that did not instantly accelerate from snooze to race. Rather it was like a freight train that seems so slow but suddenly has momentum.

Before I knew it, I was fastening the buckles of my harness and the beautiful bird was falling off its perch, clinging to the air, rising on a column of light beaming out of its underbelly.

I listened with pilot ears to the calm, professional communication first from Mike to Clearance, then Mike to Tower, then Mike to ATC.

There is one frame of the moment that is frozen in my mind. Tune, sitting backwards in the jumpseat, began to pass around rubber gloves. He held the cardboard box like a communion tray offering up the holy sacrament of BSI, body substance isolation, reminding us by his actions that, in this day of AIDS, the stakes are incredibly high. In the dimmed light of the cabin, the box went around like snacks at a horribly ghoulish party.

"Jim?" Tune queried his partner up front via scratchy intercom. "Is this a BLS or an ALS run?" (He wanted to know if this was basic life support or if we needed to break out the advanced life support cardiac drugs.)

"Don't know yet. We have the paralytics in the airway kit. 'Guess we'll have to play it by ear."

"Mike, I'm outta my belt," Tune advised Mike that he was up and moving in the back so that Mike could warn him of any unexpected maneuvers. Tune's hands played the equipment kits like a master at a medical keyboard.

Then we went back to waiting.

Suddenly there was a thump. It came from nowhere and everywhere.

"Did you guys hear anything back there?" It was Mike, a tiny voice in the headset.

And with that, we were all certain that if the other guy had heard something, perhaps, no, definitely, we had heard it too.

I heard a rattle or thought I did. Being unfamiliar with what is normal made everything sound abnormal.

Mike began to look for a friendly runway and found one off our one o'clock position. He negotiated with the local tower and, in an instant, the big bird was settling to the ramp at Signature Flight Support.

Mike was out and probing, flashlight in hand.

Nothing.

No open fuel doors, no dangling parts. Just a few snowflakes floating in the beam of the flashlight, reminding us how cold this night would be.

There looked to be a bit of blood under the right engine. It must have been a bird strike. Enough of this. We have customers waiting.

I-70 splits the prairie and the United States in two. Okay, you could argue that the West is larger but it is also nearly empty until you get to the coast. So if I-70 splits the United States not quite down the geographic middle, at least it separates the U.S. citizens pretty much in half.

Our target tonight was a young man who himself had been nearly split in half.

He said that he had been driving and probably fell asleep. I can't quite figure that one. There wasn't a car in sight, sort of asleep at the wheel without the wheel! Unless, maybe he ran off the road and collapsed or, perhaps was hit when he walked back to the highway looking for help or, maybe someone stole the wreck? Who knows? All I know for certain is that he was definitely the center of attention.

A small but well-lighted fire truck straddled the south bound lanes, a bully in red daring anyone to move. A sea of headlights backed up against the truck. From our vantage point, we watched the first small trickle of lights begin to ooze off the highway, then speed along the access road.

Mike expertly set the chopper right on the centerline. Gut instinct told me to hurry but I remembered the football and thought about my head. I decided that someone had to be out last and it may as well be me. Besides, the sound effects alone are enough to send the heart racing. Sirens and engines, whirling blades and voices in the darkness. Spooky. A thrill.

"How 'ya doin?"

"Pretty good."

It seems that emergency crews talk calmly in part to reassure themselves.

"Whatcha got?"

A female EMT Basic was standing near the stretcher in the back of the well lighted box. She turned and rattled off her report. It was a testament to training as she spoke. Every word counted, creating as near perfect a picture as could be delivered in not more than ten seconds.

"Eighteen-year old male. Has extensive lacerations to the face. Major head wound frontal region. Says he was driving and lost control. We haven't found the car. Possible hit and run. He's PEARL (pupils equal and reactive to light, something you would want to know with a head injury) and has a blood pressure of 126 over 65. Checked extremities and back with no further injuries noted. How're ya'll doing tonight?"

Thank you, ma'am. That was pretty. And you sure have done a nice job of packaging. (I only thought this. I was too wrapped in the moment to do more than what was necessary.)

"His name is Robert. Here are what's left of his clothes."

The patient was on a backboard with foam head blocks. The face, if there was one, was so completely bandaged that we had to take her word that there was someone under all the gauze. He was naked except for his jockey shorts. When you are in an accident and sustain major trauma, you can pretty much bet that you are going to lose your shirt, and pants, and socks, and...your mother was right!

Emergency medicine is a matter of quick detective work. Unconscious patients can't tell you where it hurts. You've gotta go looking. If there is trauma, you've gotta look everywhere. Front, back, everywhere. The clothes come off. Snip, snip, find us a sheet. Lookee here!

You might get to keep your shorts, but if you are a guy,

someone's going to look to verify if there is suspicion of spinal injury. Break the back and the old manhood gets a reaction that is completely out of character for the circumstance. Just the facts, please.

Stuart tells a story about a drunk who had been in a car accident and sustained all kinds of interesting lacerations, abrasions and you name it. In the emergency room, they started to cut his clothes away to check for additional trauma.

The drunk started to fight, kicking and screaming, just the kind of pleasant fellow you want to dedicate years of study to helping. First the shirt came off, snip, snip. Then the pants and Mr. Congeniality spit (or is that spat?) on the nearest nurse as he yelled, "Cover me up! Cover me up!"

She got a suture towel. Do you know what that is? It's a towel, with a hole in it!

She covered him up.

"There! Are you happy?"

Looking at Robert lying all bundled on the stretcher made me think of the pizza we had just ordered. The tones had begun. We looked for the pizza man and, seeing no one, stuffed a twenty in the door and hit the road or the air or whatever.

"Hello, Robert! How old are you?"

Somewhere under the gauze, a brain was still turned on. The muffled answer seeped out. While Jim was taking charge, other hands were getting ready for the transfer. The O_2 bottle was laid on the stretcher between Robert's legs. He didn't notice and he wouldn't have cared.

The bag of personal effects was passed out the back door. Our stretcher was wheeled into place and Robert was unceremoniously passed like a human baton in an ungodly Olympics played at the 45 mile marker on I-70.

The stretcher whipped around. Jim stepped off the back of the ambulance saying, "Nice job, folks" and, unbelievably, "thanks for allowing us to help."

"Robert! You take care, buddy. I'll call your mom."

"Tell her I'm okay."

"I will."

If there was more conversation, it was lost in the night.

Mike was stationed at the football, Robert slid neatly into the cabin and we locked him in place with a solid-sounding click on the stretcher.

We were airborne in an instant. Tune and I rechecked the vitals. Robert was getting straight O_2 via a non-rebreather mask. No major bleeding.

I decided that this was no place for an EMT. And no place for me.

Too boring. Wait all day and then, when you do happen to get a customer, he's already pre-packaged. And if there was a major problem, I'm not sure that at a thousand feet in the back of this bouncing bus that I would be the right guy to handle it. I decided then and there that if I had to make my living in this business, I would want to be at least a paramedic and I would want to work in the emergency room with lots of customers, lots of variety, no waiting, thank you very much.

Tune offered a report to Jim. No medical history, no meds, no allergies, last oral intake was Boston Chicken for lunch. And, yes, Mr. Tune was well aware that Boston Chicken was a superfluous fact but I guess we were all pretty hungry.

In seven minutes or so, we were sitting on the landing pad at a trauma center. We had passed one center because the crew didn't have faith in the service.

I like emergency rooms and this one was no exception. We passed an abandoned gurney spotted black with activated charcoal, another druggie at work. This bed had a hurt toe, this one maybe food poisoning, over here a broken arm. This place was fun!

Robert was whisked into the last curtained room where a team of medical students and maybe a real doctor would hit him like white on rice. The scene was surreal. One witch, one set of pumpkin earrings, one I wasn't certain was really in costume. Three at the head, two on each side, a pretty young woman was the odd person out so she opted to fit Robert with a catheter. Hey, she was there, he was there. Perfect.

Robert had his vital signs taken and retaken. The head blocks were gently removed after approval by the resident in charge. The head was gently palpated. Yep, one big head trauma and Robert was probably hurt a whole lot worse than he sounded. Could be that he was lucky.

As I dropped his bag of cut-off clothes onto the cold chair at bedside, Robert was reciting his name, address, and social security number. He may have been bent but this kid wasn't broken. He was AOX3, alert and orientated times three; knows who he is, where he is, and what day it is.

When we got back there was pizza, cold as a door nail, waiting on the porch.

Why would someone take a job like this? The hours certainly aren't that hot and the pay? Well, it's good but maybe not worth the aggravation. Of course, if you are a pilot, well, I guess you've got to go where there are aircraft.

And rarely do you see the results of your work. It's too often a simple matter of load and go.

Stuart told the best story.

While on duty in Kerrville, a man ran into the office shouting, "He's dying, he's dying!"

"Who's dying?" asked Stu, jumping to his feet.

"A young man in the street!"

Stu raced into the street, discovered a fellow in full arrest, began CPR and in record time, had the old Timex ticking again. Stu and his partner hustled the patient to the nearest ER.

Six weeks later, there was a knock on the door.

"Can I help you?" said the dispatcher, surprised to see a walk-in customer.

"I'm looking for the two paramedics who saved my life. I was in full arrest right out here in the street and two guys ran out and brought me back. I'd like to see them."

Stu and Steve were doing the EMS thing, waiting in the day room. They heard the conversation and came around the corner just in time to catch the rest of the conversation.

"I'd like to invite them to my college graduation, if it's all right."

It is all right. And maybe it's the thought of graduations and weddings made possible that make this work seem all the better.

I asked Randy, "Why do you do this job? "

"...because I like to fly. I like the professional freedom. We get to do things the other guys wouldn't dream of."

I like working with pros and Randy is a pro with passion. He burns over this stuff.

"You experience a lot of chaos, a lot of stress," said Jim as if he had a specific scene in mind, some far away gathering of fate and skill and equipment. "We give people second chances."

In the morning the fog was gone, replaced by cold, crisp air made especially for flying. I cranked the Little Girl to life and let her do the work that she loves to do. We took off to the south and then, banked to the right, assigned a vector by ATC almost as if to return to the field for another chance to fly with the med-evac crew. Almost, but not quite. Besides, we had to go.

We have one more dream to borrow.

19

Home for the Moment

Eight days on the road. And, even though they have been spent in the lap of luxury, I am ready to be home. Only one day. I have to leave in the morning for the last adventure. But this day, this one day is for me except for any work that is waiting in the office. Stu will come in and shoot the video clips that are to be inserted in the speaking demos on request by potential clients. Mom will have books to be signed, lined up on the work table near her desk. Bailey, the dog, will be waiting near the door where she will roll over onto her back and strike her glamorous pose until I rub her belly.

This is going to be about food.

The steak in New York was wonderful. The fish in Tampa, que magnifique, but it wasn't from home.

While waiting for the cool, stilted service in one so-called fancy joint, I kept thinking that I would rather have my boots under a table at the Cowboy Steakhouse, the only place in the world where I will sit in the smoking section. I do this just to be waited on by Nancy who treats me and everyone like someone special.

The last time we were in, I said no to a glass of wine. I was flying in less than twelve hours and I'm a real careful kind of guy. "No, thanks. I'll just have a swallow of Melanie's." Well, my 'swallow' of wine came in a glass of its own, just enough for a taste and more than enough for me to feel special.

Last night Melanie and I worked until too late and too tired. So we slipped off to the Cypress Creek Inn in Comfort just a few miles from home for a little dinner.

The little town was warm and inviting in spite of, perhaps because of, the cold air that skulked so close to the ground, running up from the river bottom, sliding through backyards and over fences. The food at the Cypress Creek Inn is wonderful. Well, perhaps not wonderful in the common sense of the word but wonderful to me.

It is just plain, good food served by friendly people. Ben may be the world's worst waiter. (Melanie wants me to finish that thought but that was it. He is the worst waiter I know. He can't remember our name, and he doesn't remember our favorites. I just get a kick out of being served by this guy! Look in the dictionary under mellow and you'll see his picture. And when I go to Cypress Creek, mellow is exactly what I am looking for.)

There isn't a recipe in the joint that didn't or couldn't have come off the side of the box. Still, the food is delicious and there's always just enough to leave you feeling full without feeling stuffed, just like home! And the prices! Shhhh! Good Lord, you can eat a full meal including dessert for less than six bucks. Pulleaze, don't tell them they are way under-priced!

If you go to Cypress Creek for fast service or gourmet food, you are in the wrong place. Comfort, Texas, is not New York or Boca Raton. And that is precisely why my pickup was parked next to the other pickups in the gravel parking lot out front.

At 47, Buns and I were still qualified to sit at the children's table. The next youngest diner was probably 65.

And there we sat, not in a hurry.

We knew Ben would get to us sometime before closing. Besides the little place was all decked out for Christmas, warm and toasty, with three Christmas pothos (healthy, green, vine-like plants) lighted in the front window.

You say you haven't ever seen a Christmas pothos? Well, they've got 'em at the Cypress Creek Inn. I guess it was a matter of, 'if it doesn't move, it gets decorated.'

Ben, the almost waiter, doesn't flit from table to table like they do at the busy places in New York. He sorta slides. He talks here for a while then there for a while. He pours a little tea, maybe busses a plate or dish but not too often and then only when he feels like it. He calls you by name or, if he has forgotten, simply makes one up. Tonight we were Barney and Barbara and who knows who we will be next time.

I ordered without benefit of menu.

"Chicken fried chicken, mashed potatoes, corn, and a glass of iced tea the size of a house. If you have the apple cobbler, set one aside for me."

Saturday, my last day before heading out again, was the best.

An errand to Wal-Mart, a little firewood cut and stacked. What mail didn't get digested Friday night, made it to the 'out' basket or wastebasket by five. And the fireplace kept the whole place toasty.

Melanie caught the spirit and made her famous chili for lunch. Chili-ground beef, tomato soup, diced tomatoes with chilies, minced onions, garlic in oil, and chili powder, not to season but burn. Oooh!

The smell of the cooking chili reached all the way back to my office and pulled me to the counter. I heaped on the jalapenos and made perfect chili, how would you say it, perfecter?

The sun never set. It was one of those seamless cold, football days except I never got to really watch any football and wouldn't have cared if I had. No, there was no sunset. Just gray to grayer and finally the day simply gave up and it was night.

Mary Patti Butters writes a Friday column in the local newspaper, our only link to the place where we reside but rarely live. Our 'on the road' houses have daily maid service and soap that comes in small boxes or sticky wrappers. Our 'garage' looks surprisingly like a hangar because that's what it is. Our car, the one we use on the road, is gray and yellow, rented by the mile. It has a lighted sign on top that turns off whenever we are in it. It turns back on when we have left it for the neighbors to use.

So on Friday, we read Mary Patti Butters' column in our hometown newspaper and discovered that Danny Smith, our volunteer fire chief, had been injured at a fire. Naturally, a barbeque chicken fundraiser was on the menu.

I would have stayed home next to the fire, eating more chili with the dog but when Mary Patti announces an event, the smart folks go. After all, home or not, this is our town and we do our part even if it is nothing more than eating chicken.

Doug, in his wheelchair snugged up to the card table, sat guard at the door of the high school cafeteria, waiting for us and everyone to arrive to pay our due. We always over-pay, a nice thing to do until we someday retire and leave the over-paying to the next guy.

Doug has one eye that's good and one eye that hides beneath a patch. Well, he may hide his eye and make light of the wheeled chair, but when there is work to be done, you will find Doug there doing his part and you can't hide that.

Eddie Taylor divvied out the barbecued bird. In his seventies, he is still a handsome man, bib overalls notwithstanding. Mr. T plopped a dark quarter onto a paper plate and teased me that he has to lick his fingers to get a better grip on the bird. Then he passed it to the right for pinto beans and potato salad to round out the offering. Someone added a ladle of sauce. Mary Patti was there to add the Texas standard, pickles and onions, before Melanie told her I'd never eat them.

Charles, that's Mayor Charles, handed me iced tea. I thanked the players, all dressed out in their Lions Club yellow vests complete with purple piping.

Dawn Wright came to say hello. That's Judge Wright when you are in her courtroom and I am not sure exactly how to address a lady Lion. Would that be Lioness Wright?

Vester Joiner sat behind us, the folks from Nonnie's Cafe to our right. The new folks from California, Bob and Mitsui looked like they had found the way to get to know folks. They were both wearing yellow and purple, caught by the Lions and converted in some secret ceremony probably every bit as scary as becoming a Moonie and being forced to hang out at airports for the rest of your life.

Harry and Cindy Holt joined us. Harry, dog tired from a long day at the local E-Z Mart, and Cindy whupped from an even longer day delivering Christmas mail.

Harry was a door gunner in Viet Nam. Tonight he was still doing his duty eating barbecue chicken, not because it was delicious, (it was!) but because it was the right thing to do. In the country, that's how things get done.

Just as Danny hurt his back helping a neighbor for nothing, the little community by the river dished out chicken and beans and did its best to say thank-you.

Lee Greenwood sings what has become our national anthem by default. He sings *I'm Proud to be an American*. Tonight I am especially proud to be an American and a neighbor.

Tomorrow we will fire up the Little Girl and point her nose west for the last long adventure. But we will be thinking of home, our home in Texas. Beautiful downtown, Center Point, Texas. U...S...of...A. It really ain't much—unless you live here.

20

Gypsy Booter

Monday. Lunch time or almost.

Seventeen-year old Jenny squirms in her seat, watching the clock as if the watching would move the hands, make it go faster, chopping a hole in the middle of a boring school day. The campus is an open campus, had been since it was built, and Jenny would be out the door like a shot, racing to her car, a Chevy Camero. The car was not new except to Jenny who had only been driving, should we measure in hours?

The barely white Camero, a seventy-three or -four, turned west in a hurry. Jenny was always in a hurry at this time of day. Now that she could drive, there would be no more hinting to schoolmates that she would like to ride along for lunch. Now she had wheels and life was good.

The day was as bright and crisp as days are made, cold, actually, when you stood in the wind. El Niño had raced through the previous day washing the smog from the valley air, brushing a little extra blue into the desert skies, pushing the clouds a little higher than usual.

We were driving 25 tons of shiny red and chrome fire truck to lunch. The group had decided on Chinese about the same time Jenny decided to turn west onto Guadelupe Road. She turned to drive past the baseball field taking just a moment to brush back her dark hair. Life was really good. Perfect hair, a perfect day. A car to call her own. Not even a zit to remind anyone that she was still a kid of sorts.

The sidewalk was full of school kids in a hurry to make the best of a too short lunch period. Everyone knows that going out for lunch is cool. Only the geeks and the mama's babies eat the junk that they slop out in the cafeteria. That's an argument even the parents and school officials must have bought when they decided to build the school, intentionally building an under-sized cafeteria knowing full well that the kids wouldn't be eating there given half a chance to break for McDonald's and freedom for even 40 minutes.

Along the endless, chain link fence moved the shadows of kids on foot, walking to lunch or maybe just walking instead of eating lunch. There were happy kids in small giggling groups and other kids who did not seem to fit. But they were all kids and it was lunch time. For some, this was as good as this day would get...

..until Jenny turned west and, for whatever reason, was unable to keep the white Camero from continuing the turn. Maybe it was drawn to the curb. Perhaps it was a remnant of evil belonging to the man who had sold her the car. Whatever it was, it was ugly.

When adults are about to be hit by a car, they turn away in an attempt, no matter how futile, to outrun the metal monster. Kids are different. When they see a car or truck heading their way, they turn toward it, looking straight into its steel face as if looking would turn it away.

At what age do we begin to turn away from our demons? Is it ten or twelve, thirteen or older? And what if we don't see or hear and are taken by surprise?

For six young shadows walking along the fence, it wouldn't, didn't, matter.

The Camero jumped the curb. It was probably confusion between the gas and the brake pedals brought on by panic when the scene in the windshield suddenly stopped looking quite right. The car lurched and jumped just as petite Suk-Chong screamed and Eric Martin choked, turning, staring, helpless to move.

The small white car wasn't so small. It took two at once; then three, four, and five, stopping at six shadows and forty feet of chain link fence.

The pretty Asian face flew up, over the bumper smashing the window on the passenger side, ruining the window and the face before the body attached rolled off the hood onto the sidewalk.

Eric. Good ole, dumb Eric, the same kid whose Mom has to remind him to comb his hair because he hasn't quite discovered girls. Eric doesn't fly, although for an instant he wants to. Eric just bounces, then rolls and skids until he is a heap of denim under the fallen fence. Eric saw it but couldn't move and wouldn't have been better off if he had. Only if the flying idea had worked; that might have a made a difference.

The big, red truck turned off the freeway. Mark, our engineer, was driving. He was looking for lunch. Mark is a big, tall guy with a Sharpei face. As friendly as they get. A guy who drove like he talked, non-stop.

We had been in Ahwatukee playing substitute firemen while the regular guys and their engine went for training. Captain Mike Sandolah fiddled with the onboard computer looking for trouble. Hey, do you remember when your mom said, "If you go looking for trouble, you might find it?" Mike must have been listening to Mom, 'cause he was intently looking and he certainly found a mess.

The radio squawked again. Like pilots who only hear their call sign, firefighters only hear their engine number and the 'good stuff.' Calls for 'reported chest pain' are largely un-noticed, not because you don't care but because you can't care. In a city the size of Phoenix, there must be a coronary incident every few minutes. Besides, they are no fun. Stick 'em on the O_2, start a line, tape on the monitor and wait for the ambulance to arrive. Maybe you'll need the AED (automated electronic defibrillation) and, if there is a paramedic on board, a shot of Epinephrine.

Nope, these calls don't even get heard unless it's your number that precedes the chief complaint.

"...school bus...pedestrians..." Two fat words sticking straight out of the radio.

"Hang a right. We're going!"

As luck would have it, we were not more than a mile away. Mike played the air horn at each intersection. Mark slipped Big Red daintily around Toyotas and Mercedes leaving their paint intact and their drivers sucking cold air through clenched teeth.

As close as we were, we were not first. There must have been a dozen bright red trucks. The scene was quiet but not for lack of noise; all the noise blended together like so much recycled paint until the air was gray with the sound of diesel engines and firemen, radio traffic and tears.

Ray, an EMT-B like myself, was sitting facing the rear, on a seat like mine on the other side of the cab. In our time together, I never noticed Ray facing any way but backwards, as if he neither needed nor wanted to know where we were headed until we were there. Stu and paramedic Manny sat in the center two jump seats, Manny on my side, nearly knee to knee with me.

The big, red truck doesn't so much stop as it simply arrives. Sometimes you don't even hear the air brakes. The thing is just there and doors are opening, people falling out boot first. It is a production on big, black wheels trimmed in chrome.

Ray grabbed a bright orange backboard and a gray case that contains supplies for trauma work. As he worked his way along the side of the truck poking first in one compartment, then another, he shopped for miscellaneous goodies not to be found in his big gray box. A c-collar, a set of head blocks and whatever else looked like it might match the moment.

Manny reached around my seat and hit the release to gain access to the drug box. Nothing in there worth stealing except the morphine. Manny's case was bright orange, perfect for keeping track of.

In seconds we were striding along an outfield fence now lying twisted on the sidewalk, blown over by a homerun hit in the wrong direction. Forty feet of chain link, four-tenths of a second of terror.

The triage officer was doing his duty, holding back the urge to rush the field and begin treatment. That wasn't his job. No, his was to act as concierge, matching bodies to arriving fire companies, loaded backboards to arriving ambulances.

The carnage had spilled northward, away from the hard concrete of the sidewalk and street. Showing no semblance of organization or thought, the bodies lay scattered about the soft, wet grass in left field.

"Paramedic engine company two-ten, how can we help?" Mike announced.

Do you know what I liked about this adventure? We didn't have to work to become part of the team. I don't know if it was the uniform or phase of the moon. From the moment we walked through the big bay doors of the station and asked to see the chief, we were one of the guys.

The first face I saw turned out to belong to Captain Mike Sandolah, a young guy with scared hair and a terminally sunny disposition.

"Come on in! The chief's not here yet. Make yourself at home!"

Stu and I dropped our equipment and I immediately began fielding questions about our project while Stu started digging out the camera. In a matter of minutes, Stu had the audio and video tape rolling and in a few minutes more, he had faded into the background. Here is the rule: The more competent and comfortable the crew, the less worried they are about video.

That's the way it is in business. Corporate politics are always borne of incompetence. Competent players play every game but politics.

Here in this station I knew in a heartbeat that we were dealing with pros.

"Camera? No problem. Shoot anything you like!"

The alarm sounded and in an instant, all casual conversation stopped. Three crews looked toward the annunciator, a lighted box mounted high on the day room wall, to see who was being called.

Mike started to the truck, then turned and said, "Hey! This one's for us. If you're going to ride, 'might as well get started." With that said, he moved toward the front of the engine. Mark, the engineer, had already unplugged the battery charger and was climbing into the cab. I hopped in behind the driver, facing backward and clawing for the shoulder harness.

Our first customers were just down the street, maybe a mile; a short trip made longer by the fact that at 8:15 A.M., we were smack in the middle of the rush hour.

One lady, whose car was banged up and abandoned in the intersection, paced anxiously at a corner 7-11. Another customer, an angry man with a child in the back seat, sat helplessly across the street, his car straddling the curb clearly not going anywhere under its own power.

The lady was as fine as fine gets when your car has just been smashed. Mike asked her if she was hurt and then, incredibly, said, "Can I get you a cold beverage?" as if we were driving a beer wagon with an unlimited supply of six-packs on ice.

She smiled, thanked him for his kindness and he was off to cross the street and work his magic again.

The pavement was quickly marked, RR, RF, LR. You get

the idea, and we cleared the intersection the old fashioned way—we pushed!

Across the street, Mike had once again offered a cold beverage, sounding more like a flight attendant than firefighter. Again the customer smiled and declined.

Mike finished his public relations. There certainly was no fire to fight or trauma to treat. He swaggered across the street back to the engine just as we cleared the intersection with the lady's car saying, as he waved the waiting traffic through the light, "Thanks, citizens!"

What the hell was that? "Thanks, citizens?" "Would you like a cold beverage?"

Who is that masked man?

Well, to tell it straight, I had a look into the secret of a fire department that has become the envy of the nation. I saw the cold beverage/thanks, citizens trick over and over before the day would finally wind to a close. Of course, the words would change as would the circumstances but in the end it was a variation of the cold beverage/thanks, citizen routine that would hold my attention.

EP 210 is what is known as an adaptive response unit. That's fancy talk for a unit that goes wherever there are holes in the coverage. It could be called to a major scene but it is just as likely to rove to a station where the home unit is out on an extended call or has moved to assist a neighboring company.

We spent the next couple of hours hanging out in Ahwatukee while the home boys were away for a short training session. Ahwatukee is Crow Indian for "place of my dreams." I can't say that it's all that accurate a description but, for firefighters, it might apply to all of Phoenix, not just this recently annexed corner. Phoenix: good pay, great training, enlightened leadership, state of the art equipment— firefighters' Heaven.

For the next couple of hours, we did the worst thing; nearly nothing except watch the latest installment of PFN, Phoenix Fire Network, a weekly television program, thirty minutes of news, training, and entertainment that was very well done.

There is a natural progression when it comes to team performance. First there is competence, you know the job and can do it. Then there is confidence, you know that you know the job and that you can do it. Finally comes comfort, you know that you can and will do the job, that you can handle whatever comes your way.

Few teams make it all the way to comfortable, maybe because there is too much turnover or, because there is too little training. I believe that too little training is the cause of too much turnover. Who wants to go to work to look stupid? (Or get killed!)

Turnover with the Phoenix Fire Department (PFD) is a whopping 1.2 percent, believe it or not!

To prove the point, our truck was better than fully equipped. This one included bicycles! The two bicycles lashed to the top of the truck were symbols of PFD innovation and training, symbols of exactly why once hired, few want to leave.

Quiet, unassuming Ray, facing backwards, taking whatever comes his way, happens to be trained in bicycle rescue. Yep, bicycle rescue.

Since Phoenix is known as the Valley of the Sun, it's natural that there will be many outdoor activities and subsequent outdoor emergencies. Take a spill down a mountainous trail and you may regain consciousness to see Ray's smiling face. On a moment's notice, the bikes come off the truck, a special trauma kit is attached, and Ray is dispatched to save your skinned backside.

He can patch you up, defibrillate your ticker or package you for a chopper ride.

There are technical rescue teams trained in mountain rescue, swift water rescue, even confined spaces rescue. Captain Mike is even training to operate heavy equipment in case there is a fire or hazardous material (hazmat) situation that requires the use of a crane or dozer. And yes, there are teams specializing in handling hazardous material incidents.

Put it in other terms and you will see that PFD has a complete menu of products, yours for the dialing of 911.

And here's one you would never imagine—palm tree rescue. Palm trees are dangerous. As the fronds die, they don't fall off; they fold down and hug the trunk. The mass of dead fronds is called the halo and, even though it doesn't look all that threatening, it is a potential killer.

Unskilled tree trimmers climb into the tree and begin to cut the fronds they can reach, the ones on the bottom. What they don't suspect is that the entire halo may be loose and, that by cutting the bottom few fronds, they are freeing the halo to slide down the trunk, trapping the unsuspecting trimmer inside where he is held tightly by the prickly fronds!

And it's more than embarrassing. The fronds can grip so tightly that their victim is unable to breathe. In Phoenix, 911 gets you official palm tree rescuers!

———————

The big red truck ran all day.

From fender bender to major accident, Mark maneuvered the rolling monster effortlessly while Mike worked his customer service magic at every turn. He even played Christmas songs on the air horn. Here we were, barreling down the turn lane in the wrong direction, turning directly into oncoming traffic, laying heavily on the air horn to clear the intersection, while Mike is executing Jingle Bells in belched-air monotone on the air horn. And 'executing' is probably not a poor choice of words!

The day was full of contradiction: terror juxtaposed against levity, laughter butting against death, tenderness in moments of cruelty; from doze to danger in zero seconds.

The day was full of nonstop calls of all persuasions. When I asked Ray how he felt about being a rover, a man without a station, he sighed and, without looking my way, melodramatically said, "We're gypsies, man. The city is our beat."

When we had a scene that required police attention, we

waited with the customers until the police arrived; not because we had to but because, as Mike put it, "It's just good service not to leave someone who is upset standing on the corner."

When we had a scene that required transporting a customer to the hospital, one or both of the paramedics rode the ambulance with us, following in the engine to retrieve them after they were certain that the transfer of care was complete.

Melanie asked about the emotions of this work. The best way I can answer is this: you handle it by handling it. You look the unpleasant straight in the eye and you talk about it. You don't look away. You deal with it then and there, probably in a light-hearted tone, but you deal with it.

The guys found us bunk space but no linens. No problem. We'll 'borrow some' at the next hospital. (It's a common practice for ambulance crews to restock linens and such when they take patients to the emergency room. Leave a sheet, take a sheet. We had nothing to leave but we did manage to take a pillow and a couple of sheets. Although the guys would tease me about security wanting to see me, I knew good and well that the sheets would be returned on the next trip.)

Out walked the sheets and in walked a crew from a chopper idling on the roof. This particular customer was intubated although the medic walking alongside the stretcher was making no effort to pump the blue bag.

"He seems to have forgotten that he is supposed to be breathing for that woman," I observed.

"She probably won't notice," was the answer and, suddenly the borrowed sheets weren't so funny.

You handle it by handling it.

In the afternoon we stopped by the district station for Mark to sign papers needed by Personnel. Behind the house, what firefighters call the station, we were treated to an impromptu demonstration of street hockey. Two young firefighters swooped and moved around the lot, the red ball serving no purpose other than to direct the skaters while the old guys, which included me, said things like, "You won't catch me doing that" even as we wished we could.

"So what are you guys up to?" The conversation began again.

"Jumping a few calls so these guys can get a look at what we do," explained Mike, his hair looking even scarier.

"You're welcome to any of our calls you want," the captain rolled his eyes before suddenly remembering, adding emphatically, "unless it's a house fire! Those belong to us!"

We had not been at the firehouse ten minutes when our number came up again. This time it was a pedestrian/vehicle encounter and we all knew, without looking at the onboard computer, who won that contest.

With lights and sirens blazing, we raced. We were on the scene in under three minutes and stunned to see one bloody mess of a human being walking around a tire store parking lot. The former cyclist was being paraded like a hunter's trophy with his arm bent across the neck of what turned out to be the driver of the truck. And, yes, the poor guy actually looked like he had been run over by a truck.

The victim, male, twenty-four-years old, with an athletic build, had been riding his bicycle when the driver of the pickup decided to occupy the same space. The truck won, no contest. Game over.

For some dumbheaded reason, the driver of the truck thought that it would be a good idea to scoop up the remains and march it around the parking lot. Man, if there is anything you shouldn't do, that was it!

We walked a backboard up to the bicyclist and gently lowered him to the ground. This guy was a real space cadet and not just because he had been hit rather hard.

"This dude wanted to take me to the hospital but he ain't got no insurance! What if we had an accident on the way, man? I'm riding with you guys. You at least got insurance!"

No, that wasn't bone sticking out of his leg. It just looked like it at first glance. Yes, that was a cut under the arm.

Monitor on, oxygen mask, start a line, immobilize the

cervical spine, tie him down and haul him off. Another satisfied customer.

The big red truck kept rolling.

Our paramedics rode with the ambulance, leaving us with only EMT-B's onboard, which meant we were no longer qualified as an Advanced Life Support (ALS) unit.

"Now that we're not an ALS unit, what happens if we get a call?"

"We're officially out of service but if we happen onto a scene, we're not driving by."

I had seen out of service units drive by a scene. I had been on these units and never felt comfortable driving by, out of service or not. I felt better knowing that we would stop this big red thing and do what we could do within the limits of our equipment and training.

Before dinner, we made seven or eight calls, some big, some just plain goofy.

One call dispatched us to a bus stop several miles from the station to assist a passenger unable to disembark.

When we arrived, our service expert bounded to the bus where a worried-looking transportation supervisor stood in support of an even more worried looking bus driver. The driver had called his dispatcher, the dispatcher sent a supervisor and the supervisor called us. The passengers were just plain puzzled.

"Hi! How can we help?" Scared hair to the rescue.

"Our lift is damaged and now we can't get this passenger off the bus."

The passenger was basking in the attention, sitting regally astride his 'Rascal' electric chair. He must have weighed three hundred pounds, a condition no doubt made worse by the fact that he walked almost nowhere.

"We can carry you off," Mike offered, half hoping that we wouldn't have to. No sense injuring a firefighter who might have greater value later.

"I can walk," beamed our little daffodil as he lightly stepped off the bus.

The supervisor turned red in an instant. The bus driver matched him shade for shade. We would have to move fast as the truth of the situation gradually dawned on the passengers who had no doubt been waiting at least semi-patiently.

Two of us lifted the 'Rascal' from the bus, a job that I am certain any one of the passengers would have gladly done twenty minutes earlier.

"Thanks for allowing us to help!"

And we were gone. Good God!

By 6:10, we were back at the house where Captain Garcia had dinner well under way. We had made several pit stops throughout the afternoon and were able to watch and smell dinner coming together. Through the passthrough between the kitchen and the day room, we watched the Booter (rookie) shred a mountain of lettuce, then slice rich red tomatoes followed by cucumbers, interrupted only by the occasional emergency run to who knows where.

Dinner seemed to draw the crews from their sleeping quarters, away from the television room and the weight room. Maintenance and paperwork came to a temporary halt replaced by the clack of dishes and the scrape of chairs.

Ed had whipped up a huge pot of mashed potatoes, an equally huge pot of green beans and a hotel-sized pan of barbecued chicken. There was fresh French bread and salad served in a bowl the size of a house.

The TV was skewering Kathy Lee Gifford again, over allegations of promoting sweatshop labor as if she could change a system held firmly in place by bargain hungry consumers, the same good folks who would be watching at other tables and passing judgment with no more thought than passing potatoes.

Conversation pretty much stopped once we were gathered around the table and the food free-for-all began. We were taking a huge risk of trying to eat at the height of rush hour and traffic accidents so dinner was wolfed.

Mid-dinner there was video of our earlier multiple-casualty scene on the news and we all turned to watch.

"Hey, Stu! Bet your footage beats that crap!"

And it did. By the time the news guys packed their scanners and made it to the scene, it was all over but the shouting. They were left to interview a numb school principal and search for tearful hangers on.

By 6:40, the table was clear and the kitchen quiet, save for the running water as the Booter rinsed the remains.

A Booter is a first year firefighter, Academy fresh and learning the ropes and hose, apparently by giving in to all the scut work that the old timers can con him into doing. Important stuff, like mopping the bays, washing dishes. You know, the stuff you hate to do at home but accept as a right of passage.

If Booter had a name, I had never heard it used. Booter. It kind of has a ring to it!

There was a short time after dinner to talk and plenty of takers.

"Why do you guys seem so happy here?"

"Look around! We work in a fireman's palace! The best equipment, the best training, and plenty of manpower to get the job done."

"And we're busy."

"You like that?"

"We love it! The worst part of this job is sitting and, at least around here, we don't sit for long."

One of the guys bent my ear about management and how they treat their crews and cited an example that he thought epitomized enlightened management in action. It seems that there is a very large firefighter who was at the moment on assignment to the Wellness Center. A Wellness Center!!

"He got so big he could hardly drive the engine. So they sent him to the Wellness Center to teach him about nutrition."

"Nutrition? This is training for a firefighter?"

"Yeah. He didn't know anything about fat grams or the difference between proteins and carbohydrates. So they're teaching him to help get his weight under control"

"At other places, they would just kiss your ass good-bye.

Here, they really care." This was said without so much as a hint of disrespect, a sign of enlightened followership!

"And they're not just changing the way he eats. They're changing the way he thinks. Pretty good, huh?"

The alarm sounded. It was ours.

This one was a simple accident. We could tell from the broken glass and sagging fenders that it probably hadn't amounted to much more than serious aggravation. Several hundred motorists who were backed up behind the intersection may have felt a little sympathy but really just wanted to get home.

"All right, guys, let's get out and make a difference!" Our service expert was at it again. We got out and we really did make a difference. Maybe that helps explain how the PFD gets world-class training and equipment. When it's time to talk about the city budget, the taxpayers remember.

With one exception, who happened to be a pretty blonde with the looks of a California surfer grown up, the guys were, well, guys. Even the blonde sported a guy's name, Barry. Barry had been quiet all day but she was easily drawn into the conversation with a simple, 'So, what do you do?' question.

In an instant, Barry's eyes lighted up. "I drive the rehab truck. It's really something." And you could tell that, true or not, at least she believed it.

We talked about this monster until, finally, she asked, "Do you wanna see it?"

"Of course! Is it out in the bay?"

"No, it's out for maintenance but I could take you to her."

Well, I wanted to see the truck but I didn't want to miss a call.

"Okay, but if my company gets a call, will you take me?"

"Sure!"

Barry and I loaded into her backup unit, a vehicle with more than a few miles on it, not at all like what I was about to see.

Rehab, it turns out, is a pretty important part of fire-fighting in this city on the desert. Here, the heat comes from more than the fire. On a 120 degree day, just keeping the fire-fighters vertical is a major task.

I remembered the hot, fall evening when I learned how to use the Jaws of Life to peel open a wreck like a can of cheap sardines. The equipment did all the work except lifting itself. But, bundled in twenty pounds of bunker gear, sweating like a pig, I could barely hoist the heavy metal jaws into place. Imagine, fighting a fire, hauling water-filled, four-inch, nylon hose in desert heat.

The rehab truck does the trick by cooling and rehydrating the firefighters so they can be quickly and safely returned to action.

Our van nudged up to a steel gate surrounding several acres of sodium-lighted staging area and repair sheds.

"Rehab ten," Barry spoke into the security monitor.

"Yes, ma'am. I'm going to need to see some ID." So said the voice from the box as the gate slid slowly open.

We rolled in, slowly, looking for the massive object of Barry's pride and joy.

There were hose trucks and pumpers, ambulances and command vehicles. The back end of a long, ladder truck poked itself out of a too short service bay revealing a neatly painted sign suspended from the rear bumper, "Ladder boys rule."

Around the back was the unmistakable shape of the rehab truck. I recognized it instantly, in spite of having never seen it before.

Barry and I climbed onboard. She worked a panel of rocker switches above the driver's seat with the precision of a concert pianist. Lights here, there, and everywhere. Instantly we were staring into the long innards of a red skinned whale, big enough to swallow Jonah and half of Phoenix.

A wide awning swings out from the side while misters cool the air. Inside, the air conditioning unit makes it possible to either cool the heat-exhausted firefighters or hang fresh meat. Take your pick.

An ALS team accompanies the rehab unit on every run, checking blood pressure and body temperature, bandaging minor wounds and double checking that the newly fit are truly fit before they are shot from the bench, launched back into the fiery fray.

The hand-held radio crackled. Our company was on the move. A violent scene, one victim, a possible knife wound. Barry fired up the van and we hit the road. I didn't want to miss a moment of the action.

En route, I asked questions by the ton.

No, she had no trouble with working so close to the guys. Yes, she had seventeen years with the department and couldn't imagine doing anything else. It would have been forestry if her mother had been successful in talking her out of pursuing a career as a firefighter. Yes, she loved driving the rehab van. She was dispatched solo and always to the biggest, baddest scenes.

"You said you were impressed with how fast the guys clear the station when they get a call."

"Yeh, it can't take more than twenty or thirty seconds. These guys really move."

"Wait till you get a fire call. That's when they run. Just wait."

It is standard practice that responding units stage somewhere near a violent scene, out of sight, until the police arrive and declare the area secure. Face it. Most of the victims of violence had at least a measure of choice in the circumstance and there is no sense exposing emergency crews to more than necessary.

The big red truck had gone into hiding in a parking lot a few blocks from the convenience store while PD, the police department, surveyed the scene. Then it rolled quietly onto the lot where a young man stood bleeding onto the pavement, his family watching complacently from their small car.

"The mother ...... bit me! Bit me!" The loser was bleeding

from bite wounds over the left eye, on the left cheek, and left jaw.

"Bit you? Why did he do that?"

"I don't know. And I just got through with plastic surgery from a bite on the right side!"

Say what you want but this guy is tasty! What is it about a human being that makes some folks just think 'snack?'

Mike tried not to laugh. Hey, the guy wouldn't press charges even though he said he knew his snacker, er, I mean, attacker. He was standing in a puddle, yeah, a puddle, of his own blood! You have to believe that there is something about a person who is not just a victim but a repeat victim of the same mondo-bizarro attack.

"Would you like the confederate style bandage or the classic toothache style?", Mike asked without so much as cracking a smile. Inside, he was rolling. Inside the engine, Stu was rolling too; the camera, that is. This was too good to miss and he didn't.

So much for compassion. This goofball has an entire crew tied up for what?

"If you refuse to go to the hospital, that's your right. But we strongly advise you to go on your own. A human bite is more dangerous than a dog bite. There are more harmful germs in the human mouth." (And inside, it had to be, 'you've gotta be kidding me!')

Back at the house, the Cowboys were getting killed, again.

"Trust me. If Tom Landry were still around, the Cowboys would have never sunk so low. He wouldn't have tolerated this trash behavior."

The talk was typical guy talk.

Mike sailed into the room, did a rather dainty pirouette and said, "I combed my hair. Are you still going to describe it as scared?"

Stuart settled in next to me. "Tyler wanted to know when is Daddy coming home. I told him that when he goes to bed and wakes up two times, Daddy will be home. Debbie asked what I said to him. He dropped the phone and ran straight to bed!"

Like Stu, most of the crew had wives and children. Most of them had part-time jobs for those long periods between shifts.

Mark is a fence contractor, a small business today but growing by leaps and bounds.

Barry raises animals and trains dogs in the German sport, schutzhund

Wild-haired Mike drives a limo. He's gotta be a stitch.

"I've been doing it for four years. I have one suit and one tie. I never untie the tie because I don't know how to tie it back again."

As I said, a stitch.

Ten-thirty and I hit the sack. The stolen sheets felt pretty good but I couldn't sleep, thinking about the next alarm. I was afraid that I might miss it.

Twelve-thirty and I had just drifted home when the lights came on simultaneously with the alarm tone. Dispatch can control station lights. Too cool!

Above my bunk, the annuciator panel glowed EP210. That's us. E10 and RH10 remained dark. It was for us all right. The voice said the magic words, "house fire" and within seconds, we found ourselves on the street racing at breakneck speed.

Mike laid on the air horn; this time with not a hint of Jingle Bells. Mark wheeled the big rig in a 25-ton solo ballet. In a flash, three companies of wide awake firefighters had cruised to the front of the house where it had been reported that flames could be seen from the street.

Nothing. Nada. Zip.

False alarm.

Fully, 30 percent of fire alarms are false. At best, it irritates the firemen. At worst, it puts a lot of people at risk all for the cheap thrill of a king-sized nutcase.

Two more calls, simple medical emergencies, and then nothing.

At six, the lights snapped on and a voice from central dispatch announced, "Good morning, firefighters. It's six A.M. on twelve-eight-ninety-seven. Have a good day."

The multiple injury scene turned out to be the big deal of the day. The most toys, the most challenge, the most opportunity to work at, what at least for some, is not as much a job as it is a calling. As we walked to the point of impact, we passed the white Camero. I know that every mind present was thinking exactly the same thought, mechanism of injury. It's a matter of training, part of what is called scene size-up. Know something about the mechanics of the trauma incident and you can infer the type of injuries that are about to be present. This isn't to shape your thinking, only to serve as a heads-up; turn possibilities into probabilities. You have to start looking somewhere and the mechanism of injury starts the process.

The passenger's side windshield was caved in. This was not a matter of a passenger slamming forward. This was a body headed in the opposite direction.

"Take that one," the concierge pointed to the nearest pile of denim. A fireman in yellow bunker gear knelt tenderly over the body, holding a hand that was all of fourteen-years old. The fireman was over-dressed, having pulled on his gear while en route to a scene he could not imagine, uncertain of what to expect, and dressing for the worst in terms of needing protection.

"What have you got here?" Manny joined the firefighter, flipping open the gray box without looking or needing to.

"I just got here. He doesn't seem to be serious. 'Says his chest hurts...'"

Zip, zip and the shirt was gone.

Manny tossed me his scissors and invited me to work in the other direction.

While Manny began assessment, paying particular attention to the head and chest, I headed for the hurt leg. Zip, zip and the pants became a useless pair of chaps.

As I cut up the right pants leg, I was startled at first. In a matter of inches, I was at the crotch. Good Lord, this kid is deformed! Then I realized that it was the sag look. Low rider pants that start at the hips were making this kiddo look like one of those bears you see at Disneyland, the ones that are all body and no legs.

I palpated the leg. Let's see, that's t-i-c, tenderness, instability, crepitus. Does it hurt? Does it wiggle where it shouldn't? Does anything sound or feel like it's scraping? Yuck!

No, no, and no. A scrape, a cut. Ohhh, this is gonna be black tomorrow but otherwise, we were looking pretty good.

"Push against my hands like they were gas pedals."

He did, as I pushed back against the soles of his feet. Good. No obvious spinal damage. Now, where are those shoes? If they fit like the pants, they could be anywhere.

Head to waist, foot to waist, we had one side under control. A pretty nasty cut under the arm which Ray and I patched up zip quick.

Now the other side. Hand over head, backboard in place. On three, let's roll him.

The backboard goes into place since we'll only be doing this once. With a little luck, there will be no treatable trauma on the back and we can slide the board into place and get this kiddo packaged.

One, two, three...four pairs of hands work as a unit. Six hands along the torso; the remaining set holding cervical spine alignment.

Now on his side and nearly naked, we check for trauma, slide the backboard into position and then gently roll him back to earth.

A blanket. Ray thinks of everything. Then the Velcro straps, each a different color so we cannot get confused as we tie him to the board.

Manny is installing head blocks, foam trapezoids that, after the white cervical collar is fastened, complete the job of totally immobilizing the head and neck. This is the most dangerous part and once we have this one firmly lashed to the board, we all relax.

Manny starts an IV, 05% saline solution, more habit than need. But it's good to have the line started in the event that some unseen problem causes the kid to crater. In that case, it would be quick and easy to shoot a drug or two.

Mike stripped away the sticky backs and plastered monitor leads on the sternum and chest. This kid was ready to go.

Behind us a chopper was landing. One of the victims, one of the kids, the Asian girl, I guess, had been declared level one, load and go. That's what the chopper was all about. Six burly firemen marched the stretcher across the soft outfield, up the backside of the pitcher's mound, and threw a perfect strike into the waiting bird.

I was thinking about all of this as we cleared the dinner table and caught the evening news. I could never be a firefighter. I can't stand the constant television.

"Hey, guys! Check out the news! That's our scene." I wanted the crew to watch and they wanted to see.

"Hey, Stu! Bet our footage is better!"

"...four remain hospitalized, two were treated and released..."

"I'd bet one of those was our boy. Man, is he gonna be pissed about those pants!"

"Station ten, unit two-ten. Auto pedestrian accident..."

Before the words fell all the way out of the ceiling, we were loaded in the engine. The massive steel doors were winding open. Mark had the lights bouncing off the bay walls.

Mike jiggled with the computer, checking the facts and address. "All right, guys, everybody buckled up? Well, then, let's go make a difference!"

And we did.

In most jobs you make a living. In some you make a life. But lucky are the few who go to work and make a difference.

21

Ours to Choose

Make no mistake about it. We are what we do.

The work we choose, in the end, chooses us.

The kid who got the job fueling small planes at the local airstrip becomes a pilot. No surprise. And how is it that the bag boy becomes the butcher, the scouts' top seller of cookies moves on to selling houses?

Was it the worker or the work? And when Grandfather puts in a good word for that job at the foundry, is he just offering a hand or acting a larger part, shaping a life for a lifetime?

Me? I would have been a doctor but I didn't think I'd have the patients. Sorry, not called for. My dad was funny and so I was shaped or maybe warped.

We all bend toward our own decisions, our choices made consciously but more likely not.

The weather was sunny in San Antonio but that was as

far west as you could fly and still be following visual flight rules. The ceiling was a thousand feet, visibility three miles (and that is the minimum allowed by the Feds for flying under visual flight rules.) Only a fool would set out in a light plane, weather like this, without an instrument rating and the instruments to go with it. Most pilots are, wisely, fair weather flyers. Why go when the weather turns raw?

We fly because we need to be somewhere on business. There are schedules to keep. This makes for many flights launched into the murk on days when I would rather be home in front of the fireplace or tucked against a pillow in my favorite chair in the office.

On this day we choose to fly. That's what the instrument rating is for, flying when you choose.

Two hundred feet and we were solidly in the gloom, disappearing into the cloud deck over Kerrville like unfortunate travelers in a Twilight Zone episode.

I trimmed the little Mooney for a steady climb to 10,000 feet and let Houston Center know that we were on the frequency.

"Houston Center, Mooney niner-five-mike-kilo is with you at two thousand feet."

"Mooney niner-five-mike-kilo is radar contact seven and a half miles northwest of Kerrville at 4,000. Climb and maintain 10,000," the controller answered.

"That's us. Up to one-zero, ten thousand for five-mike-kilo."

For the next 500 miles, there would be only the occasional glimpse of Mother Earth, and that only for a moment and only the parts of her that are barren and brown.

Just east of Fort Stockton, a military re-fueling operation, code-named Turbo three-six, checked onto the frequency asking for a block altitude from 8,000 to 12,000. We were at 10,000, cruising between layers of cloud, the highest layer marking gentle shadows on the layer below. The one shadow I did not want to see was the shadow of a military aircraft or two, or more.

(That's a great reason for choosing to fly under instrument rules. You are under the constant watch of the controllers, almost always in radio contact. But with choices come consequences. You can't fly instrument and just point the airplane in any direction. You have to bend to traffic and rules. In the end, the trade-off is a good one.)

The controller advised Turbo three-six that there was traffic at 10,000, east of Fort Stockton. That was me and I knew it. But, he said, the traffic is fast and as long as the refueling operation would break off by Fort Stockton, the traffic should be no factor. Oh, how I wish airplanes had rear-view mirrors!

We peeked at the oil fields near Fort Stockton, caught a wisp of Interstate Ten as it wafted along the desert near the Pecos River, then said good-bye to the ground and Albuquerque Center when we slipped below their radar and out of reach of the radio for 50 or so miles of loneliness.

Our flight took us to FST62, a funny little bend in the Victor airway between Fort Stockton and the Hudspeth VOR. I have no idea why the airway arrows 62 miles into the desert from Fort Stockton before making a three or so degree jog to the right. But I follow the rules and the airway with the idea that if, while we were radio and radar lost, something should happen, we would be easier to find.

At Hudspeth I always look to see why there is a place called Hudspeth and there is never anything to see. So I just call El Paso Approach and get on with the business of flying. By Hudspeth we have picked up the automated weather report, learned the hourly code and advised El Paso that we are "checking in at 10,000 with Echo' or Delta or Romeo or whatever is the code de l'heure.

We taxied to Cutter Aviation where the line guys are always hustling even when the hot winds of the desert in summer are baking the tarmac and anything that ventures onto it. These tough, mostly Hispanic guys should give a lesson to the sometimes lethargic crew that owns the tarmac where we stop in Phoenix. This time we were marshaled to a spot close to the building, next to a brightly painted tail-dragger, a high wing plane that sported yellow and red paint, looking perfect in a shaft of sunshine that had found El Paso and nowhere else for several hundred miles in any direction.

From the other side of the yellow bird, a forty-ish fellow in a T-shirt and jeans, sauntered over to have a closer look at five-mike-kilo, inquiring about her pedigree and the weather to the east. His plane, a high wing fabric-covered, two-seater that was not equipped for instrument flying, had been resting in El Paso for two days. I told him that I hoped he liked El Paso and recommended Forti's Mexican Elder Restaurant, a barrio hideout of hot Mexican food and warm Southwestern hospitality. I also recommended that he give El Paso at least another day as this was no day to venture across so much open space under so much closed in weather.

His face fell at the news just as a pair of blue-jeaned legs scooted out from under the yellow bird.

"What's the word?" asked a perky blonde with braided hair that matched her airplane.

"He says he hopes we like El Paso."

"Oh." The legs slid back under the plane to continue the work. It may not fly in weather but at least it looked good.

If there is one thing that sticks with me from all our adventures, it is this idea of choosing our destiny. Why do some, too many actually, persist at work that does not fill them up and make them whole? Why?

And worse, why do folks make choices that are actually destructive?

I walked into the local convenience store and was soon lost in the act of looking for an item Melanie needed to finish our dinner. Suddenly, I looked up to see a young man walking up the aisle toward me.

He was dirty from greasy head to barefoot toe. He wore no shirt, only several tattoos. The outfit was completed by a cigarette dangling from his mouth. By the time he made it halfway along the aisle, a woman, surely his physical counterpart, walked the aisle in the opposite direction, except that she wore a shirt, albeit a dirty one. She was dressed identically to the fellow.

"Where's your old lady?" she dragged on the cigarette.

"Awww, she's in jail."

"Oh."

Oh? Oh? You don't know me from Adam but if I wrote at the end of this book that it was dedicated to my wife who is currently in jail, would you think, 'oh?' I think not.

So I am left with this question about choices: I know that we are the sum of our choices but are we able to actually choose? Isn't being aware that there are options part of the choosing?

One of the most important stories in the Bible is the first one, the Adam and Eve apple in the garden parable. It is the story of how God gave us freedom. Without the freedom to choose, we are no different than animals. It is the freedom to choose that makes us whole. And the story of these adventures is the story of choice and choosing.

Riding in a cab to LaGuardia, we enjoyed talking with our Haitian cabbie. You know, say what you want about cab drivers and joke about their inability to speak English if you will but, driving a cab is in many instances the very essence of the American dream. What better way to learn a new language and the customs of a new country than to drive a cab?

We've met some of the most thoughtful, hard-working individuals ever while riding in cabs. People who have an education. People who often have had the courage to flee repressive governments. People who have a dream and have chosen to follow it.

This cabbie was no different. He was the father of two girls and was working towards a degree in pharmacology in his few off hours. He told us about bringing his younger brother to New York and taking a precious day off to make a proper impression.

The cabbie drove his brother all over the city showing him exclusive residences balanced by a tour of areas rife with poverty, drugs, and aloholics.

At day's end, they stopped for coffee and the delivery of the punchline: In America you can choose. You can wind up with the druggies or you can live with the wealthy. And it is all a matter of choice.

In Dallas I met an attractive saleswoman with a mysterious accent.

"I can tell you are not from around here. I'd bet you're from Alabama," I joked.

"I am from Russia," and she wasn't joking.

"I kinda figured that. Tell me, what is it that brought you to Dallas?"

"I have degree in pediatric psychology. Here I can choose good job. Government does not choose for me. It is simple."

Simple? Perhaps. Easy or obvious? Not for some.

Flying is nothing more than a series of choices, usually involving weather.

Inside I talked to the weather guys and got the news. Another day in El Paso would also be good for Mooneys but not good for business. So we elected to launch with the idea that if things got really rough, we could and would do the most important of all aerial maneuvers, a 180 that would take us back to the barn.

I filed for 12,000 feet and in 15 too-short minutes was climbing over Mexican airspace anticipating a turn to the west and a hand off to the controllers in Albuquerque. Once at 12,000, we could see nearly forever and the sight wasn't all that encouraging. Although the Stormscope was clear, (no dancing green crosses that promised connective activity) the windshield was full of disappointment and black, black skies just off the nose.

I requested a descent to 10,000 which would keep us out of the clouds. The idea was that below the cloud bases, we could see the rain cells and fly around them. This worked for nearly a hundred miles as we zigzagged first north then south, before the mountains grew and the storms began to settle, hunkering lower to suck power from the earth below.

We asked to climb and were cleared to 16,000. I watched

the airspeed drop as the little Mooney stuck her nose up and gamely began her climb. Outside the air temperature was ten below zero and falling. I hoped that we had made the right decision. If the lifting action of the storms carried warmer moisture, it would freeze in an instant on the cold skin of the Mooney. I pulled open the cabin heat, double-checked the defroster, and switched on the pitot heat so that moisture hitting the pitot, (the air speed sensor) would not freeze rendering it useless.

At this altitude the air is so thin the little Mooney sips fuel since there is not enough oxygen to drink deeply. The same for us. We broke out the canulas and sniffed the clean, clear gas that hissed from the tank suspended behind my seat. All the while we hoped that we would reach the tops and be able to see the larger cells so we could steer clear.

That was our choice but Mother Nature dealt a different hand. In it she held ice, the bane of aircraft large or small.

"Center, Mooney niner-five-mile-kilo. Pilot report. We have light, clear ice passing through 15,000."

No de-ice. No hot prop. No turbo-charging to zoom us to the tops.

We could sense the tops. We could hear about them as a King Air reported that he was just grazing the tops at flight level two-zero (20,000 feet.) We could dream about it but we couldn't go there.

All we could do was hope. Hope follows choice, never the other way around.

About 20 miles shy of the Totec intersection, an imaginary point in space some 40 miles south of the Phoenix Sky Harbor airport, we broke out into the clear at 10,000 feet.

Well, almost clear. We were looking at a wall of thunderstorms that stretched from horizon to horizon. There were choices here. Fly through; fly under and through; or maybe take a shot at that little hole just to the north, the one that appeared to be closing between too dark sheets of solid falling water.

We'll take the hole, not the curtain. Phoenix Approach

gave us the option, a choice we would not have known was ours to make had we elected to remain in the clouds at 16,000.

Funny thing about choices. They are all around us but so often we are in the dark in the clouds, unable to see them. Robert Frost and his road less traveled could maybe have come even closer to truth had he mentioned that it is the choice unknown that makes all the difference.

In a matter of minutes we were through. A few minutes more and we were in the sunshine taxiing to parking at Scottsdale Airport. By evening we were at the DoubleTree enjoying a reception with the client. By morning we would have enjoyed game four of the World Series and be breakfasting in the southwestern elegance of the hotel.

But wherever we are, whatever we would be doing, could never be more nor less than the sum total of our choices.

And who would say that the gardener who swept the walk before us would not have been piloting a Mooney had the choices been different?

And just as it is ours to choose, perhaps it is ours to honor the choices of others. There but for the grace of God, and I will add the grace of my choices, go I.

22

N95MK

She's a beauty, all decked out in the tackiest paint job on the planet. I decided that if we were going to spend more on an airplane than we did on our house, well, I want to be noticed. And, no doubt, taxiing to the ramp in niner-five-mike-kilo definitely gets one noticed.

The cowling is deep blue, accented by a rather large silver star. The blue sweeps back along the underbelly and past the landing gear before turning up toward the tail. A gold streak caps the blue along the tail and, what the Mooney folks describe as Really White, is the color of the top and vertical stabilizer.

Mooneys are known for having a vertical stabilizer, the tall part of the tail, that looks like it has been installed backwards. Funny or not, that oddity of design plays a major role in improved performance.

There is a bit of magic about the tail number of this airplane. The tail number is also the radio call sign. Controllers who have time to think beyond their busy screen sometimes try to figure out the meaning behind tail numbers much as the rest of us attempt to decipher vanity license plates. One drug dealer that I know of had the tail numbers of his plane changed to 131MS which stood for his birthdate and initials.

Niner-five-mike-kilo is extra special. The 95 signifies the year the aircraft was manufactured, M is for Mooney and K represents that I'm flying the 10,000th Mooney. And I am. Mike-kilo is a commemorative edition that is really something special. If Mooney knew how to build it into an airplane, they put it on Mike-kilo. This baby is all dressed up with someplace to go!

Inside, the little plane looks and sits like a Ferrari. It costs about as much as a Ferrari, too! There is more avionic hardware crammed onto the panel than you can say grace over. Every inch of panel space is owned by one instrument or another. The little Mooney may be pricey but the darned thing will practically fly itself.

Learning to fly is an interesting exercise in teamwork from which many corporate executives could take a lesson. The instructor, known as a CFI, must balance command against empowerment. He or she has to know when to take the yoke and fly the plane. Instructors, though, are a lot better than most business folks when it comes to knowing when to let go. You've got to remember that, for an instructor to let go, requires them to get completely out of the airplane and stand helplessly on the ground as their student, their airplane, and their reputation leave the ground without them.

Too many businesses are run by folks who only get half of the equation. They grab the yoke but they never let it go. Not only is this a sure-fire way to hold back corporate growth, it leads the boss straight to an early divorce, heart attack, or grave.

The Mooney people have their act together when it comes to selling an airplane. You can buy a new Mooney but they won't give you the keys until your ability to fly the darned thing is checked out by an independent training company, FlightSafety International.

If you are a relatively low time pilot and aren't at least a bit intimidated to transition from a slow flying, high-wing aircraft to a low-wing, high performance, complex aircraft that is faster than the devil, you're an idiot. Period.

I must be brilliant because I was scared half to death!

FlightSafety International does for Mooney customers exactly what we try to help our corporate clients do for their internal customers: Teach them everything they know to safely and confidently fly solo, no matter what the task. It doesn't much matter what is the task or industry. Folks fly best when they are comfortable. And folks who are not competent are never comfortable (or at least shouldn't be.)

At twelve thousand feet, flying solo, there is only one leader in the plane. You. You've got to know your stuff. There is no one to take the yoke in an emergency.

The leading cause of accidents involving airplanes is over-confidence preceded by under-competence.

When you pick up your Mooney, one thing is for sure. You can damned well fly the thing!

First you get familiar with the plane and its systems. You learn a little about the aerodynamic principles that keep it from falling like the ton of metal that it is. Then you gradually take on greater and greater responsibility until one day, your instructor says, "Take me back to the hangar. I think you are ready."

When your heart falls out of your throat and you can breathe again, you take the little booger out and you fly! Free as a bird! Your instructor's every word echoes in your ear as you make each turn in the pattern and finally announce that you, king or queen of all that soars, are "on final for runway one-two. Full stop, Kerrville!"

Why doesn't everyone who punches a clock feel like they are flying?

The FlightSafety program is an advanced version of the first course in flying; A lot about the plane, more about the design characteristics that influence its performance and then lots of gear up/gear down practice until, finally, the instructor hands you the keys and invites you to stop by for coffee the next time you are in the neighborhood.

If you don't mind, a word of thanks. First to John and Martha King. If it weren't for their wonderful video taped series, chances are, I would still be just thinking about flying. I've spent hours and hours watching John and Martha on videotape as they made the sometimes rather complicated lessons of flying uncomplicated and interesting.

If you want to do more than dream about flying, order a set of the King tapes and plant yourself in front of the VCR.

There is one more rather unusual thank you and it goes to the guy who sells the other brand of aircraft. I live in a little nowhere town well off the beaten path. I run a little business. No corporate flight department, no fancy reception area although Mom is a pretty fancy receptionist.

So I called the 'other guys' and asked if they had time to talk to me about buying an airplane. They sent information to get me off their back. Mooney sent a salesman to answer my questions.

When I called with questions and to perhaps schedule a demo, the other guys took forever to return my calls and finally, told me that because they had other, more expensive planes to sell, they would give me a call when they could work me in. Mooney promised a demo at my convenience and delivered on the promise.

Now, I know that a Mooney is not a multi-million dollar Citation jet but, at three hundred thousand buckos, this represented a serious purchase to me.

One afternoon, the phone rang. It was the 'other guy.'

"Scott? If you happen to be in our town next week, we might be able to give you that demo flight you requested."

"I'd love that! Should I fly down in my new Mooney?"

"Pardon?"

"I bought a new Mooney three weeks ago. She's beautiful!"

"I guess I should have gotten back to you sooner," came the rather sheepish reply.

"Well, I understand. You have planes that cost in the millions to sell. I guess it's pretty easy to lose track of the little ones."

Dumbhead.

About the Little Girl:
Engine: Continental IO-550-G
Propeller: McCaully, 3-blade, constant speed, 73"
Seats: 4
Length: 26'9"
Height: 8'4"
Gross weight: 3,368 lbs
Wing span: 36'1"
Max cruise speed: 190 kts at 9,000 feet
Range: 1,130 nm/6.7 hrs at 9,000
Rate of climb: 1,200 feet per minute
Horsepower: 280 MCP
Useful load: 1,143lbs
Usable Fuel: 89 gal
Stall speed (flaps extended, gear down): 59 kts
Climb gradient: 703 feet per nm
* for more information: www.Mooney.com

23

Carpe Diem!

I f I never wrote a single word about these adventures, if I never deliver a single keynote or seminar based on our travels, I will still be a better person for having gone in search of a borrowed dream or two.

I learned a fistful of things about work that paint the face of work and workers more vividly than anything I have read or heard before. About life, these adventures have been life in a glass, a metaphor in two years, good for an age of learning.

Like the rocks that grow in the yard, it is taking a while for the lessons to pop to the surface. I guess that for years I will be dredging up one lesson or another as circumstance and time shine new light on our experiences.

Here's what has revealed itself so far:

ABOUT WORK

Power of the First Day

In the course of the adventures, I experienced one first

day after another. In my real life as a presentor at conferences and conventions, I had lost, in the blur of a hundred 'first days' a year, the powerful importance of an employee's first day on the job. It is on this day that new employees, new members of the team, get the heaviest dose of values and culture. Sometimes this dose is fatal and new employees decide not to return. Worse, they often decide to return but only until they can find something else.

Most first days are little more than invitations to hang out with a reluctant old-timer. Too many first days are studies in awkwardness.

In my personal business life, I promise (to me) to never forget the power of the first day. On that day I will make certain that new team members feel welcome and important, and that they know who we are and exactly what it is that we are about.

Spirit Killers

I haven't seen too many happy union shops.

That's not to say that there aren't happy union shops. Only that I haven't seen many.

I can walk into a conference center and tell you in a matter of seconds if we are dealing with a union crew. The first time I hear "That's not my job," I can tell that a union is at work. Unions are too often spirit killers. Human beings are not designed to go an entire day without thinking. And the moment you stuff a human being into that little tiny box called a job description severely restricting both thought and activity, you've got unhappy workers.

In non-union shops if I need a different microphone or need to have the lighting adjusted, the usual answer is "no problem." That's rarely the case in union environments.

Wherever we have man functioning as a machine rather than a living, breathing problem-solver, we have unhappy work.

My message to employers: Instead of dummying down jobs to make them idiot proof, consider complicating things and stand by to be surprised at how creatively your crew rises to meet the challenge.

My message to unions: I know that you think tightly limited job categories protect jobs and perhaps they do. But, long-term, while you may have a few more jobs, the cost that the worker must pay in terms of boredom and mind-numbing repetition is too high. Lighten up!

Artificial, Substitute Experience

Maybe I'm the last to notice but there really are techniques for artificially giving work teams experience. In pre-hospital emergency care the favorite approach is one that I call 'Scenario.' Students are constantly given scenarios and asked to describe the appropriate actions.

"You arrive at a scene and discover that a small car has hit a light pole. The windshield is smashed on the driver's side. The driver is still in the vehicle. The door is open. The driver is a woman in her mid-twenties and she appears to be in late term pregnancy. She is bleeding profusely from her forehead and does not seem to be conscious. What do you do?"

Let's not get sidetracked by fooling with the response to the above scenario. For now, just notice how such a scene immediately kick-starts the thought processes and imagine how something similar could work for you. It could be customer service situations, economic or political situations, even mechanical or procedural situations.

The only way people learn is by doing.

Training is a matter of arranging for people to do as many things as possible while under the supervision of a mentor. Scenario allows the learner to artificially experience as many situations as possible.

There are two other important techniques, routine and example.

In the best of all worlds we would always have time to think through our actions. Well, sometimes we are called upon to make decisions before our intuition has sufficiently developed to carry the moment. For those situations we need a routine, we need canned responses that are likely to work even without our complete understanding of the moment.

For example, pilots are told to run through the GUMPF (Gear, Under-carriage, Mixture, Prop, and Flaps) check prior to landing. This simple routine helps us avoid those embarrassing moments of landing with the wheels still tucked into the belly or having the engine die short of the runway because we forgot to switch fuel tanks.

Routine is a substitute for intuition and is especially important when there are other distractions clamoring for attention at critical moments.

EMS personnel use SAMPLE and AVPU as gentle reminders of information they need to gather regarding a patient's history or level of consciousness.

Finally, we learn from example. All the training in the world doesn't substitute for a real-life example that you can imitate.

For too long, while learning the skills of an EMT-B, I carried around a small notepad for taking patient information. Can you imagine trying to administer oxygen and taking a blood pressure reading while writing on a tiny pad resting on the patient's stomach? Then I noticed an arriving paramedic transcribing my information onto his latex glove. Duh!

Now when I am on scene, I make my notes on my disposable glove and no longer have to chase a small notepad across a quivering chest! Example!

Sum of Choices

This is an easy one. We are the sum of our choices. Looking back at all the jobs we have worked, I can honestly say that I could have easily made a lifetime of any of them. Not because they would have been my choice but because of how easy it would have been to have chosen any of these jobs as a career.

You may think that people who do technical work are smarter than the average bear. Well, I think not. Oh, there is some matter of aptitude, I guess. But more, it is a matter of choice. Choose this road and there are you are, down that road with little or no excuse or explanation.

Allen Turner, a guy I used to cook with at Denny's, would often sigh about mid-shift and say, "Remember, no matter where you are, that's where you are."

Fine, Allen. The question is, how did you get there? And the answer is—you decided. You did. Not your mother or your teacher or the government—you did.

And the surprise is how few people realize that they are where they are by choice and that they can choose themselves to be someplace else.

Truck-Computer-Match

Whoa! It was a smack of reality to suddenly realize that so much of work is at odds with the way man is constructed. We probably would have expected it had we thought about it. But seeing man as a machine was a shock.

We like the metaphor of truck-computer-match to describe how some folks go to work. Some are used as machines, turning and twisting, lifting and lugging in endless repetition for eight, ten or twelve long, dreary hours. We were even more surprised to discover that some people had learned to like it!

Other workers are more like computers, being used to solve problems. These seem to be a happier group, using their brains and sometimes their bodies to solve problems, reacting to the unexpected, and delivering time and time again a solution.

But the happiest of workers did not seem to be the problem-solvers. Nope, the happiest were the problem causers! People who, having completely solved themselves out of one problem, had the total freedom to actually create whole new sets of problems.

I have come to believe that man was created to solve problems and that left without a meaningful problem, man will create new problems just for the sake of the game.

That same compulsion I think is what drives folks to totally screw up their lives. Something that is working, or could work, we tend to jump in and jumble it up. It seems to me that half of our problems we make up and the other half we simply hang on to for comfort.

Drown in an Inch

What a surprise to discover that so many folks who are expert at what they do can be complete goofballs when it comes to something others might find simple.

I'm the same way. I have no fear of an audience. It doesn't matter if it is several hundred or several thousand. I can be flawless...if you give me a microphone. But talk to me one-on-one at a party and I can't get my name straight.

So it is with many of the folks we worked with. We would often watch them struggle with problems that we saw simply and quickly handled in other venues. It's funny to think that we can get so narrowly focused that we often fail to see that someone else has already come up with a simple, sometimes elegant solution.

As we crossed each adventure off our list, we watched in amazement at how our experiences in previous adventures shed unexpected light on the adventure of the moment.

For example, my experience of using GPS to navigate the little Mooney enabled me to quickly point out a few GPS features that the crew of the Arco Juneau did not know their equipment capable of.

Thinking about how the workers in the foundry had a little trouble connecting with their customers, the farmers, it seemed only natural to recommend to the chefs on Amtrak that they take a quick walk through the dining car so that they could connect directly to their customers.

Working in the emergency room was fun for me because I treated it like working in a fine restaurant and immediately recognized that while no one likes waiting, you can easily make the wait more bearable by keeping the families informed.

Everywhere there are lessons to be learned, cheap, easy,

maybe free lessons, that you can learn from folks completely out of your business and yet instantly apply.

From now on, when I have a problem, I am going to ask for advice from people completely out of the field. (Unless it's a problem that I am enjoying having!)

The Techno Blur

We're starting to see the marvelous blending between high-tech and high-tough work. No, high-tough is not a typo. I intended to use the word tough.

It used to be that there was thinking work and muscle work. Dummy work or master work. White collar or blue.

Not any more.

Now we are seeing that much of the muscle work requires a little brain work as well. We watched foundry workers at John Deere manipulate sophisticated test equipment. We've seen firefighters attach automatic defibrillators and perform medical miracles while carrying a stretcher across a soggy field. Even flying the little Mooney is a toss of aerial ballet and sophisticated navigation.

What else could we do to put technology into the hands that also do the heavy lifting? When we do, we'll be surprised at the brilliance of the common man.

Competence-Confidence-Comfort

I learned this a long time ago. First you are competent, then you are confident and, finally you become comfortable with what you do and who you are. Get the order wrong and confidence becomes cockiness.

This simple truth applies to entire organizations as well as it applies to individuals.

Do you know what is a flail segment? It occurs when a rib or rib section is broken in two places creating a segment that is not attached at either end. The result, in addition to plenty of pain, is what is known as paradoxical movement. In other words, as the patient breathes, the rib section moves in and out but not in synch with the rest of the chest.

Point? Organizations are like individual patients in their response to trauma. When the organization is hurting, it often does things that are the opposite of what a healthy organization might do.

And sometimes, to keep from doing the wrong thing, the organization simply does nothing at all.

A patient with a flail segment or any other type of painful injury is likely to exhibit a guarding behavior. Holding a cracked rib so that it cannot move, limping to protect a damaged foot, ankle, or leg. You get the idea.

Organizations, like patients with trauma, tend to guard when they are in pain.

When you see an organization guarding or resisting movement, it is not the guarding that is the problem. That is only a symptom of something deeper.

Usually the problem is a matter of not knowing, a matter of competence.

In incompetent organizations, there is a lot of guarding that is often manifested as politics.

One definition of mental health is the ability to take intelligent risks. Organizations that are guarding are not about to take risks, intelligent or otherwise, and that puts them at a decidedly competitive disadvantage. "We've always done it this way," is an expression of organizational guarding.

Another sign of guarding is politics. When players start playing the blame game, you can bet that someone (or some ones) are incompetent and, rather than be discovered, they attempt to throw off the scent of stinking thinking by pointing in another direction.

Know this: Corporate politics are a sign of fear. Fear results from not knowing how to cope. Call it incompetence. Whenever you see politics, look deeper and you will discover an underlying fear borne of incompetence.

Pre-flight

It's easy to miss but great teams have frequent pre-game skull sessions. On Southwest Airlines before every take-off and every landing, the captain and the first officer brief the procedure. No matter whether they have been in and out of the same airport several times that very day, they always brief the procedure so that in the event that something goes awry, there will be little doubt about both response and individual responsibility.

At the Ritz Carlton you can watch them line up prior to serving a banquet. Questions about the service order and the menu are answered. And can't you imagine how much more comfortable the waitstaff must feel, knowing that they are fully informed and that there will be no unpleasant surprises? Who wants to look stupid? No one! And the line up pretty much guarantees that every server will look and feel like the fully informed, fully involved team player that they are.

But the biggest plus must surely be that the entire team is now pointedly focused on the goal. In this case, happy customers.

On the Arco Juneau even the routine deck work began with a crew muster that included an outline of the tasks at hand as well as a mini-safety briefing covering any tools or materials likely to be used. When walking across a lonely expanse of heaving deck, it gives you confidence to know that you are working a well-thought plan and have all the important details and knowledge necessary to do your part.

I never fire up the baby Mooney without first completing a multi-page check-list. Could I go without it? Sure! Some pilots simply, "kick the tires and light the fires" and head into the wild blue. But why? Especially when I may be faced with a complicated SID (Standard Instrument Departure route.) Why be surprised?

Be prepared to the point that you are never surprised. That's playing a thinking game and it's a matter of playing the game instead of letting the game play you.

Stu made the interesting observation that there really isn't such a thing as flying solo, that even when I am alone in the soup, picking my way through the murk, the controllers are part of the team. Good point.

Who is an unseen but important part of your team who might need to be included in the pre-flight briefing?

The question for you is simple. How could you pre-flight your operation?

Individual Lessons
The Game You Play Is Playing You.

If you think the work you do doesn't change who you are, you aren't paying attention! Put the firefighters from Phoenix in the same room as the laundry workers from Dallas and the sailors from Alaska and the farmers from Iowa, and then try to tell me you can't tell who is who. Nonsense!

I knew it the moment I saw the gray men standing next to their gray machines at John Deere. I knew it the moment I climbed aboard the Life-Net helicopter in Kansas City. Different breeds of cats, none of them the same, all of them different. And the difference came not so much because of who they are as it was what they do. The work you do is working you and there is no escaping it.

If the foundry seemed dark and dreary to me, it did not to the men who worked there. Perhaps it is what my dad used to say about the restaurant business; when you use the back door day after day, you eventually stop seeing the business from any other perspective. Like buying a new car, it is bright and shiny the first day and pretty much the same on the second. But there comes a day when you suddenly realize that the baby you drove fresh and pretty off the dealer's lot has become a clunker and it's impossible to remember when exactly that happened.

The guys in the foundry have been going to work in the same place to do the same things for so long, they no longer noticed. I cannot help but wonder if, when they finally retire to the Winnebago, they will notice that a life had been spent, living on autopilot while they sheared and stamped one greasy, gray part after another.

For me, the lesson is clear. The work you do is working you. If you are what you eat, then it must be doubly true that you are what you do. The big voices and their rough language, the unshaven sometimes toothless grins, surely weren't requirements for the job. Somehow, along the line they came from the foundry, molded and stamped permanently into the soul.

Look closely at what you do and ask if you can love it. Because if you cannot, perhaps it's time to make a change before you are stuck with yourself and not liking it!

What Gets Rewarded Gets Done.

There are careers and there are jobs. Working in the paint department is a job. It does not fill you up. It does not make you better. It only pays the rent.

Now, that's not all bad, especially if you have rent to pay. And, there are surely worse jobs in far worse places. There isn't much in the way of danger and, even though you live an entire day without so much as an awareness of daylight or dark, the yellow glow, green paint, and gray noise certainly won't hurt you.

The pay is handsome.

You hardly get dirty.

I didn't even sweat.

You could wear the same jeans a couple of days in a row.

The work sucks. Hang this part, put that one on a pallet and bet your paycheck that they will be gray going out green coming back. The computer counts parts, a sophisticated adding machine that eventually connects directly to your paycheck. Work faster, get paid more. It is as simple and sinful as that. It's work that must be done. Not important in itself but without which the world would cease to eat so it isn't all that frivolous.

This is a classic example of work leading to reward. A job that's just a job. Not all that important unless you have rent to pay. And don't we all?

All Work Done Honorably is Honorable Work.

Talk about respect and there is no point in mentioning

the carnival. It's fun for an afternoon. Cheap thrills made not so cheap by regulation and threat of tort. But still cheap in the sense that it's unusual and beyond garish with a lot of lights, blaring music, and exaggerated motion served up by an army of the odd.

Carnies don't look too friendly and why should they? They may have slept under a truck, again. And God knows, that even though their money is good, it doesn't spend quite so well as when it comes from a Gucci purse. Nope, the carnie is part of the show.

Half freak, half low-life servant, the carnie is just there, like part of the ride, a piece of the equipment. And like equipment, there is no need to baby it. You can leave it out in the rain or sun and it won't really be hurt. Carnies are used to it. They're fugitives, right? Don't they owe child support in Kansas or something?

Well, no.

The fugitives work in office buildings and hide behind huge pieces of useless furniture. The fugitives will wait for your annual review and get even.

Carnies, on the other hand, will tell you to '—— off' and go about their business.

You think not?

I walked into a meeting with a client where we were about to present a training program. Now, we're talking a Fortune 500 company, and right near the top of the list. Only this company with billions in sales and tens of thousands of employees doesn't have a training program. They've got politics and corporate intrigue. They've got a dictator living in the executive suite who can call a supplier and 'request' a fully crewed jet and tickets to Broadway but they don't have so much as a plan for training the new kid how to find the washroom.

My client was brilliant. His presentation should have warranted a standing ovation and all the funding necessary to get started on training.

All he got was a blank stare.

Actually, the stares were directed to the boss sitting,

(occupying, actually) the end of the massive conference table.

There was not a word from the knights in dull-witted armor sitting cowardly around the table, not so much as a nod of support for the fellow who wanted to do the right thing even as the competition was building stores, surrounding and dominating a market these guys had built and now were surrendering by default.

We started out of the room. Defeated.

"Scott." My name came from the power end of the table, more a command than request. "You haven't said a word. What do you have to offer?"

"I didn't say a word because Bob made such a wonderful presentation. Anything I could have added would have just been opinion. Are you asking for my opinion?"

"Yes," came another command from a face tanned from too much golf or tennis and not enough time in the stores where the obvious would have been seen.

"Well, first of all, I can't imagine that a company of this size would not be a leader in training already. That you are just now thinking about training is quite a surprise.

"Second, your guy presented you with a plan that is first rate and critical if you intend to stop the competition. Yet, not one of the folks sitting around this table voiced any kind of support at all. Instead, they looked to see what you would say and you didn't say much.

"Finally, I can guess from the way you have your arms folded, that you aren't really buying these ideas."

The pause was long and thick. I felt that for once, honesty was not a particularly good policy. The corporate demigods waited without breathing on the chance that a breath might attract the attention of little Hitler at the end of the table. By now the tanned face had turned from brown to bright red.

"So just who do you think is so hot?"

"How about Southwest Airlines? They wouldn't dream of letting untrained employees experiment on their customers."

"Cattle call airline," George Hamilton's stunt double hissed.

"OK. Wal~Mart. They have an incredible corporate culture that, more than low prices, is making them the retailer of choice."

"Amateurs," he pronounced. "Let's take a break."

Outside the room, in whispered voices, the semi-brave few, those with guts or low mortgages or without kids in college, let Bob know that they believed that he had a great plan, "something we desperately need," yet not a single one of them had spoken up.

Do we want to look at the folks who carry the water and even imply that there is no honor in doing the grunt work when in so many office buildings even a grunt is too big a statement to make?

Carnies are just like you and me, only dirtier and more tired, and used to it.

The carnie lives in a Third World country and understands how it is to live inside a PBS documentary that the gentle folks can watch without being embarrassed, the one the people in front of the camera will see. When you get to the unpleasant parts, turn the damned thing off.

All work done well is honorable work.

In cold rain or blistering sun, it doesn't matter. The carnival work gets done. And it is good work because it is done well.

Freedom is a Powerful Motivator.

If there is a most powerful motivator, it is not money. Nor is it title or office. Nope, the big one is freedom. Watch the one act play that repeats itself nightly on the U.S./Mexican border and you quickly catch the theme. Freedom. The Mexicans want it, the border rats want it. No matter which side of the game, a great score is measured in kilos of freedom. The drug smugglers want economic freedom. The illegals want the same, only they are willing to work harder for less. It is not a matter of morals.

The striking thing is that the border patrol agents also want freedom of sorts. They want to play the game their way. They want to 'lay-up' and wait in dark canyons, free to catch the bad guys. They thrill to the hunt where the rules are theirs for the making.

For the longest time I mistakenly thought that freedom was something that only mattered if you lived on the wrong side of a border. I was certain that the reason people pushed themselves across rugged mountains in the dark of night was simply a matter of economics. Jobs are scarce in Mexico and it seemed only natural that people with ambition would do whatever it takes to make for a better life for themselves and their families.

No, crossing the border is not so much about bucks as it is about freedom, freedom to wring as much out of life as possible. I can't say that if the situation were reversed that maybe I wouldn't do the same. Actually, I hope I would have that much courage.

The real surprise is that freedom was a theme in more adventures than the one we played along the border. Everywhere we traveled, we met people who used work not as a end in itself but rather a means to an end. In many cases we experienced work as a place holder, a matter of biding time or trading it in exchange for things that really mattered. And I suppose that if you can't do what you love, the next best thing is to do things that eventually allow you to chase a dream of your own.

Wouldn't it be perfect if our work and our dreams were one and the same?

Freedom to play the game your way may be the ultimate choice.

When Workers Connect with their Work, Work Becomes Art.
When the small man with dancing eyes peers from under a tall chef hat and says, "I am the Cookie man," you know that work can become art. It is not the work that is art. It is not the cookie baked or house constructed. It is not the

presentation given or prognosis drawn. No, they are, at best, mere expressions of the art. The art lies in the connection between the worker and the work. It is more act than product and watching a middle-aged man lovingly remove another hundred chocolate cookies from an oven at five o'clock in the morning is all the proof necessary that art is a matter of context rather than content.

When the work and the workers are able to connect with the end users, magic happens. They don't have to know them or see them or even hear from them, although that helps. Work never becomes art until the work has purpose. When the worker cannot see or at least imagine how the fruits of the labor will be used or enjoyed, there is no art, only work.

We've seen dirty laundry become pure art. We've watched a carefully bandaged wound and a tanker of Alaskan oil delivered without incident become art. The worker and the work must connect.

If you are not connecting with the end user of your work, do it now. Find out how what you do makes a difference because, then and only then, can you move from worker to artist extraordinaire!

Sign your work!

Shared Experience Enhances Team Intelligence.
There were big lessons I learned in the hotel laundry. Working with Lorena, following her hands, lifting one sheet after another onto the endless belt and feeding them into the press, I learned a lesson about learning. One chief lesson is this: When people begin to work as a team, magic happens. It is not that they learn to think alike. It is that they learn to trust the decisions made by their team mates. They may not be able to predict what or how their team mate will decide, only that the decision will be a good one, faithful to experiences previously shared.

Lorena's hands knew where my hands would go even before either of us could have verbally made the prediction. And there is more. Shared experiences, whether or not they are relative to the matter at hand, contribute to the collective intelligence of the team. It is as if knowing that the person at the other end of the table or the other side of the office, also has children or likes to dance or whatever. It is this knowing that allows us to think not alike but together.

And one other thing. It was in the laundry that I first noticed something interesting about becoming a member of a team. It was something that I began to look for and notice on all the other adventures. There is a moment when the new kid finally becomes part of the family.

Always there is one moment, one very obvious moment when the last barrier falls. You can learn to watch for it and you'll see it, too. And once you know, you can begin to create situations so that the barriers fall sooner rather than later.

My moment in the laundry came when Sammy offered me gloves and I declined. I'll remember his words always, spoken with a smile as the head housekeeper raced to offer me gloves. "It's all right, Evelyn. He don't need no gloves. He's just like us."

I learned these things while washing sheets.

A Shared Obstacle Causes Teams to Bond.

Two adventures, one lesson. It was instantly apparent. The similarities of work on the oil tanker out of Valdez and the passenger train out of Lorton, Va., were striking.

"We can't get off," was the word for word explanation given for why teams riding either sea or rail tend to bond so quickly and completely. Teams of individuals who would, left to land and their own devices, would never wind up at the same party, would, at work, come together without so much as a moment's discussion.

Oh, sure! Even under tough conditions, it takes a little while for group confidence to develop. But beyond waiting for confidence to build, give a team a common unforgiving obstacle like the sea or a dark night on iron rails and magic happens.

All great performing teams have an enemy. It could be the weather. It could be a competitor. It could even be imaginary. But, real or not, if you don't have an adversary, get one. If your enemy is benign, paint a wicked face on him and puff him up to your troops because we've seen it time and time again. Teams don't really gel until they come to see such bonding as necessary for survival.

Even the big players like Southwest Airlines and Wal~Mart like to think of themselves as little guys fighting for survival. If they didn't have competitors, they would invent them. And so should you.

When the Worker is in Control,
the Work and Worker are Indistinguishable.

I had been on the road for a solid week. The big iron took me to Kansas City where I spoke to a thousand or so enthusiastic Wal~Mart managers. The next day the wheels had barely touched the runway in San Antonio before I was speaking to a computer hardware company. By mid-afternoon, Melanie and I were in the baby Mooney surfing a strong tailwind to Atlanta. Then we were on to Beaumont and home again in thirty-six hours. And it was back to big iron for flights to Aspen and Victoria, Canada.

Was this the way man was designed to live and work? I don't think so.

What was the week's highlight? Well, that was Sunday when I took the dog, fatso Bailey, for a three mile walk into the hills near our home. We then took the little John Deere down along the creek bottom and cut firewood. Bailey stood guard, sniffing and poking, looking for trouble and wandering in and out of the clear, icy creek that runs along the back of the property.

By dinner time I was hot and sweaty in spite of the cool air of mid-February. First the gloves came off, then the vest. The hat got tossed onto the hood of the tractor, soon joined by the shirt. I hoped that Melanie would ring the triangular-shaped dinner chime if she needed me rather than look over the bank and spot me without a shirt. There would be hell to pay for that!

Dinner was roast pork and mashed potatoes with rich brown gravy. There was some other vegetable stuff but who remembers that?

The house smelled wonderful.

I tossed a log on the fire and headed for the shower. The dog and I showered together. I lifted off her scarf and she patiently took her place under the stream of well-water.

When Melanie came in to dry the dog and toss me a fresh towel, she didn't need to ask how my day was. She could look at my jeans lying on the tile floor and tell from the sawdust and leaves sticking to the faded denim, I had had a great day. The reddening scrape on my ankle was unneeded further evidence that this had been a day well spent, doing what man is intended to do—sweat.

When I work on our property, it is never without a plan. But it is a plan that changes. If I am walking to the well-house, I may carry along a hoe or chainsaw if I think that later I will be working over there and need the tools.

If I am hauling brush to the burn pile, I may carry stones for the fire pit on the return trip.

The dog and I may do trash duty along the road, check the mailbox on the way back down the drive, pick up a few large stones that have risen to the surface in the grass along the edges or stop for an impromptu wrestle and chase over by the warehouse. That is the way man began to work. Hard work but without form. Tough, physical work but self-directed.

When I have had civilization up to my neck, I need to cut firewood, burn brush, mow in endless parade along the perimeter of what passes for my yard.

On the farm, you get to do two things that are critical to health, mental and physical. First, you get to work without direction, thinking all day. Second, you get to take intelligent risk.

Farming is one big risk after another softened by the knowledge that you have choice.

Sure, there is the possibility that there won't be a paycheck at the end of the season but it is your possibility, borne out of a million decisions that you made along the way.

Hard work is good work. Work that makes you sweat, that makes the muscles burn, beats anything you can do riding a machine or climbing endless steps to nowhere.

Human beings are designed, built by our Creator, to work independently...and, to sweat.

Responsibility Breeds Responsibility.

If you saw them on the street, you would be surprised to see that the men and women who ride the flying metal monster to one rescue after another look so ordinary, and so young. Why, these are kids who carry with them the magic potions of life, of triumph over trauma, and wield them as powerful weapons for good!

They don't look like doctors (however it is that doctors are supposed to look.) And they are not doctors. They are something better, specialists at saving lives, experts who swoop from the sky in a huge whoosh, whoosh of whirling metal blades and flashing lights.

What is amazing is how these young people are free to make such huge decisions. Don't big decisions need to come from behind a desk? How about from a computer?

Bringing order to chaos, happy endings to sad days, the folks on the med-evac chopper wield more than medicine. They decide. And the decisions come in an instant, in a literal heartbeat. And they are good, responsible decisions made by people who are more responsible because of the trust that some unseen medical director, the guy with the desk and the computer, has placed in their bag of tools.

How much more responsible do we become when we are forced to look death in the eye? How much more responsible could and would the average person be if stripped of the enabling hand-holding of mom or dad, boss or friend.

If there is a lesson to be learned at 1,500 feet, it is that responsibility begets responsibility. We rise, or fall, to the moment.

Variety and Fast Pace Contribute to Rewarding Work.
Have you ever been exhausted but not tired? Wiped out but not beat up? When we finally said our good-byes to the Phoenix Fire Department, we had been "rode hard and put up wet." Tired but full, as if we had done something that mattered, as if the day had been spent, used up but not wasted.

Our lives are measured by the silent passage of moments. Some are large and memorable. Most are small, forgotten almost before they are born and instantly hauled off by boredom and neglect.

When work makes a difference, when moments count, each and every one, then it is not just the moment that mattered but us. When we make a difference, when we are able to thoroughly fill a day to the bursting, we matter. Boredom kills men, not by destroying our bodies but by rotting our souls.

When I die, I hope that they will say I was thoroughly used up, spent. Every moment. And there was nothing left but the memory—and it was good. All of it.

Carpe Diem!

Index